D0783102

the web of words

29

LIBER GENERATIONIS

the WEB OF WORDS

structural analyses
of the old english poems
vainglory, the wonder of creation,
the dream of the rood, and judith

with texts and translations

BERNARD F. huppé

state university of new york press
albany

Published by State University of New York Press
Thurlow Terrace, Albany, New York 12201

© 1970 by the Research Foundation of
State University of New York. All rights reserved
ISBN 0-87395-057-7 / LC 70-91202
Printed in the United States of America

Designer: Rhoda C. Curley

To Anne, Alex, Geoffrey
My Charlotte's Web for them

contents

pREфace

Like Pip I began work on this study with great expectations. I hoped to make a detailed analysis of a large body of Old English poetry. After a few months when I found myself still enmeshed in the intricacies of *Vainglory*, which I had assumed would present few problems, I realized that my study would have to be selective rather than comprehensive. Therefore, for intensive study, I selected four poems: two of these, *Vainglory* and *The Wonder of Creation* are short, reflective poems; one, *The Dream of the Rood*, is a vision poem of moderate length; the last, *Judith*, is a long biblical narrative. Together these four poems appear to me to be generally representative of the varieties of Old English religious verse. The method of analysis, which is developed through the study of the four poems, seems to me to have general applicability, and the judgments I have made seem to me to have general relevance.

The Old English texts and accompanying translations have a purely utilitarian function as providing easy reference for the reader involved in following my detailed analyses. In addition the texts suggest the rhetorical form of Old English poetry, which is implied by my method of analysis; the translations reproduce faithfully (nakedly?) the form that my understanding of the poems takes.

The first draft of this book was completed during a sabbatical year, 1964–1965. I then returned to my duties as chairman, and the draft mostly sat, except as I tried out the ideas in it on my graduate seminars, and as sporadically I found time for revision. References to literature after 1965 are to specific works which seemed to me to have significance when they appeared.

Mrs. Jane Kroetsch and Mrs. Judith Marsh gave me valuable assistance in preparing a typescript. Mrs. Elsie Oakley, Secretary of the English Department, did much of the final copy, and supervised the production of the remainder. I wish here to acknowledge my debt of gratitude to her for her services to the department and for her many kindnesses to me. Mr. Fred Jones of our department read the MS. carefully and fruitfully; for his detailed suggestions I am most grateful. My graduate students provided me with many useful questions and suggestions. I thank them for being responsive, though captive and willing. I wish also to acknowledge the helpfulness of Mr. Norman Mangouni, Director of the SUNY Press. His services in the cause of scholarship are of great importance. My debt of love to my children I have acknowledged in my dedication; I acknowledge here my deep debt of love to their mother.

introduction

Old English poetry achieves a considerable variety within the confines of its generally didactic or homiletic aim and its basically uniform metrical and rhetorical structure. The four Old English poems proposed for study in this book were selected as representative of this variety attained by the manipulation of uniform structural elements for a purely didactic end. The translations which accompany the studies were not part of the original intention of the book, but somewhere along the way they proved useful in providing a point of departure for the exposition of the method of structural analysis set forth in the studies. In effect, the explanation of a word or syntactic structure in the translation appeared helpful in explaining the analytical procedure which impelled the choice. Because the translations thus take on a considerable importance in the exposition, a word about what they are intended to be is in order. Quite simply, the translations are intended to be faithful; what they are faithful to, however, needs some definition.

The mechanics of the translations are governed by certain rudimentary facts about Old English verse, i.e., that it is accentual and alliterative. Each line of verse consists of two half-lines, each a metrical unit consisting of two naturally stressed syllables (three in expanded lines), and two or more syllables which are unstressed or have secondary stress. The two half-lines are linked by a pattern of alliteration which requires that the first stressed syllable of the second half-line, the "key stave," alliterate with one or both of the syllables receiving natural stress in the first half-line: "*Téarful Wíllie tíred quíckly*," or "*Téarful Tómmie tíred quíckly*." The second stressed syllable after the key stave is excluded from the alliterative pattern: thus "*Téarful Wíllie tíred tótally*," and "*Téarful Tómmie tíred tótally*," are not permissible alliterative patterns. Infrequently, however, a cross pattern is allowed: "*Téarful Wíllie tíred wíllingly*," or "*Wéary Tómmie tíred wíllingly*."[1]

1. The account of Old English metrics is a simplification, but not an oversimplification. The systems of Sievers, or A. J. Bliss, on the one hand, and then of Heusler, or Pope, even

Gerard Manley Hopkins, and the modern poets who learned from him, have accustomed the contemporary reader to a metrics not too unlike some reconstructions of Old English, except that alliteration remains an occasional adornment, not a pattern of recurrent linking. W. H. Auden begins a poem with a line taken from the Middle English prose of the *Ancrene Wisse*, which, when arbitrarily divided, provides a metrically sound line of Old English verse:

*D*oom is *d*ark   and *d*eeper than any sea *d*ingle

But Auden wisely abandons the regular alliterative pattern after the first lines, such pattern appearing inevitably forced and unnatural to the contemporary ear. Auden's example suggests that a modern translation of an Old English poem may imitate its metrics but not its regular alliterative pattern. However, if imitation and not re-creation is the aim of translation, some kind of alliterative pattern has to be employed, otherwise there would be a loss of faithfulness to the original.

These rudimentary facts govern the mechanics of the translations. No attempt is made in them to imitate the device of the key stave; rather the aim is at the simplest alliterative pattern, regular, but not demandingly obtrusive. The pattern of the translations is for one naturally stressed syllable of the first half-line to alliterate with one in the second, regardless of position: "Yet *l*ying there   for a *l*ong while," where the alliteration on the key stave is given no preference over such a line as, "There on the *m*ount   I endured *m*any," where alliteration is not the key stave. Alliteration of both stressed syllables of the first half-line with either one, but only one, of the stressed syllables of the second has been very sparingly permitted, "to *f*ell these *f*oes yet I stood *f*ast." Expanded verses have been imitated simply by the addition of one stressed and one or more unstressed syllables, "great and *g*allant he ascended   the *g*allows abject height."

Although vocalic alliteration was normal in Old English verse, it is not satisfactory in Modern English, and the alliteration aimed at in the translations is almost entirely consonantal; furthermore, only single consonants

---

the excellent recent study by Robert Creed (*PMLA*, 53 [1966], pp. 23–33) appear to me to suffer as hypotheses in being more complex than the material to be explained. As one example, Sievers' five patterns can be maintained only by recourse to the principle of the "resolved stress," a contradiction in terms, in effect, a syllable being either stressed or not, quite independently of the length of the syllable. Two short syllables may have the duration of one long syllable, but the stress falls on one; it does not hover over both. I believe the Old English poet was free to place his two stresses where he wished in the half-line, within the limitations of his language which did not allow much possibility for concluding with two stressed syllables (ˣ ˣ ′ ′). He could, of course, produce a very weak half-line like *missenlice*, where a secondary stress serves in place of a full stress; he could expand his line by the addition of unstressed syllables up to the point where a third stress had to occur, in which case, the "expanded line" resulted. At any rate, this simple hypothesis will do for me until a better one comes along—as I hope it will.

followed by vowels, or consonant clusters are considered to alliterate. Thus, "Then none will be *found free of all *fear*" is preferred over "Then none will be *free of the sense of *fear*."

Two other obvious facts about alliteration bear mentioning. It is the initial *sound* (phoneme) not the *spelling*, of the stressed syllable which governs the alliteration. "To his *k*ingdom he ascended from whence he will *c*ome," provides an obvious example: *k* and *c* have the same sound (or more strictly speaking are allophcnes), and thus alliterate; whereas the *c* of *ascend* does not alliterate with the *c* of *come*. The same is true of "pro*f*oundly schooled in the pro*ph*etic teachings," or "unprotected through his *s*ins I could dis*c*ern," where the spellings *s* and *c*, *f* and *ph* disguise the actual alliteration. These lines illustrate also the obvious fact that alliteration depends upon the identity of initial sounds of the stressed syllable, which is not necessarily the first syllable; thus the prefixes of *discern* and of *profoundly* and *prophetic* are unstressed and play no part in the alliterative scheme. Or again, "Listen to my revelation of the special vision" does not provide the satisfactory alliteration of, "Listen as I reveal the special *v*ision."

Although they imitate the mechanics of Old English verse, the translations are not intended to stand by themselves as equivalents in Modern English of their originals; rather the translations are ancillary to the studies in providing a basis for exposition of the structural analysis of the originals. However, because the translations are meant to be readable, the frequent serpentine involutions of the Old English verse have not been followed; a natural word order has been substituted within the limits of line-by-line faithfulness to the original, but the translations are cheerfully awkward in syntax, where smoothness could be gained only at the expense of faithfulness.

Similarly, a fairly standard Modern English vocabulary is employed in the translations, except where the aim of faithfulness to the original made the use of "poetic" and unusual words as well as manufactured compounds necessary. The use of such words could not be entirely avoided since the Old English poet not only used stock metaphors (kennings), as well as words found only in poetry, but also had as perhaps his chief verbal resource the "open-ended" compound. These supplied him with an inexhaustible treasury of coinages for special contexts, but without loss of ready recognition since the substituted element in the compound remained hinged to a "formulaic" base. Thus when the poet of *Creation* needed an adjective signifying the golden brightness of the sun, he manufactured *goldtorht* (or apparently did so, since it is uniquely attested in Old English verse) either on the model of a compound with *torht* as the second element, (*wlitetorht, wuldortorht*) or with *gold* as the first element, (*goldbeorht, goldwlanc*). The "right" word in the translations is the one that approximates the denotations and connotations of the poet's usage, even if the modern word appears strange, clumsy, or ineffective. Finally, to make clear what the translations are not, the pattern of stress and alliteration has not been violated knowingly, but if to achieve the pattern, loss of faithfulness had resulted, the pattern would have been sacrificed. Line-by-line faithfulness to the original is the overriding rule in the translations.

This disclaimer of any literary merit in the translations seems to forestall any possibility of finding fault with them; unfortunately, it seems also to suggest that there was little point in attempting them since they attempt nothing themselves. The disclaimer, of course, has been a little too disingenuous, for the faithfulness aimed at in the translations is not that of an interlinear gloss. If this had not been so there would have been no reason for the considerable effort involved in achieving a metrical and alliterative translation. An attempt was made in the translations to be faithful to the spirit, as well as the substance, of the originals. Thus the translations try to suggest the allusiveness and the richness of meaning of the originals: their combination of starkness and richness, of ornament and moving simplicity, of word play and sober doctrine. The attempt is halting, but perhaps it will succeed in encouraging the reading and rereading of the originals, which after all is the purpose of this book.

The translations also attempt to suggest the quality of the rhetorical structure of the originals. Since the rhetorical structure of the Old English poem exists as the vehicle for thematic development, the terms rhetorical and thematic structure are almost interchangeable—yet must be distinguished. The theme is something understood between the poet and his audience; it has the quality of doctrinal axiom. The development of this theme in the rhetorical structure of the poem tends, to the contrary, to be serpentine, elusive, difficult, puzzling. The reason is not hard to understand: with the destination of the poem, its theme, being known, the interest lay in the topography of the journey, in the delight of the maze, where the known goal can be discovered only by finding the rational route that leads there, whatever the distractions. The rhetorical structure of an Old English poem is complex, involved, and yet at bottom clear and rational.

The process by which the essentials of structure are perceived in Old English poetry is more like finding the way in a maze than it is like solving an equation. This is simply to say that it is good—very good—poetry which is at issue, and living things take uneasily to purely logical analysis. A method for the structural analysis of an Old English poem can be described, and the description can be useful, as long as it is recognized that it is not the description of an actual process of appreciation, but the discrimination of the rational thread— and only of the rational thread—in a complex search of hit and miss, where intuition and sensitivity to nuances are more important than logical deduction.

The Old English poem does not move in a straight line: at its simplest it is pyramidal; at its most complex it is like one of the great signature pages of the *Book of Kells*, where the eye first sees only a maze of serpentine lines until suddenly the initial stands out in sharp relief. (See frontispiece and plate I.) The grammatical rigidities of modern punctuation, responsive to the analytic charac-

ƀⳑⰵⱀⰵⱃⰰⱅⰹⱁ

Reprinted, by permission of the Board of Trinity College Dublin, from the *Book of Kells*.

PLATE 1. XPI a(utem) generatio

ter of Modern English, tend to obscure, rather than to clarify the synthetic character of the Old English sentence. Certainly modern punctuation tends to hinder the grasp of the syntax of the Old English poem which is responsive more to rhetorical than to grammatical structure. By way of example, the first lines of *Vainglory*, lines 1–8, suggest the difficulty of trying to impose a modern system of punctuation on the essentially synthetic and rhetorical structure of an Old English poem, for the syntax of the lines, at least our modern sense of it, and their rhetorical structure are in apparent conflict.

> Hwæt, me frod wita   on fyrndagum
> sægde, snottor ar,   sundorwundra fela!
> Wordhord onwreah   witgan larum
> beorn boca gleaw,   bodan ærcwide,
> þæt ic soðlice   siþþan meahte
> ongitan bi þam gealdre   godes agen bearn,
> wilgest on wicum,   ond þone wacran swa some,
> scyldum bescyredne,   on gescead witan.

The modern editor sees in the first two lines a simple, exclamatory sentence, with a compound subject, and a predicate with direct and indirect objects:

$$\text{Hwæt} / \left.\begin{matrix} \text{frod wita} \\ \text{snottor ar} \end{matrix}\right\} / \text{ sægde on fyrndagum } / \text{ me sundorwundra fela } /!$$

He sees lines 3–8 as a complex sentence, the predicate governing a compound direct object and completed in a result clause introduced by þæt:

$$\text{Beorn boca gleaw witgan larum } / \text{ onwreah } / \left\{\begin{matrix} \text{wordhord} \\ \text{bodan ærcwide} \end{matrix}\right. / \text{ þæt ic, etc.}$$

The punctuation adopted by the modern editor seems to the modern reader entirely unexceptional, but in fact it distorts the actual rhetorical structure of the lines. The first two lines do not constitute a sentence, for their meaning is actually completed, through restatement, in the next two lines. Thus lines 1–2 are rhetorically linked to 3–4. The punctuation should suggest this linkage, not a separation into two sentences. A comma, not a period, appears appropriate, particularly if the use of the comma is restricted to the function of indicating a linking division, and is not used, as in Modern English, to indicate apposition, restriction, etc.

The remaining lines, 5–8, which appear grammatically to constitute a result clause dependent on the predicate in lines 3–4, are no more related to this predicate than they are to that in lines 1–2. In fact they state a conclusion which is at least equal in importance to the statement made in 1–4, and which completes a single statement of cause and effect: (1–4) what the wise man has said has resulted (5–8) in an increase of awareness in the *persona*. The structure of the complex sentence in Old English was much looser, and more ill-defined, than in Modern English, so that, in effect, the result clause was not felt to be as tightly dependent on the main clause as in Modern English. To reveal the rhetorical, that is, the essential structure of lines 5–8 in *Vainglory*, they must be shown not as dependent upon lines 3–4, but as separate, and yet related, to the repetitive statement of lines 1–4, which they complete. The rhetorically independent value of lines 5–8 as an element in a compound, not a complex structure, is suggested by translating *þæt* as "thus," and by the use of the semicolon after line 4. As translated the passage appears in the suggested punctuation as follows:

> Lo! a wise messenger   old in wisdom
> revealed many mysteries   to me long ago,
> he opened a locked tale   the herald's foretelling
> this man informed   in prophetic teaching;
> thus truly ever since   I could perceive
> through secret song   the son of God
> welcome among dwellings   and also the weaker man
> I could discern   unshielded through sins.

In addition to the problem of modern punctuation, which, responsive to Modern English structure, has the effect of obscuring the essential rhetorical structure of the Old English poem, there is the further problem of there being no agreed upon definition of the basic rhetorical units which form the Old English poem. Thus, except for the "verse paragraph," there is no terminology by which these units may be designated, so that it is necessary to adopt a set of rhetorical terms to define and designate the rhetorical units, except for the verse paragraph.

The smallest unit is obviously the half-line, but the basic rhetorical unit is usually made up of a cluster of half-lines, as in lines 1–2, 3–4, 5–8 of *Vainglory*. This basic unit may be designated arbitrarily, in the absence of a conventionally agreed upon term, as a "clausule." If in the rhetoric of Old English poetry the half-line may be likened to the phrase of modern grammar, then the clausule may be said to serve in rhetoric a function analagous to that of the clause in grammar. The clausule, in other words, is a rhetorical statement which contains a predicate, but which is incomplete in itself and requires the presence of one or more additional clausules to make an independent rhetorical statement. A clausule may be simple or compound. The latter contains two or more simple clausules together making a statement the meaning of which is, in turn, completed by one or more additional clausules. Lines 1–4 of *Vainglory* constitute a compound clausule consisting of the simple clausules of lines 1–2, 3–4. The meaning of this compound clausule is completed in the simple clausule of lines 5–8. The simple clausule may be punctuated by the comma, the compound by the semicolon. Reference in the studies to clausules is by small letters for simple clausules, and by small letters and superscripts for compound clausules. Thus lines 1–8 of *Vainglory* consist of a^1, a^2, b.

Together, the compound or simple clausules which, for example, make up lines 1–8 of *Vainglory*, constitute the next higher rhetorical unit. This may be designated as the "period," and punctuated accordingly. Reference to periods is by small arabic numbers. The period makes a single complete statement and may consist of two or more clausules, simple or compound—as in periods 1, lines 1–8, and 3, 13–21 of *Vainglory*—or may consist of a single clausule—as in period 2, lines 9–12 of the same poem.

The next higher unit is the verse paragraph, which consists of one or more periods together making a fully developed statement. A verse paragraph may consist of several periods or of one. In *Vainglory*, lines 1–21 constitute a verse paragraph of three periods making a single developed statement about the learning process of the *persona* through his instruction in secret song. On the other hand, the concluding lines 82–84 constitute a verse paragraph of only one period, which, in turn, consists of a single clausule. Verse paragraphs may obviously be indicated by indentation and spacing, and for convenience by small Roman numerals. Verse paragraphs may be grouped to form the "parts" of reflective poems like *Vainglory* and *Creation*, or "scenes" in a narrative poem like the *Dream of the Rood*. In long narrative poems like *Judith* these scenes may be further grouped into "episodes." Parts or scenes will be indicated by large Roman numerals, and episodes by capital letters.

If the process of division and subdivision seems pedantic, so must Dante's divisions of the poems in the *Vita nuova*. Tastes change, and a poem of the Middle Ages cannot be appreciated fully until the contemporary reader has been willing to share for a moment an older view of literary convention and reality. What seems to be an encumbrance may later be shuffled off, but at one time a sympathetic effort must be made by the reader to participate in an experience for which his own literary habits provide little guidance. The structural analysis of an Old English poem by reference to the rhetorical building blocks with which it is constructed helps us to catch a design which may otherwise escape us entirely.

The elements of structure which have been described may be diagrammed:

| clausules | $\left\{\begin{array}{l}a\\b\\ \\c\\d\end{array}\right.$ | periods | $\left\{\begin{array}{l}1\\2\\ \\3\\4\end{array}\right.$ | verse paragraphs | $\left\{\begin{array}{l}i\\ii\\ \\iii\\iv\end{array}\right.$ | parts or scenes | $\left\{\begin{array}{l}I\\II\\ \\III\\IV\end{array}\right.$ | episodes | $\left\{\begin{array}{l}A\\B\\ \\C\\D\end{array}\right.$ |

The diagram is purely schematic, for in any of the rhetorical units the number of immediate components may vary; i.e., a period may comprise several clausules or only one, a verse paragraph several periods or only one, and so forth.

The clusters of components which make up any of the rhetorical units more often than not are distinguished by some form of rhetorical design, even in the smallest units where the element of design is variant or incremental repetition of key words or phrases, as in clausules a^1, a^2, and b of period 1 of *Vainglory*: a^1

frod wita . . . snottor ar, a² *beorn boca gleaw;* a¹ *sægde,* a² *wordhord onwreah;* a¹ *me,* b *ic;* a¹ *sundorwundra,* a² *bodan ærcwide,* b *gealdre.* Adeline Bartlett has shown the considerable frequency of employment in the verse paragraphs of such elements of design as envelope and parallel pattern, etc.[2] These elements of design are also extended frequently to the structure of periods, as in period 3, lines 13–21, which is framed by an envelope pattern through the repetition of *þonne* clauses at the beginning and end. Larger unity of part or scene, and episode is achieved by pyramidal clustering; by the interlocking of verse paragraphs through repetition and variation of motifs, key words and phrases; also frequently by the interweaving of a thread or threads of allusion or metaphor throughout the poem. Quite often the first verse paragraph serves to establish the primary thematic or metaphoric motif upon which the development of the poem is based.

The translations attempt to imitate, as far as possible, the rhetorical design of each poem by suggesting the echoic variations and incremental repetitions which are essential to its structure, and to follow carefully any metaphoric pattern which may exist as a unifying force.

Concerning thematic structure only a few points need to be made.[3] Chiefly, the reader must be alert to, and prepared for, the "metaphysical" level which supports seemingly unmotivated transitions; frequently, a basic metaphor which is varied and disguised in the course of development, provides, once grasped, the clue to the unity of the poem. For example, there was no obscurity for the poet of *Creation* in moving without warning from the idea of the diurnal journey of the sun to that of the journey of creation from its beginning in time to the end of time, and from that, in turn, to the idea of man's life as a journey to eternity. The association of these journeys existed on a "metaphysical" level present in the minds of the poet and his audience, for poet and audience shared a common body of doctrinal truths, represented symbolically by a number of commonplace metaphors deriving ultimately from patristic interpretation of the Bible. An Old Testament figure like Judith, for the Old English poet who celebrated her, was representational more than she was historical; that is why she was for him a historical character of the Old Testament, who yet embodied Christian virtues and who prayed to the Trinity. The level of the symbolic was pervasive, and united what otherwise would have been a series of disparate units. Since the Old English poet was dealing with revealed truths, his rhetoric was supported by their axiomatic and metaphysical presence; in turn, his rhetoric served to build a verbal structure to make these truths living realities through the reader's effort to follow the difficulties of the text to its theme. The poet's intention was not to represent flatly the words of the preacher, but to excite the mind to a fresh per-

2. See the very important study by Adeline C. Bartlett, *The Larger Rhetorical Patterns in Anglo-Saxon Poetry,* New York, 1935.

3. See Bernard F. Huppé, *Doctrine and Poetry,* Albany, 1959; D. W. Robertson, *Preface to Chaucer,* Princeton, 1963.

ception of the preacher's truth. What the poet sought in his elaborate structures, metaphors, and word creations was not to have his audience wonder at his skill, but to heighten their awareness of truths which they acknowledged in common. The formal and thematic structure of Old English poetry is always clear, but its clarity is encrusted with patterns of deliberate obscurity and with words of conscious ambiguity.

To translate is to attempt to understand. The studies to which the following translations are ancillary give an account of the difficulties, other than mechanical, met along the way, and provide explanation of how the difficulties were resolved. The explanations, if they are successful, should shed light on the poets' methods, their practice of deliberate obscurity, of obscure allusiveness, of a style, in short, which is always logical, but never direct, which achieves simplicity by means of elaborate artifice.

I. two reflective poems from the exeter book

a: OFERHYGD

Godes bearn—Feondes bearn

I

i　Hwæt! me frod wita　on fyrndagum
　　sægde snottor ar　sundorwundra fela,
　　wordhord onwreah　witgan larum
　　beorn boca gleaw　bodan ærcwide;
5　þæt ic soðlice　siþþan meahte
　　ongitan bi þam gealdre　godes agen bearn
　　wilgest on wicum　ond þone wacran swa some
　　scyldum bescyredne　on gescead witan.
　　Þæt mæg æghwylc mon　eaþe geþencan,
10　se þe hine læteð　on þas lænan tid
　　amyrran his gemyndum　modes gælsan
　　ond on his dægrime　druncen to rice.
　　Þonne monige beoð　mæþelhergendra
　　wlonce wigsmiþas　winburgum in
15　sittaþ æt symble　soðgied wrecað
　　wordum wrixlað　witan fundiaþ
　　hwylc æscstede　inne in ræcede
　　mid werum wunige;　þonne win hweteð
　　beornes breostsefan　breahtem stigeð
20　cirm on corþre,　cwide scralletaþ
　　missenlice.

ii　　　　Swa beoþ modsefan
　　dalum gedæled,　sindon dryhtguman
　　ungelice.　Sum on oferhygdo
　　þrymme þringeð,　þrinteð him in innan
25　ungemedemad mod　—sindan to monige þæt.
　　Bið þæt æfþonca　eal gefylled
　　feondes fligepilum　facensearwum,
　　breodað he ond bælceð　boð his sylfes
　　swiþor micle　þonne se sella mon;
30　þenceð þæt his wise　welhwam þince
　　eal unforcuþ　—biþ þæs oþer swice

a: VAINGLORY

Son of God—Son of Satan

I

  i Lo! a wise messenger   old in wisdom
revealed many mysteries   to me long ago,
he opened a locked tale   the herald's foretelling
this man informed   in prophetic teachings;
5   thus truly ever since   I could perceive
through secret song   the son of God
welcome among dwellings   and also the weaker man
I could discern   unshielded through sins.
Readily any man   may reason of this
10   who does not let   lust of the spirit
and overpowering drunkenness   impede him in his thoughts
in the little span   of this transitory life.
When many men   are merry of talk
the warlike idolators   in the cities of wine
15   sit lofty in symposium   recite the truth-song
interweave discourse   seek to discover
what field of strife   may find a dwelling
among men in the hall;   when the wine heats
human senses   a hue arises
20   clamor in company,   speeches clash shrilly
in disharmony.

  ii   Thus human souls
are divided in twain,   men in value
are not alike.   One leaps for glory
in his insolence,   inside him swells
25   an immoderate soul   —of such there are too many.
He is entirely filled   with envious thoughts
through the darts and treacherous   wiles of the devil,
he swells and belches   and boasts of himself
more than does   the better man;
30   he supposes his manner   appears to everyone
not entirely infamous   —it will turn out otherwise

þonne he þæs facnes   fintan sceawað.
Wrenceþ he ond blenceþ   worn geþenceþ
hinderhoca,   hygegar leteð
35   scurum sceoteþ   —he þa scylde ne wat
fæhþe gefremede—   feoþ his betran
eorl fore æfstum,   læteð inwitflan
brecan þone burgweal   þe him bebead meotud
þæt he þæt wigsteal   wergan sceolde.
40   Siteþ symbelwlonc   searwum læteð
wine gewæged   word ut faran,
þræfte þringan,   þrymme gebyrmed,
æfæstum onæled   oferhygda ful
niþum nearowrencum.   Nu þu cunnan meaht
45   gif þu þyslicne   þegn gemittest
wunian in wicum;   wite þe be þissum
feawum forðspellum   þæt þæt biþ feondes bearn
flæsce bifongen,   hafað fræte lif
grundfusne gæst   gode orfeormne
50   wuldorcyninge.

II

i   Þæt se witga song
gearowyrdig guma   ond þæt gyd awræc:
"Se þe hine sylfne   in þa sliþnan tid
þurh oferhygda   up ahlæneð
ahefeð heahmodne   se sceal hean wesan,
55   æfter neosiþum   niþer gebiged
wunian witum fæst   wyrmum beþrungen."
Þæt wæs geara iu   in godes rice
þætte mid englum   oferhygd astag
widmære gewin;   wroht ahofan
60   heardne heresiþ,   heofon widledan,
forsawan hyra sellan   þa hi to swice þohton
ond þrymcyning   þeodenstoles
ricne beryfan   swa hit ryht ne wæs
ond þonne gesettan   on hyra sylfra dom
65   wuldres wynlond;   þæt him wige forstod
fæder frumsceafta   —wearð him seo feohte to grim.

when he discovers   the consequences of his iniquity.
He writhes and evades   envisions ensnarements
many and base,   shoots shafts of malice
35   lets them fly in showers   —he knows no shield of guilt
for the harm he has done—   he hates the better
man through envy,   lets the darts of malice
break the bastion   the battle sanctuary
which the Master   commanded him to guard.
40   Insolent he sits at feast   befuddled with wine
lets his words   go forth with wiles
press contentiously,   fermented with pride
full of vainglory   he is afire with envy
with malice and treachery.   Now if you meet
45   a lord like this   living in the dwellings
you may know him;   take heed by these
few intimations   that he is the fiend's
son incarnate,   incorrigible is his life
his soul hell-bound   without sustenance of God
50   the Prince of Glory.

II

i   The eloquent prophet
sang about this   recited this verse:
"That one who stands   too stiffly high
through vainglory   in the time of vexation
lifts himself in pride   will be brought low,
55   after the journey of death   will be bowed down
to dwell in torments   entangled with serpents."
It was long ago   in the kingdom of God
that vainglory   and vaunted strife
arose among the angels;   they raised conflict
60   fierce incursion,   they defiled heaven,
treated with contempt   their Better when treacherously,
as was not right   the mighty Ruler
of glory they thought   to reave of his throne
and then to win   the joyful land of wine
65   to their own law;   the Lord of creation
prevented this in battle   —for them the strife was too bitter.

ii   Þonne biÐ þam oþrum   ungelice
     se her on eorþan   eaÐmod leofaÐ
     ond wiþ gesibbra gehwone   simle healdeÐ
70   freode on folce   ond his feond lufaÐ
     þeah þe he him abylgnesse   oft gefremede
     willum in þisse worulde   —se mot wuldres dream
     in haligra hyht   heonan astigan
     on engla eard.   Ne biþ þam oþrum swa
75   se þe on ofermedum   eargum dædum
     leofaþ in leahtrum   —ne beoÐ þa lean gelic
     mid wuldorcyning.   Wite þe be þissum
     gif þu eaÐmodne   eorl gemete
     þegn on þeode   þam biÐ simle
80   gæst gegæderad   godes agen bearn
     wilsum in worlde   —gif me se witega ne leag.

iii   Forþon we sculon a hycgende   hælo rædes
     gemunan in mode   mæla gehwylcum
     þone selestan   sigora waldend.   Amen.

ii   Then is it not alike   for the other who lives
his life humbly   here upon earth
and stands ever   in steadfast peace
70   with his neighbors in the land   and loves his enemy
though he did him   many times harm
wilfully in this world   —he to wonderful joy
from hence may ascend   in the happiness of the saints
to the land of the angels.   Not alike is it for the others
75   who in fullness of pride   for their offensive deeds
live wickedly   —their rewards are not alike
with the King of glory.   From these things learn
if you meet a prince   of humble mind
living in the land   to that lord ever
80   is a guest conjoined   God's only Son
delight of the world   —unless the prophet lied to me.

iii   Thus, in mind ever considering   saving counsel
we must remember   every moment of time
the veriest good   the God of victories.

VAINGLORY has not excited much critical discussion, probably because it has seemed uncomplicated, unexciting, and unrewarding, its theme shopworn, and its structure banal.[1] (What could be more lackluster than the poet's apparently arbitrary reference to an unspecified prophet to mark the beginning, middle, and end of his poem!) Yet an attempt at meaningful translation at least dispels the notion that it is actually an easy or simple poem. Its syntax turns out to be frequently puzzling, and its vocabulary unfamiliar and obscure. The unfamiliarity and obscurity of its vocabulary have a ready explanation: in the eighty-four lines of the poem there are twenty-one otherwise unattested words, six which occur only once outside *Vainglory,* and one that is unique in poetry, but attested in prose.[2] Of course, in the extant body of Old English verse the uniquely attested word is common, in part because the extant body represents but a fraction of the whole, but chiefly, it must be supposed, because the Old English poet had no theoretical objection to the hapax-legomenon, and because in writing a type of "formulaic" verse, whether oral or not, he would tend to form new words, particularly compounds, to fill the traditional frames. Although the hapax-legomenon was common in Old English verse, the number of uniquely attested forms in *Vainglory,* relative to its length, is exceptionally high, which would suggest that the poet had some originality in word creation.

However, unless the coined compounds can be shown to play a part in a metaphorical design essential to the structure and thematic development of the poem, they—along with the frequently difficult syntax—may only suggest an

---

1. *Vainglory* is the Modern English title given by Krapp and Dobbie, *Anglo-Saxon Poetic Records* (New York, 1936), 147 (*ASPR,* III). The title has been accepted here for the translation, but the sub-title to suggest the balanced themes. The OE texts are presented for convenience, and to illustrate the effect of the proposed system of rhetorical arrangement upon the usual printed appearance of OE poetic texts. They are eclectic; usual and obvious emendations have been silently incorporated; unusual emendations, or emendations of special interest are explained in the studies and accompanying footnotes.

2. The uniquely attested forms are: *sundorwundra* (2), *ærcwide* (4), *wilgest* (7), *mæþelhergendra* (13), *æscstede* (17), *ungemedemad* (25), *fligepilum* (27), *breodaþ, boþ* (28), *blenceþ* (33), *hinderhoca, hygegar* (34), *inwitflan* (37), *symbelwlonc* (40), *þræfte* (42), *nearowrencum* (44), *forþspellum* (47), *grundfusne* (49), *ahlæneþ* (53), *neosiþum* (55), finally *bælceþ* (28), which is given by C. W. M. Grein in *Sprachschatz der angelsächsischen Dicchter,* revised by Köhler (Heidelberg 1912), and by Bosworth-Toller in *Anglo Saxon Dictionary,* Oxford 1882, as a unique form, but may represent only an unusual usage. The forms attested here and only once elsewhere are: *soþgied* (15 and *Seafarer* 1), *scralletaþ* (20 and *Fates of Men* 83), *þrinteþ* (24 and as *aþrunten* Riddle 37.2), *facensearwum* (27 and Psalm 55:1), *gearowyrdig* (51 and *Gifts of Men* 36), *abylgnesse* (71 and Psalm 68:25). *Widledan* (60), preterite of *widlian,* is attested in prose, but not in poetry.

ineffectual poet's surrender to expediency. Study of the poem provides convincing evidence to the contrary. *Vainglory* is no *Psalm of Life*, soon exposed as the work of a sententiously pious non-poet. The difficulties in *Vainglory* are intentional, and the vocabulary and syntax provide an effective "metaphysical" design, as part of the poet's purpose of inculcating a time-worn truth in such a way as to make it vivid, touchable, impressive.

The larger structure of *Vainglory* presents few problems. The poem has two major divisions.

I lines 1–50
    Paragraph i,   lines 1–21, thematic, the two types of men
    Paragraph ii,   lines 21–50, descriptive, the vainglorious man
II lines 50–84
    Paragraph i,   lines 50–66, thematic, the words of the prophet, interpreted with reference to the fallen angels
    Paragraph ii,   lines 67–81, descriptive, the good man
    Paragraph iii, lines 82–84, thematic, the remembrance of God.

The poem begins simply enough. In period 1 of paragraph i, 1–8, the poet's *persona* tells that he has learned from a scholar how to interpret the words of the prophet. Even the first of the poet's many unique compounds, *ærcwide*, "foretelling," in clausule a², line 4, is perfectly straightforward, but in clausule b, 5–8, the description of what the poet has learned to perceive in the "foretelling" presents an immediate stumbling block.[3] Not only is the clausule too elliptical to be immediately clear, but also a key phrase, *scyldum bescyredne*, translated "unshielded through his sins," is in fact, ambiguous, *scyld* meaning either "sin" or "shield." The possibility of confusion is real since Bosworth-Toller translate, "separated from protections [shields]," Mackie and others, "deprived of his sins."

A decision depends on determining the meaning of *wacran*, "the weaker man," the noun which the disputed phrase modifies. Through the wise man's teaching the poet is able to perceive in the prophecies *godes agen bearn*, "God's own son," and also "the weaker man." "God's own son" may signify Christ, for it is he whom the prophet foretold. The reading "separated" or "cut off from sins" would be appropriate to Christ, born without sin, but "weaker man" must

3. Although the meaning of *ærcwide* is plain, its grammatical function is not. It may be either accusative or instrumental: if instrumental as with Bosworth-Toller, the phrase *bodan ærcwide* is to be taken as parallel to *witgan larum*; if accusative, as with Grein and the *ASPR*, the phrase is parallel with *wordhord*. The latter reading is preferable since we would expect the main object to be defined by repetition and since there is agreement in number between *wordhord* and *ærcwide*.

then also be an epithet for Christ, recalling perhaps, although with some contriving, his incarnation in human flesh ("man, but without original sin?"). But "weaker man" is more naturally taken as referring to a man other than Christ, a fallen man, where the phrase meaning "separated from protections" might be appropriate. This reading would establish a contrast between "God's own son," [4] the good man who lives in the imitation of Christ, and the "weaker man," the sinner, who is without the protection of the Father. In this event, the meaning "deprived of sin" would have to be ruled out, since the sinner cannot be so designated. The rest of the poem supports the contrast, for the poet distinguished the two human souls, the son of God and the son of the devil (see lines 22–24, 47–48, 67, 78–80). But the reading "separated from protections," which is implied by this context, seems forced and ineffective, since the concept of sin is essential to the definition of fallen man, in contrast to the son of God. The translation, "unshielded through sins," is not merely an attempt to force upon the phrase a meaning it ought to have. It derives from the hypothesis that the poet, aware of the two meanings of *scyld*, created an unusual phrase, playing on both meanings of the word: with the noun in the instrumental it means "cut off through sins"; in the dative, "cut off from protections"; and in combination, "deprived of protections through sins," that is, "unshielded through sins." All that can be argued against the reading is that the use of the instrumental is unusual, but in a poet seemingly given to word creation, this is no argument. That word play is involved simply strengthens the likelihood of the reading, for word play was highly esteemed by medieval poets.

This, as the Friar said, is a long preamble to a tale. But it has seemed worthwhile to let the reader follow the tortuous track to the translation, by way of suggesting that the verbal difficulties of *Vainglory* result from a conscious effort at density of meaning, designed to serve a thematic development. As I have elsewhere tried to show, the Old English poet was as addicted to ambiguity as is the contemporary poet—if for different reasons.[5] The ambiguity here seems deliberate—and appropriate. The poet has been instructed in the prophetic mysteries by a wise man, a message bearer, well-schooled in the prophetic books, in short, an exegete. It is appropriate that the poet should phrase the gist of his discovery in the elliptical and allusive style of the prophetic writings. The matter may be put in a way that would have been familiar to the biblical scholar of the poet's age, that is, to the man instructed in the prophetic teachings. The poet has perceived that the messianic prophecies, *bodan ǽrcwide*, "the herald's message," have a tropological meaning relevant to fallen man: Through God's son we are again made God's children; without him we are weak and lack God's protection because through sin we are cut off from him. To derive the meaning, the poet's words must be read with attentive imagination; that is how he would have

4. See Eucherius' allegorical dictionary, *s.v. filius*, PL, 50, 755.
5. *Doctrine and Poetry*, Albany, 1959.

PLATE 2. The Ravenna Cross

Reprinted, by permission, from Paul Thoby, *Le Crucifix, des Origines au Concile de Trent* (Bellanger, 1959).

wanted it, seeing poetry as an exercise of the faithful imagination, a means of grace.

Without some such explanation of what the poet had in mind, it is difficult to make the jump to period 2, lines 9–12, which is a transitional generalization turning from what the poet has understood to what the reader may understand, "Readily any man may reason of this." Yet not really "any man," for "any man" is now restrictively modified, though again in a puzzling way (lines 10–12). From what is stated in period 1, we should suppose that it would be a son of God who could perceive the message of the prophecy. The MS., however, appears to give precisely the wrong meaning, as Mackie translates, "On this can every man easily reflect who, in this fleeting life, allows wanton pride and drunkenness too strongly to mar his understanding." Such a reading clearly does not make sense, and the Columbia editors have followed Cosijn's suggestion and supplied a negative [*ne*] *lætan*, "does not allow." Yet emendation, always a last resort, is not necessary.[6] The verb in Old English as yet later in Hamlet's "I'll make a ghost of him who lets me" is ambiguous: it includes in its meanings its own inversion "allow" and "prevent." (See Bosworth-Toller sv. *lætan*, especially meanings I and II.) The poet's use of the verb is probably deliberate, but because the verb in Modern English is no longer ambiguous, it has been translated "prevents." The verb "prevents" governs the remainder of the period:

$$\text{prevents} \begin{Bmatrix} \text{vanity} \\ \text{drunkenness} \end{Bmatrix} \text{hindering—him.}$$

There is editorial uncertainty about the relation of these lines to the next, 13–21. No break is made by the Columbia editors until line 19; Mackie makes a break at the end of line 13. The difficulty rests in the suddenness of the poet's shift from exposition to description. The rhetoric of the poem is, however, unambiguous. Characteristically, the passage, 13–21a, is marked off by "envelope" repetition, for the period consists of two clausules, each introduced by *þonne*, "when"; (13 and 18); further, the first clausule, lines 13–18a, is marked by an

---

6. A good example of justifiable emendation is that of *druncen* (12) for the MS. *drucen*, as suggested by Grein and followed by other editors. Accepting the emendation are we to treat *druncen* as a noun or as a past participle, with *weorþan* understood, the ellipsis of the infinitive following *lætan* being common? With the latter some such emendation as that suggested by Klaeber, *to ricene* would be in order since *to rice* would be adverbial. However, it seems best to treat *druncen* as a noun parallel to *gælsan*, and *to rice* as an adjective phrase, formed on the model of *to lytlum, to strang, to hraþe, to swiþe*, and meaning "too great," or, as in the translation, "overpowering." The difficulty of the passage is suggested by Mackie's translation (*EETS* 194, London 1934) where this careful translator is forced to treat the reflexive *hine* as a possessive, and to make the direct object of the infinitive *lætan* the dative plural *gemyndum*; to wrench *to rice* from *druncen*, having it modify *amyrran*; to make *monige mæþelhergendra* parallel with *wlonce wigsmiþas*, both subjects of *beoþ*, (13), leaving *sittaþ* without a subject, a fact disguised by translating as a relative clause, "who sit at the feast."

incremental, zeugmatic verb pattern: *sittaþ—wrecað—wrixlað—fundiaþ*, which
is completed in the second clausule, 18b–20a, by *scralletaþ*:

(a) idolators $\begin{cases} \text{sit} \\ \text{recite and interweave discourse} \\ \text{seek strife} \end{cases}$ (b) speeches clash.

In this carefully contrived third period the poet defines descriptively the
life of the "weaker man," the one who does not reflect on the message of the
prophet because vanity and drink obsess him; thus in the translation the passage
is treated as a period having thematic relation to the first period. The period consists of a set description of men at the feast, couched in conventional heroic, or
Beowulfian, terms. This description is an extended metaphor descriptive of the
life of the "weaker man." The first clausule is introduced by a "when" clause,
"When many men are merry at talk." The key word here is the uniquely attested *mæþelhergendra*, literally "speech-praising," but translated freely "merry
of talk." The Columbia editors follow Grein in emending to *mæþelhegendra*,
"holding converse," an attested form. They argue from context, but this argument seems rather to support the unique form. The men here pictured do not
merely converse; they praise speech, find it delightful, are merry in it. The
introductory lines of the poem have shown the real value of speech, which lies
not in speech itself but in the perception of the truth in speech, *in verbis verum
amare, non verba,* as Augustine puts it. But these men praise talk in a worldly
symposium, wine-talk, as the balanced "when" periods of this verse paragraph
suggest (13 and 18): "When men are merry of talk . . . When the wine heats
human senses . . . ." This is why the conversation of such men leads not to
the peace of God but to the world's welfare, *æscstede*.

The poet's epithet for these men, the compound *wigsmiþas* (14), is found
only in poetry and is of limited occurrence. The first part of the compound,
wig, is again a homonym, meaning either "war" or "idol," so that the compound
may mean either "maker of war," that is, "warrior," or "maker of idols." The
latter meaning is certain in *Psalm* 113:12 of the *Paris Psalter*. The meaning
given by the lexicons to the word in *Vainglory* (as well as to its two other
occurrences) is "warrior," but the evidence is not as unambiguous as general
agreement would make it appear. The first occurrence of *wigsmiþ* would be
Genesis A 2703, where, as in the *Psalm*, it is used to designate the Egyptians; if
wigsmiþ, "idol-maker," is taken as a kenning for "idolater," this meaning would
be as appropriate here as "warrior," perhaps more. The last occurrence is in
Brunnanburh 73 where in a concluding flourish the poet declares Athelstan's
triumph over the heathen vikings to be the greatest since the Angles and the
Saxons, *wlance wigsmiþas,* overcame the British (*Wealas*). Here the simple
meaning "warrior" seems inescapable until one reflects that the *Brunnanburh*
poet was speaking in historical perspective, making, in fact, a comparison between
heathen vikings and the Anglo-Saxons in their former unregenerate state, "these

heathen conquerors," as Bede had long before called his ancestors. It is precisely of *idolatrous* warriors that the *Brunnanburh* poet is thinking in his comparison.

One is tempted to trace an historical thread of literary borrowing. The poet of *Genesis* A, who was fond of word play as I have tried elsewhere to show, created a portmanteau compound, *wigsmiþas* to be read "idolatrous warriors." He may have been influenced by *Psalm* 113; at any rate the translator of the psalm apparently borrowed his word. For reasons which will be made clear, the *Genesis* poet's word was one the poet of *Vainglory* wanted. Later, the *Brunnanburh* poet, an omnivorous borrower, took the whole phrase from *Vainglory*, *wlance wigsmiþas*, because it served compendiously to designate the Anglo-Saxons of the time when they were like the heathen Vikings.

For the poet of *Vainglory* one meaning of the compound, that is "war-maker," was clearly appropriate to this picture of a feast which leads to strife, but equally appropriate was the meaning "idolater," not only to designate the "men merry of talk" as unregenerate, but because an important Pauline image would have given sharp point to the word "idolaters" as designating these feasters; in I Cor. 10:

> 7. Neither be ye idolaters, as were some of them; as it is written, the people sat down to eat and drink, and rose up to play. . . .
> 14. Wherefore, my dearly beloved, flee from idolatry.
> 15. I speak as to wise men; judge what I say.

Again in Phil. 3:

> 19. Whose end is destruction, whose God is their belly, and whose glory is their shame, who mind earthly things.
> 20. For our conversation is in heaven.

The men described by the poet are idolaters in the Pauline sense, at war with each other and with themselves. Thus, in the translation the kenning "idolater" is given the preference, modified by "warlike"; the adjective *wlonc*, "lofty" is placed in the next line (15).

The feasters are said to live *winburgum in*, (14) translated literally "in the cities of wine," that is, "where wine is drunk." The compound is limited to poetry, but is of fairly frequent occurence. It designates heathen cities—for example, the imperial cities Rome and Babylon—but also Jerusalem. This would suggest that the word has a double reference: to the holy city and to the city of the world. In fact the word has a single level of meaning, since the reference to Jerusalem (*Daniel* 58) is to the city in its fallen state when it becomes captive to Babylon.[7] *Winburh* designates, then, the worldly city of

7. The use of *winburh* in *Daniel* 58 implies in context that Jerusalem is a doomed city which flickers in vainglory, because they were abandoned by God, *þenden hie let metod*; interestingly the poet seems to play, like the *Vainglory* poet, on the two meanings of *lætan*,

false delight, doomed to destruction through its own folly. Thus the word is only apparently ambiguous.

The next key word of clausule a of period 3 is *soþgied,* (15). This is also a compound of rare occurrence, being found only here and *Seafarer,* 1, but it is unambiguous: it can only mean truth-song. This very lack of ambiguity sharpens the irony of its use here. (It is an irony like that of *Daniel,* where having described the Hebrew people falling into evil ways, the poet declares, *þæt wæs weorc gode.*) The voices of the feasters are, in fact, raised in self-deception. The truth can be found only where the son of God is "welcome among dwellings," but the inhabitants of the "cities of wine" do not make him welcome; the song they sing is not charity, but strife; not love, but hatred of neighbor. Their natural desire for companionship is perverted into enmity. The truth they sing is false; they are self-deceived.

The poet describes the worldly symposium in an incremental chain of phrases, the verbs of which, as we have seen, form a zeugmatic pattern which cannot be successfully imitated in translation: sit, recite and interweave discourse, seek the place of strife; speeches clash. The truth they seek is the *æscstede,* 17, a word apparently specially created by the poet. Some see the word as a kenning for "fortitude," others more literally as meaning "battlefield." [8] There is little reason to consider the word as a kenning, for its function is to define what the worldly make of the "winburh." Yet there were several words for "battlefield" available to the poet; he probably chose to create his own word because the first element of the compound "spear" establishes a basic metaphor to designate the maliciousness of the wicked man. As will appear, the poet develops from the image of the "spear-place" a whole series of interlocking images involving the idea of "spear."

In the second "when" clause introducing clausule b, 18–21, the poet defines the wine of the worldly cities—it is the wine which excites the human mind to

---

"abandon," "let." In Psalm 79:12 the context is a song of exile, a lament for God's wrath over his city, a context almost identical with that in *Daniel.* In *Andreas* 1636 and 1672 the word has reference to the heathen city of the Myrmidonians. In *Daniel* 622, the word refers to Belshazzar's dissipated and doomed Babylon. In *Widsið* 77 (as in *Vainglory*) the word appears in the plural and refers to the dominion of the Roman empire. Here again the context implies worldly power (with perhaps an accompanying sense of doom?). The word, finally, in the dative plural, as in *Vainglory,* appears in *Juliana* 83, again with the connotation of evil worldly power: Juliana's father swears he will give Juliana over to punishment, as he may find protection of Heliseus, *winburgum in.*

8. Grein glosses *æscstede* as a kenning for fortitude: H. Marquardt, *Die Altenglishchen Kenningar* (Halle, 1938), 215, treats the word as a kenning: "Das bisweilen auf die Halle als Schauplatz des Wortstreits bezogene *æscstede* Mod 17 ist wahrscheinlich im Wortsinnen als 'Stetigkeit, Eschenfestigkeit' zu verstehen, doch war ein Anklingen an kriegerische Kenningar vielleicht beabsichtigt." Bosworth-Toller and Mackie treat the word literally as meaning "place of battle." Since the entire action is, in a sense, mental, more is involved than the mere invention of a kenning; an entire metaphoric frame of reference is created by the poet.

clamor and noise. He concludes by returning to the zeugmatic verbal pattern of the a clausule, *cwide scralletaþ / missenlice*, translated "speeches clash shrilly / in disharmony" (20–21). The verb is found only here and in *The Fortunes of Men*, 83, where it has reference to the sound of the harp string. The root of the verb seems related to Modern English *shrill*, plus the causative verbal ending *ettan*, so that "to make a shrill sound" would appear a suitable translation. The sound of worldly voices does not rise in harmonious unison, praising God like the harp of the Psalmist, but confusedly in disharmony. The effect of the poet's summarizing phrase is to suggest the inversion of the psalmist's song of praise, the song of the disharmonious harp.

Verse paragraph *ii* of *Vainglory*, 21–50, is concerned with a closeup of the "devil's own son." It is introduced by a brief thematic period distinguishing the two kinds of men, 21–23. The poet's use of the introductory connective "thus" seems arbitrary since in i he gave only a picture of worldly men. However in i it is said that through reading of the prophets both the son of God and the weaker man can be discerned. In the world what is chiefly visible is the false, in particular, vainglory which needs to be exposed in order for the truth to appear. Only by seeing the world in the light of revelation does the worldly man appear for what he is, the doomed son of the devil.

The paragraph presents some difficulties in syntax.[9] The problems, which have to do with shifts of reference, are largely solved once the structure of the paragraph is grasped. Two brief periods, 1 (21–23) and 6 (44–50), frame periods 2–5 (23–44). Period 1 provides an introduction, 6 a conclusion to periods 2–5, which develop a description of the vainglorious man. Periods 2, 3, and 4 include parenthetical clausules, which serve as commentary:

1 (21–23)		Thus men are not alike
2 (23–25)	(a and b)	In man vainglory swells (c)—too many are like this
3 (26–32)	(a^1 and a^2)	The vainglorious man is a glutton, but thinks his manners are approved (b)—he is unaware of consequences.
4 (33–39)	(a)	He is tricky (b)—he is unaware of his vulnerability —(c) he is full of hate
5 (40–44)		He feasts, swells, bursts with malice.
6 (44–50)		Such a man is a son of the devil.

The syntactic difficulties in periods 2, 3, and 4 arise largely from the sudden shifts from clausules of description to parenthetical clausules of comment: in period 2, description in a and b, comment in c; in period 3 description in a, comment in b; in period 4 description in a, comment in b, description in c.

The syntactic difficulties are compounded by the difficulties of unusual diction; these, however, are resolved once the metaphoric structure of paragraph

9. *ASPR* III, 299.

ii is understood. The inner consistency of the images in ii is revealed in observing that the poet has picked up images already started in i, 3, the description of the worldly men: images of drink, of strife, and in particular, the image of the "spear-field." This pattern of images leads subtly to the recognition that the vainglorious man lives in the image of his master the Serpent. Like him he twists and turns, seeks to wound, only to wound himself.

Of particular interest is the piling up of uniquely attested words in periods 2, 3, 4 of ii, which describe and comment on the vainglorious man. In 2 (23–25) the poet uses *þrinteð*, "swell," and *ungemedemad*, "immoderate," both unique except that the past participle of the former, *aprunten*, is attested in *Riddle* 37.2. The poet's use of these special forms seems to mark his intention of establishing in the concept of "swelling" and "lack of moderation" a base for a metaphoric picture of the vainglorious man as drunkenly gluttonous (cf. *druncen to rice*, 12). This picture is developed in period 3, 26–32, in which are clustered four unique words: *breodað, bælceð, boð,* and *fligepilum*.[10] The first noun in period 2, *æfþonca*, "malicious thought," is of infrequent occurrence and is sufficiently ambiguous in form to occasion its identification by Grein as nominative singular, "envious one," (?) and by Bosworth-Toller genitive plural, "grudges." The latter is clearly right. The subject is *þæt*, "that one," "he," described as filled with *æfþonca*, "malicious thoughts," through the devil's wiles. An image is involved: in effect, the swollen and immoderate soul of the vainglorious man is filled with malice through the flying darts (*fligepilum*) of the devil. The poet presumably created *fligepil* to give emphasis to the image of the spear. The inter-locking image of drunkenness is picked up next in the series of unique and difficult verbs. For the first of these, *breodað*, two conflicting identifications have been made: Grein gives it as from *breodian* (?) "to call out;" Sedgefield, and others, from *bredan* (i.e., *bregdan*), "to trick, lie." My translation presumes still a third possibility: *breodaþ*, i.e., *bredaþ* from *bredian* (?), "to broaden, to swell." This supposition occasions some uneasiness, and Grein's solution "to cry out" as a variant of the next verb *bælceð* would be entirely acceptable, if it were not that the meaning "swell" is effective in context: the concept of "swelling" seems involved, for the verb *bælceþ* appears to be unique only in form and is from *bælcettan*, "to belch," as in Psalm 44:1, *Min heorte bealceð god word*, where *bealceð* translates *eructavit*. (Compare Chaucer's use of the verse from the Psalm in the *Summoner's Tale* in wry comment on the Friar's hypocritical gluttony.) The poet describes the vainglorious man as distended with malice through the devil; he belches not good words, but evil ones; he belches and boasts (*boð*) of his superiority to the better man. Metaphorically he is the drunken man, deceived into thinking highly of himself. His god is his belly and it produces the belch of boasting. To put this in an even more homely way: he suffers from indigestion caused by the devil's darts which fill his stomach like wine; in his

10. Grein, followed by Bosworth-Toller, read as *fligewilum*; the error was subsequently corrected.

drunken arrogance he thinks himself the object, not of disgust, but of admiration.

In the clausule of comment 3b, 31–32, which indicates the vainglorious man's blindness to retribution, the poet uses the word *fintan*, literally "tail," that is, by extension, "consequences." His use of the metaphor seems a deliberate means of suggesting the image of the serpent, the devil, whose poisoned tail wounds himself. The consequences, *fintan*, for the deluded man will be the sting of the devil's tail.

In period 4, 33–39, the poet further develops the metaphoric picture of the vainglorious man becoming like his serpent master, particularly in describing how "he writhes and evades," *wrenceþ he ond blenceþ*. *Blenceþ* is an otherwise unattested word, the meaning of which, is however, unambiguous, being preserved in Modern English *blench*. In addition the poet emphasizes the spear image by employing two unique compounds, *hinderhoca* and *hygegar*. The first of these, literally "low (i.e., base) snares," is effectively rich in connotations. The base hooks are in context the snares by which the evil man hopes to catch the unwary, the poor fish. In another sense they are hooks which pull a man low; that is, the devil's hooks, as in the *Blickling Homilies*, *ðonne bið he geteald to þære fyrenan ea and to þam isenan hoce*. In creating *hygegar* as still another variant for "spear," (cf. *æscstede*, *fligepilum*) the poet gives incremental emphasis to the fact that these are the spears of the depraved mind; the *hygegar* are literally "mindspears," translated "shafts of malice." In effect, the poet locates the "spear field," *æscstede*; the *fligepilum* fly into and from the mind of the devil's captive.

In the clausule of comment, 4b, 35–36, the notion of the proud man's folly is again interjected. The poet seems here to repeat his play on the two meanings of *scyld*, "guilt," and "shield." (Cf. line 8.) In not knowing his guilt, the evildoer does not see his true shield, the protection of the Lord.[11] The translation of 35–36 attempts to suggest the play on words by a fairly loose rendition. It is, in fact, remorse or shame which enables a man to see sin for what it is, and thus provides him a shield against evil. In developing the concept of self-destruction the poet echoes period 3 of i, with its generalized metaphorical picture of worldly life. He does this chiefly through skillful choice and invention of words. The first uniquely attested word is *inwitflan*, "darts of the mind" (37), translated "darts of malice." This is a variant of *hygegar* (34) emphasized by chiastic phrasal repetition (*hygegar leteþ: læteþ inwitflan*.) *Inwitflan* thus forms part of a metaphoric chain which begins with *æscstede*.

Particularly notable is the poet's creation of a very bold image keyed on two compounds, *burhweal*, literally, "wall of the city," translated "bastion,"

11. Cf., the definition of *scutum* in Eucherius' allegorical dictionary *PL*, 50, 738, "*Scutum*, protectio Domini. in psalmo: *Domini, ut scuto bonae voluntatis tuae coronasti nos* (*Ps.* 5:13). Compare also the OE version (*ASPR* VI, 22) of Psalm 34:2, *Gegrip gar and scyld and me georne gestand in fultum wiþ feondagryre.*

(38) and *wigsteal,* "place of battle" or "altar place" (39). These are what the vainglorious man is described as breaking with his *inwitflan,* "darts of malice." Curiously, these darts are described as breaking the *wigsteal* which God commanded him to guard; that is, his own soul. However, in the light of the poet's development of the concept of self-wounding, the apparent reversal of the imagery of the darts causes no difficulty. It is seen as a bold bringing together of a set of images begun in the description, i, 3, of the idolaters at feast who create the *æscstede. Burhweal* and *wigsteal* are of fairly frequent occurrence and seem to have been selected by the poet because they echo in combination leading words from the earlier description, i.e., *wigsmiþas, winburgum* (14). Of particular significance is the poet's choice of *wigsteal,* where he repeats the earlier word play made possible by the two meanings of *wig,* "war," and "idol." Both resulting possibilities are attested for the compound: first, "bastion"; second, "place where the altar stands in a church." In the translation the word is rendered "battle sanctuary." By means of the implicit word play the poet brings together in one forceful image the concept of the worldly man, the *wigsmiþ,* turning the *winburh* into an *æscstede.* Here the vainglorious man is pictured emitting malice like darts, which are intended to destroy others, but in fact return to destroy his own soul, the bastion, the shield, which God gave him to protect. His soul is a holy place. In it should live the son of God. When he protects his soul by making it an altar place, it in turn becomes a bastion of protection against the darts of the devil. When he places in his soul the false idol of worldly vanity, he destroys the sanctity of the altar place and pierces the security of the bastion. It should be noted that the poet's image serves not only to recapitulate the thread of the introductory description, but also picks up by implication the image of the son of God, described as *wilgest on wicum,* "welcome among dwellings" (7).

In period 5 of the descriptive insert, 40–44, the poet returns to the image of the feast, beginning with the first word, *symbelwlonc,* "insolent at feast" (40). Specifically this unique compound is a chiastic reflection of *"wlonce wigsmiþas . . . sittaþ æt symble"* (14–15). The word *præfte* (42), also uniquely attested, is of doubtful meaning, but seems probably to be the instrumental of a word meaning "contention" or "quarrel," best translated as an adverb, "contentiously." The word reflects the concept of strife central to the introductory picture of the way of the world. The phrasal combination, *præfte þringan, þrymme gebyrmed,* "press contentiously, fermented with pride" (42) echoes the introductory descriptive passage *þrymme þringeð, þinteð . . . ungemedemad mod* "leaps in glory, an immoderate soul swells" (24–25). *Gebyrmed,* "fermented," (42) is the metaphoric equivalent of *þinteð,* putting in a homely image what is implied by the swelling of the immoderate soul: the vainglorious man is a vat of fermenting, swelling malice; he gives off the barm of evil.

The final word of the period, *nearowrencum,* "treacheries" (44, translated in the singular), is also a unique word, approximated in the unique *nearusearwe* of *Elene* 1109. From the latter we may gather that the connotation of *nearowren-cum* is "imprisonment": these are the tricks, wrenches, which cause imprisonment. With this connotation the word serves as an incremental variant of *hinderhoca* (34), those hooks which serve to snare the one who employs them. The second part of the compound, *wrencum*, echoes the verb *wrenceþ*, "writhes" (33) with its connotations of devil-like wiles. The compound is given special emphasis by its concluding position and by the rhetoric of its phrasal combination, *niþum nearowrencum*, for *niþum* may be a noun used as an adjective, or the phrase, as Kock has suggested, may be an example of asyndetic parataxis. The latter is the reading favored in the translation, "malice and treachery," where, however, both *niþum* and *narowrencum* are translated in the singular, without any attempt at rendering the rhetoric of the original syntax. Thus, along with echoes of the imagery of the feast, the poet includes echoes of the spear imagery in the final periods of the descriptive insert.

In the sixth and concluding period of ii, 45–50, the poet addresses the reader directly in remarks which echo the first period of paragraph i. There the poet says that he has learned to perceive in prophecy the son of God, welcome among dwellings; here he tells the reader that he, in turn, may recognize through the intimations the poet has given (in periods 2–5 of ii) the son of the devil living among the dwellings. The verbal parallel is close, and two of the variants which link i,1 and ii,6, *ærcwide* and *forðspellum*, are found only in *Vainglory*: *ærcwide/ . . . meahte/ ongitan . . . godes agen bearn/ wilgest in wicum;* (4–7) *cunnan meahte/ . . . wunian in wicum/ . . . forðspellum/ . . . feondes bearn* (44–47).

In ii, 6 the son of the devil is described as *flæsce bifongen*, literally "enveloped in flesh," translated "incarnate." As Christ took the form of man, but through the prophecies could be known as the Son of God; so the vainglorious man is made in the image of God, but may be seen through proper understanding to be the son of the devil in man's flesh. Finally, he is called *grundfusne gæst*, "a soul bound for hell" (49), the adjective being another form found only in *Vainglory*. He is also described as *gode orfeormne*, "without sustenance in God." Both phrases reaffirm his bondage to the devil: he is caught by the devil's hooks, and stuffed with malice, he is without the sustenance of God. More importantly, the two phrases serve to provide a transition to the ensuing description of the fallen angels, the subject of the second period of paragraph i of Part II. The transition is logical: in the description of the vainglorious man, we have glimpsed his master, the devil; we shall now see how man's sin reflects the first satanic sin. The poet, in effect, provides two balancing descriptions, the second of which completes the spiritual understanding of the first.

To introduce the description of the archetypal fall, II, i, 50–66, the poet again refers to the words of the prophet, as at the beginning of poem; except here, 52–56, he cites what purports to be a biblical verse, although what verse it is difficult to say. The lines do not appear to be a translation or close paraphrase of any specific verse of the prophets, unless, as is possible, one has eluded identification. Psalm 35:12 (Vulgate) is not very close, but for reasons which will appear, may have been in the poet's mind:

> *Hi ceciderunt omnes qui operantur iniquitatem;*
> *expulsi sunt nec potererunt stare.*

> There all who work iniquity are fallen; they are
> cast down, and shall not be able to stand.

Even as loose paraphrase, the lines in *Vainglory* are not especially close:

> That one who stands   too stiffly high
> through vainglory   in time of vexation
> lifts himself in pride   will be brought low,
> after the journey of death   will be bowed down
> to dwell in torments   entangled with serpents.

However, the context of the poet's introductory affirmation that he had learned to interpret the prophets suggests a look at patristic commentary, where, indeed, a nexus of ideas emerges which at least tells something about the collocation of ideas found in the poem. The psalmist's verse lacks, of course, the poet's specific interpretation of the fall as signifying damnation, but this interpretation is found in the commentaries of Ambrose, Augustine, and Cassiodorus. Moreover, if we, quite legitimately, look beyond the verse to the entire psalm of which it is part, the commentaries provide a significant set of parallels to the leading themes and images found in the poem. Specifically, we find in the commentaries: 1) the arrangement balancing the evil against the good; 2) the perception of a reference in the Psalm to Christ, his sons, and their fallen brethren; 3) the theme of vainglory; 4) the concepts of self-wounding, self-deception, deceit linked with the image of the serpent; 5) the metaphor of the worldly as drunkards and idolators; 6) the fall of the angels and their human followers, specifically derived from interpretation of verse 12.

For ease of reference, excerpts translated from the introduction to Cassiodorus' commentary, and from the commentaries of Ambrose and Augustine [12] are grouped under these six headings, and are included here not because they establish a source, but because they are instructive in providing a background for understanding the workings of the poet's mind, his leaps of association, his imagery.

---

12. Psalm 35 is Psalm 36 in the modern Vulgate and King James versions. My numbering of verses is in accordance with the modern Vulgate, which does not include the inscription as verse 1. Cassiodorus, *Expositio Psalmi, CCSL,* 97, p. 317ff. (my translation); Ambrose, *Enarrationes in XII Psalmos Davidicos, PL,* 14, 998–1012 (my translation); Augustine, *St. Augustine on the Psalms,* translated by Hegbin and Corrigan (London), 1961, Vol. 2, pp. 223–248. See also *CCSL,* 38, pp. 322–336.

1) *Arrangement by balanced opposition of good and evil.*

This arrangement of the psalm is suggested in the introduction to Cassiodorus' commentary:

> Concerning the order of the Psalm, the whole is spoken by the *persona* of the prophet. [Cf. the poet's use of *persona*.] In the first section he vigorously accuses the despisers of the law . . . [Later] he commends more vigorously the portion of the good.

Cassiodorus also notes the extreme "subtlety" of the Psalm. He has apparently followed Ambrose in his commentary:

> The Prophet about to say in the next psalm [36] what is the form of the just, first expresses the form of the unjust. For we cannot understand what the form of justice is, unless we understand what the appearance of iniquity is; for they are to each other opposite and contrary.

2) *The perception of a reference in the Psalm to Christ, his sons, and fallen man.*

Ambrose:

> In the whole extent of the psalter the title of this psalm is unique, which declares the psalm to be written by a servant of the Lord. Who that servant of the Lord is we may see; what the sequence of the psalm signifies; to whom the psalm is said. We hear to whom it is spoken: *Lord,* he says, *in the heaven of your mercy, etc.* . . . To whom this, unless it is spoken to the Son of God? Unto this end, therefore, this psalm is directed, so that we may become servants of justice, not proud ones of arrogance. For the wages of obedience are liberty, of arrogance, death. . . . [verse 7] *Sons, however of men* . . . that is, not a generation of vipers, but sons of men, who live in the image and likeness of God; who are gathered not in herds, but in fellowships. . . . [verses 11–12] Therefore first he exposited the life of the unjust, afterwards he added the sacrament of divine understanding. . . . *And let not the hand remove me.* For as the saints are members of Christ, so the impious are members of the devil.

Augustine:

> [Verse 6] *Men and beasts wilt thou preserve, O Lord.* . . . Having already spoken of *men and beasts,* the Psalmist afterwards speaks of the *children of men.* . . . Who are the sons of men, then? Those who put their trust beneath *the covert of his wings.* Men, so called, rejoice like the beast in material things, but the sons of men rejoice in hope. . . . And if you wish to learn the distinction between the two classes of men, you may begin by

considering two men, Adam and Christ. . . . When we bear the likeness of earthly men, we are men; when we bear the likeness of the heavenly **man,** we are the sons of man; for Christ was called the Son of Man.

3) *The theme of vainglory.*

Augustine:

[Verse 6] . . . *Thy judgments are a great deep.* The Psalmist applies the name *deep* to the depth of sin into which a man sinks by despising God. [Cf. lines 29 and 61 of *Vainglory.*] . . . From what cause? From pride . . . It is from pride the Psalmist implores us to be delivered when he says [verse 11]: *Let not the foot of pride come to me, and let not the hand of the sinner move me.* . . . What does the hand of the sinner signify? The working of a seducer to evil. Have you become proud? He who persuades to evil will corrupt you.

Ambrose:

[Verse 1] [Having compared the evil man's likeness to that of Satan, Ambrose continues.] Vain indeed the show of boasting; but the criminal spirit of pride does not fear with reviling to profane divine majesty.

4) *The concept of self-wounding, self-deception, deceit linked with the serpent imagery.*

Augustine:

[Verse 2] . . . The Psalmist speaks not of one man, but of the whole race of the ungodly, who injure their own selves by refusing to understand and live aright in consequence. . . . *There is no fear of God before his eyes.* He plots his deeds of deceit, then. Perhaps he is unaware that God can see within? . . . *For in His sight he hath done deceitfully.* In whose sight? In the sight of One whom he fears not in his hypocrisy. *That he might find out his hypocrisy and hate it.* The cheat has acted in such a way as not to find it out . . . [verse 7] . . . Because they were self-confident and ungrateful, they deserved to be enslaved by the passion of their own heart and became a great abyss, so that they added hypocrisy to their other sins, for fear they might come to a knowledge of their iniquity and hate it.

Ambrose:

[Verse 1] Whatsoever the unrighteous man says is unrighteousness, which is brought back to its author, like the offspring of the viper, which rends at once its parents . . . . For just as thorns are borne in the hands of a drunken man, as Scripture declares, Proverbs 26:9, likewise in the talk of the unjust is born what wounds the speaker . . . . The serpent penetrates others with his venom, the unjust himself.

5) *Metaphor of the worldly as drunkards and idolaters.*

Ambrose: See the reference to Proverbs immediately above.

Augustine:

There were some among the Jewish people, at any rate, who understood and cherished the hope of one day receiving the mercy which is in heaven. There were others among them who longed for nothing but bodily comforts, with earthly and temporal bliss. These men slipped so far that they fashioned, or at any rate worshipped, idols. *They shall be inebriated with the plenty of thy house.* The Psalmist was looking for a word from human experience to use in speaking; and since he beheld men soaking themselves in drink, taking wine to excess and losing their reason, he saw the image to use.

6) *The fall of the angels and their human followers, specifically derived from interpretation of verse 12.*

Cassiodorus:

The psalm is concluded briefly in the destruction of the evil.

Augustine:

It seems as if the response, [12] *There are all the workers of iniquity fallen,* were given to show that they have come to that deep of which it has been said: *Thy judgments are a great deep;* they have sunk to that abyss to which haughty sinners have fallen. *Are fallen:* what first caused this fall? *The foot of pride* . . . . Because every wicked man today has fallen through pride. . . . When warning the Church to be vigilant, the Lord spoke thus: *She shall watch thy head, and thou her heel.* [Gen. 3:15] The serpent is watching when the foot of pride approaches you, so that when you falter he may throw you headlong.

Ambrose:

[Verse 12] *There are all the workers, etc.* We can also understand *There* in the future, that is, *There will be weeping and gnashing of teeth* [Matt. 13:32], and *Naked then I go forth* [Job 1:21]. How brief is the going forth, how great the conclusion. . . . For we fall in this world, but we arise in Christ to whom be the honor, the glory, for ever and ever, now and forever, world without end, amen.

There is a sufficient paralleling of ideas between the commentaries on Psalm 35 and the poem to suggest that the poet may have had this, or a similar set of ideas in mind in citing the "words of the prophet." In any event, his citation focuses attention within the poem on the spiritual history of vainglory, its beginning in Satan's sin of pride, and its terrible end in Satan's hell.

The poet suggests this dire history metaphysically by juxtaposing a created compound, *neosiþ*, "journey of death," (55) literally, "corpse-journey," against a formulaic phrase for hell torments, *wyrmum beþrungen*, "entangled in serpents." (56) The end of the twisting and turning of vainglorious men is the lonely journey, outside God's protection, to be wrapped in the actuality of his serpent-like nature. Their fall is the result of their having lifted themselves up in pride, a concept given emphasis by the uniquely attested, *ahlæneð*, (53).

Because in the fall of the angels the spiritual truth about the vainglorious man is set forth the poet carefully builds the second period of II, i, which describes the evil angels, so that it echoes the earlier descriptions of vainglorious men, I, i, 3; ii, 2–5. As they made of the *winburh* a place of strife, the angels transformed the *wynlond* (65) into a place of strife through their *heresiþ* "warlike incursion" (60). The vainglorious angels and men are both described with echoic word play as treacherous, but self-deceived: the result of what the angels *to swice*, "treacherously," attempted in despite of *hyra sellan*, "their Better," (61) is other than they anticipated; The vainglorious man who is filled with *feondas facensearwum*, the "devil's treacherous wiles," (27) has contempt for *se sella mon* (29), but with a result *oþer swice*, "different" (31) from what he expected.

In the next paragraph, ii, 67–81, the poet gives a contrasting picture of the son of God, who is humble as the other is proud. (Compare Augustine's remark in his commentary on Psalm 35; "Through pride we have so fallen as to arrive at the perishable state of mortality; and since it was pride that wounded us, it is humility that heals us.") The contrast is further marked by the poet in his emphasis on the harmony of the humble man, who from strife achieves peace, loving his enemy though he try to harm him. Thus he will not "be brought low" (54) like the proud man, but will "ascend" (73). A specific contrast is made between the two types of men. Lines 21–22, "Thus human souls/ are divided in twain," which introduce paragraph ii of I, are echoed at the beginning of II, ii, 1, "Then it is not alike for the other [the son of God]," (67) a statement contrastively repeated to introduce period 2, "Not alike is it for the other [the son of the devil]," (74) and finally to conclude period 2, "Their rewards are not alike" (77). in the incremental chain of thematic statements the contrast stated in I, ii, 1 is thus balanced against the contrast made between periods 1 and 2 of II, ii. Further emphasis is given to this balance in period 3 of II, iii; the direct address to the reader, "From these things learn/ if you meet," (77–81) clearly repeats I, ii, 6, "Now if you meet . . . Take heed" (44–50).

The echoic pattern is given even further elaboration. Thus the structure of

I, i, period 1, which includes mention of *godes agen bearn* (6), is closely imitated in II, ii, 1; the structure of both in turn stands in repetitive contrast to I, ii, 6, containing the reference to *feondes bearn* (47). In I, i, 1, the son of God, *godes agen bearn*, is described as *wilgest in wicum* "a welcome guest in the dwellings" (6–7). In II, ii, 1, the humble man who *simle*, "ever," keeps peace, who loves his *feond*, "enemy," [13] though he do him injury *willum in þisse worulde*, "wilfully," (70–73) is described as having *simle gæst gegadered godes agen bearn, wilsum in worlde*, "ever conjoined, a guest, God's own son, delight of the world" (79–80). In contrast to these descriptions, in I, ii, 6, the vainglorious man who is met *wunian in wicum*, "living in the dwellings," is *feondes bearn flæsce bifongen . . . grundfusne gæst*, "the fiend's son incarnate . . . his soul bound for hell" (46–49). The chin of incremental, contrastive repetition hinges on its final deployment in II, ii, 3 (77–81) where the poet skillfully establishes the concept of the indwelling of the spirit (*gæst gegaderad* vs. *flæsce bifongen*), the key to earlier crux in interpreting *wigsteal*. The soul of the son of God is inhabited by the Son of God, whose altar is the human soul; when God is not welcome in this dwelling, the man becomes a son of the devil, and the altar of his soul becomes a place of battle. One who turns the *winburh* into the *æscstede* shares the fate of the angels who desecrated the *wynlond* (65) and thus dwell in torments, *wunian witum fæst* (56). The image of the indwelling of the spirit is held in suspense; it is developed by incremental repetition of *bearn*, *wunian* and finally by contrastive play on the homonym *gæst*, "spirit/ guest." The son of the devil does not have as his *guest* the Son of God; that is why he becomes a hell-bound *ghost* (to use the Modern English word which retains traces of the Old English homonymy). One small but significant detail may also be noted; the repetition, in describing the good man, of the adverb *simle*, "ever." The concept of eternity is thereby linked to the good man, as against the vainglorious man who lives in worldly time.

The repetitive scheme concluded in II, ii serves as a metaphorical frame for the whole poem, and is enforced by the final phrase of the paragraph, *gif me se witega ne leag*, "unless the prophet lied to me" (80). The spiritual insight the poet has gained through study of the prophet, 1–8, may seem belied by the *soþgied* (15) of the worldly man, but the "words of the prophet" (52–56), reveal that worldly truth is falsehood, and that the prophet does not lie. Through the prophet we learn to discriminate, *on gescead witan* (8), between the two types of men, the old Adam and the new; from observing men of the world in the light of this spiritual understanding we may learn, *wite* (46 and 77), the truth of the prophet's words.

The poem concludes with a simple deductive formula setting forth the truth to be derived from the considerations educed in the poem: we must be mindful of salvation, remembering always the best, *þone selestan*. By choosing

13. For MS. *freond*, following an emendation accepted by the Columbia editors as demanded by the sense.

the superlative, the poet with great economy achieves an effective summarizing phrase. Both the vainglorious man and the disobedient angels despised their better, *sella* (29), *sellan* (61). Their error was to forget the superlative goodness of God with whom there is no comparison.

The evidence of conscious design in the poem seems sufficient answer to any initial doubt about the actual degree of creativeness involved in the poet's unusual vocabulary. Moreover, the poet has apparently used his new formations with an eye to overall design, for it seems not by chance that the uniquely attested forms in the poem are clustered in the first section of the poem, where the fiction of ambiguity in discriminating between the two types of men is maintained, and where the ambiguous self-deception of the vainglorious man is described. In II only two unique forms appear, *ahlæneð, neosiþ*, words used in the verse from the prophet, i, 1, and in their contrast suggesting the folly of the vainglorious man's journey in life. In the remainder of II, i, and ii, there are no unique forms. The poet thus sharply distinguishes the balanced halves of his poem: II presenting the spiritual truth about the false life pictured in I. The evidence for the poet's extraordinary attention to detail and for his rhetorical subtlety seems complete.

The design of the poem is at the service of its meaning; it demands of the reader a willingness to follow a subtle metaphoric thread. It exemplifies effectively the high artifice of the Old English poet, consciously practicing the rhetoric of the difficult in order to intensify the reader's intellectual excitement in rediscovering the truth in words, which he and the poet shared. We may not share his truth, nor enjoy his artifice; we would be naive to patronize either.

FIGURE 1. The Crucifixion (Pierpont Morgan Evangeliary, 9th c.)

Reprinted, by permission, from Paul Thoby, *Le Crucifix, des Origines au Concile de Trente* (Bellanger, 1959).

B: WUNDOR FORÞGESCEAFTES

Heofonas bodiað godes wuldor

I

 i Wilt þu fus hæle fremdne monnan
  wisne woðboran wordum gretan,
  fricgan felageongne ymb forðgesceaft,
  biddan þe gesecge sidra gesceafta
5 cræftas cyndelice cwichrerende
  þa þe dogra gehwam þurh dom godes
  bringe wundra fela wera cneorissum.
  Is þara anra gehwam orgeate tacen
  þam þurh wisdom woruld ealle con
10 behabban on hreþre hycgende mon
  þæt geara iu gliwes cræfte
  mid gieddingum guman oft wrecan;
  rincas rædfæste cuþon ryht sprecan
  þæt a fricgende fira cynnes
15 ond secgende searoruna gespon
  a gemyndge mæst monna wiston.

 ii Forþon scyle ascian se þe on elne leofað
  deophydig mon dygelra gesceafta,
  bewritan in gewitte wordhordes cræft,
20 fæstnian ferðsefan, þencan forð teala
  ne sceal þæs aþreotan þegn modigne
  þæt he wislice woruld fulgonge.

 iii Leorna þas lare! ic þe lungre sceal
  meotudes mægensped maran gesecgan
25 þonne þu hygecræftig in hreþre mæge
  mode gegripan —is sin meaht forswiþ?
  Nis þæt monnes gemet moldhrendra
  þæt he mæge in hreþre his heah geweorc
  furþor aspyrgan þonne him frea sylle
30 to ongietanne godes agen bibod;
  ac we sculon þoncian þeodne mærum

B: the wondeR of cReation

The heavens declare the glory of God

I

i Wayfaring man   welcome the stranger
give words of greeting   to the wise seer,
question the far-wanderer   about the first creation,
ask that he speak   of the spacious creations
5   of their life-renewing   natural powers
which every day   under the destiny of God
bring many wonders   to the race of men.
Each is a sign   a clear symbol
to one who in wisdom   holds the world fully
10   in his mind's grasp   the man contemplating
what in time past   through power of harp
men often expressed   in songs of prophecy;
they firm in reason   could rightly unfold
what best of mankind   these men ever questioning
15   and professing   understood fully
and had ever in mind   —the web of mysteries.

ii Therefore the man who lives   his life courageously
in contemplation ought search   the secret creations,
inscribe in his wit   the word-hord's power,
20   make firm his mind,   consider fully;
the vigorous man   will not then be vexed
in completing wisely   his earthly way.

iii Learn this lesson!   with no lingering I shall speak
of the Creator's majesty   which is mightier
25   than you through wit   though wisely skilled
may grasp in your mind   —is your might sufficient?
It is not the measure of man   mover of the dust
that he may through wit   the work on high
mark any further   than the Master
30   will give him to know   God's very law;
for thank we must   the mighty Lord

awa to ealdre   þæs þe us se eca cyning
on gæste wlite   forgiefan wille
þæt we eaðe magon   upcund rice
35   forð gestigan   gif us on ferðe geneah
ond we willað healdan   heofoncyninges bibod.

II

i   Gehyr nu þis herespel   ond þinne hyge gefæstna!
Hwæt! on frymþe gesceop   fæder ælmihtig
heah hordes weard   heofon ond eorðan
40   sæs sidne grund   sweotule gesceafte
þa nu in þam þreatum   þurh þeodnes hond
heaþ ond hebbaþ   þone halgan blæd.

ii   Forþon eal swa teofanade   se þe teala cuþe
æghwylc wiþ oþrum;   sceoldon eal beran
45   stiþe stefnbyrd   swa him se steora bibead
missenlice gemetu   þurh þa miclan gecynd.

iii   Swa hi to worulde   wlite forþ berað
dryhtnes duguþe   ond his dæda þrym
lixende lof   in þa longan tid,
50   fremmaþ fæstlice   frean ece word
in þam frumstole   þe him frea sette
hluttor heofones weard,   healdað georne
mere gemære.   Meaht forð tihð
heofoncondelle   ond holmas mid,
55   laþað ond lædeþ   lifes agend
in his anes fæþm   ealle gesceafta.

iv   Swa him wideferh   wuldor stondeþ
ealra demena   þam gedefestan
þe us þis lif gescop.   Ond þis leohte beorht
60   cymeð morgna gehwam   ofer misthleoþu
wadan ofter wægas   wundrum gegierwed,
ond mid ærdæge   eastan snoweð
wlitig ond wynsum   wera cneorissum.
Lifgendra gehwam   leoht forð biereð
65   bronda beorhtost,   ond his brucan mot
æghwylc on eorþan   þe him eagna gesihð

in endless time   so the eternal King
may suffer to give us   comeliness of soul
that readily hence   to the kingdom on high
35 we may ascend   if we are sufficient of mind
and willingly keep   the law of the heavenly King.

II

i   Hear this adventurous song!   Be resolute of soul!
Lo! in the beginning   God the Father
the treasure's high Keeper   created heaven and earth
40 the sea's vast depth   the visible creations
which now in hosts   lift high and raise
the holy praise   through the Lord's hand.

ii   Therefore in fullness of knowledge   he fastened all together
each with the other;   all had to keep
45 strict direction   as the Steersman commanded
the various measures   through mighty nature.

iii   So through length of time   the legions of the Prince
declare to the world   his clear comeliness
the glory of his works   his gleaming praise,
50 steadfastly work   the Master's eternal word
in the first thrones   which the Master fashioned
heaven's resplendent Keeper,   and hold gladly
the sublime course.   The candles of heaven
his might sends forth   along with the seas,
55 the Holder of life   directs and leads
in his embrace   the whole of creation.

iv   So the glory abounding   abides forever
in the most loving   merciful Judge
who created this life for us.   And this light brightness
60 comes every morning   over the misty darkness
traversing the waters   wonderfully adorned,
and at daybreak   dawns in the East
radiant and beautiful   for the races of men.
Brightest of torches   it tenders light
65 to each of the living,   and all may delight in it
who have been entrusted   by the true King of triumphs

sigora soðcyning   syllan wolde.
Gewiteð þonne mid þy wuldre   on westrodor
forðmære tungol   faran on heape
70   oþþæt on æfenne   ut garsecges
grundas pæþeð   —glom oþer cigð,
niht æfter cymeð—   healdeð nydbibod
halgan dryhtnes;   heofontorht swegl
scir gescyndeð   in gesceaft godes
75   under foldan fæþm   farende tungol

v   Forþon nænig fira   þæs frod leofað
þæt his mæge æspringe   þurh his ægne sped witan
hu geond grund færeð   goldtorht sunne
in þæt wonne genip   under wætra geþring,
80   oþþe hwa þæs leohtes   londbuende
brucan mote   siþþan heo ofer brim hweorfeð.

vi   Forþon swa teofenede   se þe teala cuþe
dæg wiþ nihte   deop wið hean
lyft wið lagustream   lond wiþ wæge
85   folde wið flode   fisc wið yþum;
ne waciað þas geweorc   ac he hi wel healdeð,
stondað stiðlice   bestryþed fæste
miclum meahtlocum   in þam mægenþrymme
mid þam sy ahefed   heofon ond eorþe.
90   Beoð þonne eadge   þa þær in wuniað,
hyhtlic is þæt heorðwerud   —þæt is herga mæst
eadigra unrim   engla þreatas;
hy geseoð symle   hyra sylfra cyning
eagum on wlitað,   habbað æghwæs genoh,
95   nis him wihte won   þam þe wuldres cyning
geseoþ in swegle;   him is symbel ond dream
ece unhwylen   eadgum to frofre.

III

Forþon scyle mon gehycgan   þæt he meotude hyre
æghwylc ælda bearna: forlæte idle lustas
100   læne lifes wynne;   fundige him to lissa blisse;
forlæte heteniþa,   gehwone sigan
mid synna fyrnum;   fere him to þam sellan rice.

with sight of eyes   to see it on earth.
The sublime globe   makes its glorious
way in company   toward the western skies
70 until at dusk   across the deep
of the ocean it comes   —the second darkness calls,
the night comes after—   it keeps the unalterable decree
of the holy Prince;   the heaven's planet
the wayfaring globe   wends in God's plan
75 radiant and bright   under the world's embrace.

v   Therefore no living man   has sufficient learning
to be competent of himself   to know where its source is,
or how the golden sun   goes under the earth
in the dark mist   under the mass of the waters,
80 or who living in the land   may in the light
find enjoyment   after it journeys over the edge.

vi   Therefore in fullness of knowledge   he fastened together
day and night   deep and high
welkin and river   land and water
85 flood and field   fish and streams;
his works do not weaken   for he keeps them well,
they stand steadfast   firmly established
with mighty bonds   in the power of his majesty
through which heaven and earth   may be lifted high.
90 They abound in blessings   who abide there,
happy is that household   —it is the greatest of hosts
the countless blessed   the companies of angels;
they see their very King   and with sight of eyes
gaze on him forever,   of each good have enough,
95 with no dark gloom   the King of glory
they see in heaven;   feast and harmony
are the pleasure of the blessed   in the plenitude of eternity

III

Therefore to serve his Creator   each son of man
must have resolve: leave idle desires
100 life's fleeting pleasure;   aspire to the delight of redemption;
leave all malice,   with the miseries of sin
let it drop away;   draw to the good kingdom.

although the vocabulary of *The Wonder of Creation* [1] is less interesting than that of *Vainglory*, its formal and metaphorical structure is more interesting. The external form of the poem is that of a logical argument based on a theme which is derived from a fusion of patristic interpretation of the first verses of Genesis (*In the beginning . . .*) and of Psalm 18.1 (*The heavens declare . . .*), both being paraphrased in lines 38–42. Upon the logical frame of the poem is woven a sustained metaphor of journey, centering on the symbolic description of the journey of the sun in lines 59–75. The meaning of the metaphor is at one with the symbolic meaning of the biblical texts.

An outline of the formal structure of *Creation* is a necessary preliminary to the study of the metaphoric and rhetorical details of the thematic development, for without a grasp of the central framework, the development of the poem in detail can become confusing. In its formal structure the poem leads by logical steps to a standard conclusion; man should aspire in obedience and humility to heaven. The poem has three parts: I, 1–36, Introductory Exhortation, advocating humble enquiry into God's creation; II, 37–97, Tale of Creation, describing the order of creation, and having as its central motif the journey of the sun; III, 98–102, Concluding Exhortation, urging as the purpose of man's enquiry his aspiration to heaven. The concluding exhortation is not elaborated, but Parts I and II are carefully structured in paragraphs which are set off by a rhetorical pattern of introductory formulas. These suggest the logical design of the poem; they consist first of the hortatory verbs, "Welcome" (1), "Question" (3), "Learn" (23), "Hear" (37); second of the logical connective, "Therefore" (17, 43, 76, 82, 98), and of the consequential connective, "So" (47, 57).

Part I, Exhortation, is framed by two paragraphs: i, 1–16, iii, 23–36, each introduced by hortatory formulas: *Wilt þu . . . gretan* (1–3), *Leorna þas lare* (23), Paragraph ii is introduced by *Forþon*, "Therefore" (17). All three paragraphs center on the theme of enquiry:

> i Welcome, question.
> ii Therefore [man] ought seek of the secret creation.
> iii Learn this teaching.

Part II, Tale of Creation, is introduced by the hortatory *Gehyr nu þis herespel* (37) and *Hwæt* (38). The introductory paragraph i is followed by five paragraphs; ii, v, vi are introduced by "Therefore," iii and iv by "So." Para-

---

1. Grein's title *Wunder der Schöpfung* is clearly preferable to the Columbia editors' *Order of the World* in view of the poet's indication of his subject by the biblical texts he paraphrases, Genesis 1.1 and Psalm 18.1.

graphs ii and vi describe creation in Boethian terms, and with the striking repetition of the introductory line of each they serve to frame paragraphs iii, iv, and v. Paragraphs iii and iv describe the journey of the sun, and v declares the insignificance of man's understanding in comparison with God's might. Paragraphs i, iii, iv, are introduced by statements which deal with the theme of God's might and his praise; in contrast paragraphs ii, v, vi are introduced by statements which concentrate on the theme of knowledge:

i Hear this adventurous song! Be resolute of soul. Lo! in the beginning . . . .
ii Therefore, in fullness of knowledge he fastened all together . . . .
iii So through length of time the legions of the Prince declare to the world   his clear comeliness . . . .
iv So the glory abounding   abides forever.
v Therefore, no man living has sufficient learning . . . .
vi Therefore, in fullness of knowledge he fastened together . . . .

Part III, Concluding Exhortation, consists of only one verse paragraph; it is again introduced by "Therefore": "Therefore to serve his Creator each son of man must have resolve . . ." (98–99). The introductory formulas of Part I center on enquiry; those of II center on the theme of God's might, and on knowing; the final formula centers on what the end of enquiry should be. Upon this logical framework is built a complex rhetorical structure.

Part I, Exhortation

Part I develops the concept of the need for man to enquire of God's creation. Paragraph i contains two periods, 1–7, 8–16, which, like much of the poem, have the pattern of question and response. The poem begins in direct address to the reader, called a "wayfaring man," *fus hæle*.[2] The reader so identified is enjoined to ask "a stranger, a far-wanderer about the first creation and about the spacious creations whose natural powers bring many wonders to the race of men" (1–7). In the context of their bringing "many wonders to the race of men," the heavens seem specifically indicated, for it is through the natural powers of the heavens that portents of good or evil are brought to mankind, and these natural powers control such wonders as the great movement of the seasons.

2. This free translation seems justified because the adjective, *fus*, has unmistakeable connotations of "preparation for a journey." Thus, Grein (*s.v. fus*) says, "offenbar zu findan gehörig, dessen Grundbedeutung 'ire' ist." The idea of "preparation for a journey" is omnipresent, as a glance at a few of Grein's citations suggests: *fus sceal feran; fus ond forþgeorn; ofer foldan fus siþian; fus on forþweg; is nu fus þider gæst, siþes georn;* finally, *fus leoþ* means "death, or parting song."

This identification is established later by the centering of the description in Part II on sidereal movement. However, at the beginning the subject of the voyager's enquiry is presented as something of a verbal mystery, with the shift from the singular *gesceaft* to the plural *gesceafta* and the uncertainty of the meaning of *cræftas cyndelice*. The "wayfaring man," otherwise unidentified, is to get his answer from "a stranger, a far-wanderer," who is identified only mysteriously as a *woðbora*, a word meaning literally "speech-bearer, witness," but in context ambiguous in its meaning, and translated by the neutral "seer." There are only five other attestations of the word, all in poetry: three times with the generalized meaning "poet" or "singer" (*Riddles* 31,24, and 80,9; *Gifts of Men*, 35); once as an epithet for those who observe a portentous comet, i.e., "astronomer" (*Death of Edgar*, 33); once as an epithet for Isaiah, i.e., "prophet" (*Christ*, 302). Since the reader of *Creation* is apparently to enquire of the heavens, the meaning "astronomer" would appear appropriate; however, the exact meaning of the word is left as part of the question to be partially answered in the second period of i, 8–16.

In effect, the second period serves to clarify the ambiguities of the first. The two periods of i are linked by means of the rhetorical device of polyptoton, repetition with grammatical variation, *fricgan*, 3, *fricgende*, 14. The voyager, bidden in period 1 to question (*fricgan*) the seer (*woðbora*), in period 2 has the example set before him of "the man contemplating" the work of former men who were "ever questioning," *fricgende*. These men "expressed in songs of prophecy" the "web of mystery" which they questioned (10–15). In plain prose, the reader is given the example of a man studying Scripture as the key to his life's way.

The second period is thus designed to answer the questions raised in the first. Concerning the "spacious creations" it declares that they become a "clear symbol" to one who has studied the prophets or psalmists. A symbol (*tacen*) is a visible sign which represents something other than itself, or has a meaning other than its particular designation. Most obviously of all created things the heavenly bodies are visible tokens, symbols of destinal and providential forces. the *woðbora* as "astronomer" would look to the heavens for meaning, but in the context of the models for the *woðbora* set before the reader—the prophets —this designation is too limiting; he must also be, like them, poet and prophet, psalmist. *Woðbora*, then, in *Creation* carries all the connotations of the word as it is attested in Old English verse—poet, prophet, astronomer. Furthermore, it is difficult in considering the range of connotations of *woðbora* not to recall the three Magi, the wise, far-voyaging astronomers who saw the star in the East and knew that it was a symbol which signified the coming of the Glory of God descending on the earth in fulfillment of the prophecies which they had pondered. ("Seer" is too colorless to suggest this richness of poetic connotations, but it does approximate the central meaning of the word.)

With the meaning of *woðbora* established, the significance of the poet's shifted repetition of *gesceaft* is suggested. The "spacious creations" (*sidra gesceafta*) are a symbol of the invisible and eternal creation of the "first creation" (*forþgesceaft*), for two aspects of creation are thus distinguished in patristic exegesis: first, the creation *in principio,* in eternity, when eternal things were created, God's heaven and the angelic hosts; second, the creation in time, for example, the heaven created on the second day, that is, the firmament, the highest visible heaven, which is in turn a symbol of the invisible heaven of the eternal creation which it represents.[3] The astronomer observes the visible heavens (*sidra gesceafta*); the prophet understands that they are but symbols of the invisible.

The search for the connotations of *woðbora* has led to the meaning, astronomer—prophet—poet. It is in the patristic reading of Psalm 18.1 that these meanings tend to coalesce. For patristic commentary on the Psalm which begins, "The heavens declare the glory of God, and the firmament shows the work of his hands," provides the collocation of ideas by which those in the poem may be understood. Thus Cassiodorus commenting on verse 1 says,

> Although declaring the glory of God can be understood literally (*ad litteram*) as when the guiding star (*dux stella*) proceeded the magi coming to Bethlehem, which star standing above his cradle showed the coming of the Lord Savior; nevertheless, we apply this better to the apostles and prophets, who in discussing his coming filled the earth with holy admonitions. In them God dwelled, as if in the heavens, who embraces all widely, not from part, but entering in the plenitude of his majesty. For part is not in God, but everywhere entire and full he is. To the impious one indeed it is said: *Who are you to declare my glory?* And *the works of his hands* follows, that is, man himself who was made with his hands. But this is said to the praise of the prophets that since they are his works they deserve to announce the awe-inspiring mysteries of their Creator.[4]

The association of ideas in the first two periods of the poem is explained by the commentary. The visible heavens in the obedient fulfillment of "the destiny of God," praise him and reveal "many wonders to the race of men" (5–7). But if man seeks to understand their mystery he must turn to the experts, the psalmist-prophets, who are themselves represented by the heaven with which they are identified because they also reveal that man's true way of life is to praise God in obedience to his decree. Of course, in the poem, the train of association is developed metaphorically, and the deductions drawn in the poem are not expository as in the commentaries; they remain on the level of metaphor.

Thus paragraph ii does not provide a plain explanation of *woðbora,* of *gesceaft,* or of why the reader is addressed as *fus hæle;* nor does it identify the men who "in time past" knew best how to explain the "web of mysteries." Although the transition (*therefore*) from i to ii is formally that of premise to con-

3. See *Doctrine and Poetry,* 112–115.
4. Cassiodorus, *Expositio Psalmorum, CCSL,* 97, p. 169.

clusion, the actual transition is intuitive, not discursive. From i it is deduced in ii that a man "who lives his life courageously in contemplation ought search the secret creation," etc., and so doing he "will not be vexed in completing wisely his earthly way." That is to say, an equation between the contemplative life and a life of fortitude is derived from the metaphoric substance of i; the equation is not deduced discursively from i as conclusion from formal premise. In view of the probable monastic provenance of such a poem as this, it is not surprising to find the monastic ideal of contemplation advocated through the striking association of contemplation with the virtue of fortitude. It is a challenge, as it were, to the ideal of the warrior society in which monasticism found sufferance. It claims for the contemplative a virtue in Christian definition to which the warrior, in his own definition, laid sole claim. Ultimately the transition from i to ii is based on an explicit chain of reasoning to be found in scriptural exegesis, but since the poet was addressing an audience for whom this chain of reasoning was merely axiomatic—not as with us something to be followed painfully—he could be sure that his structure of metaphor would be meaningful without discursive explanation.

Paragraph iii, 26–36, which repeats the introductory hortative pattern of i, introduces a new admonition, that man in his search must be humble, recognizing the immeasurable contrast between his understanding and God's. The contrast is cleverly marked by the epithet for man chosen by the poet, *mold-hrendra* "mover of dust" (27), as against the designation of the heavens as *cwichrerende* "life-renewing" (5). The contrast between God's understanding and man's is suggested in Cassiodorus' commentary on Psalm 18.1, "To the impious one indeed it is said, *Who are you who declare my glory?*" With this question, compare line 26 of *Creation*, "Is your might sufficient?" [5] The idea of humility in meditation is also suggested in the Psalm itself, the last verse, *Let the words of my mouth, and the meditation of my heart be acceptable in thy sight, O Lord, my strength and my Redeemer.*

In paragraph iii is also introduced the concept of man's goal in life: man obeys the Lord and gives him thanks so that he may ascend to the heavenly kingdom. The idea of the eternal kingdom is implicit in the symbolism of the visible heavens which represent the invisible, and the concept of salvation, the heavenly reward, is implicit in the address of the final verse of Psalm 18 to the Redeemer. Obviously to serve God is to praise him; and the heavens, which praise God in serving him, represent by symbolic extension the saints who in word and action sing God's praise in serving him. In emulating the saints man will ascend to the heavens. The concept of salvation, like that of the contrast between man's understanding and God's, is also marked by the repetetive varia-

5. The reading of the half-line as a rhetorical question is that of Bosworth-Toller (*s.v. forswiþ*).

tion, *cwichrerende–moldhrendra,* for the stirrer of dust may become like the heavens stirring life by imitating the saints who are symbolized in the heavens.

Logically, the definition of man's goal as the ascent to heaven provides the explanation that the "wayfarer" was to seek from the *woðbora.* Metaphorically, the ascent to heaven, in paragraph iii, is a link in the symbolic development of the journey theme established in the diction of the very first lines of the poem, where the metaphor is suggested in the poet's addressing the reader as *fus hæle,* "wayfaring man." The man preparing for voyage must enquire the way, as it were, from the *woðbora,* who is identified, in relation to the journey metaphor, as *fremdne* [6] and *felageongne;* that is, a stranger who has come on a far journey, a "far wanderer." He is one who has, then, experienced the wayfaring life (like the Magi? like Paul?). It is obvious that the man preparing for his voyage, *fus hæle,* will be asking directions from the experienced traveller. Since his journey will be guided by his knowledge of the heavens which show his path, he is told to ask about the "life-renewing natural powers of the spacious creations," that is, the heavens.

The poet by his use of *woðbora,* and by his suggestion of the symbolism of the heavens, establishes the metaphorical meaning of the *fus hæle.* He is the man desiring to be a pilgrim to the Lord, seeking his guidance from one versed in the meaning of the heavens through scriptural revelation. In turn, the pilgrim to the Lord must seek to understand the typology of the life-giving movement (*cwichrerende*) of God's creation; this reveals that his journey should be an ascent to heaven in the imitation of creation which praises its Creator. The conclusion to paragraph ii makes the significance of the metaphor clear in a figure of speech describing the result of the proper contemplation of the heavens; a man so occupied "will not then be vexed/ in completing wisely his earthly way" (21–22). Here the concept of life as a spiritual journey, with spiritual goals, is made metaphorically explicit.

The basic structure of Part I is a dialectic of question and response, with the *persona* of the poet addressing directly the *persona* of the reader as "wayfaring man." In i he admonishes him to question the far-wandering seer; in ii he deduces the need for the contemplative life; and in iii, speaking in the first person ("With no lingering I shall speak," 23), he admonishes the "wayfaring man" to learn the lesson of humility in searching out the goal of his journey. Superimposed on this framework is the proposed dialogue between "wayfaring man" and "seer" which is to have as its subject God's creation, specifically the movement of the heavens. The "seer" has as the object of his study the psalmists-prophets, who are typified by the heavens which declare the glory of God. To question the seer is in effect to question the saints (prophets, evangelists, magi, etc.): both heavens and saints declare the glory of God, and reveal the

6. Grein glosses *fremde,* "*alienus, peregrinus.*"

journey home. The answer, then, to the proposed question is given in the metaphor of journey: the voyager should embark on a pilgrimage which has as its end the right completion of life on earth, followed by the ascent to heaven.

Part II, Tale of Creation

In paragraph i, the introduction to Part II, the lesson which the voyager is to hear from the poet is called a *herespel,* a unique compound, glossed by Grein, "rede," and by Bosworth-Toller "noble tale." Neither provide any explanation. In his unique compounds, the poet tends to provide a straightforward set of meanings, usually quite literal,[7] and since the first part of the compound, *here,* "military," is unambiguous it is difficult not to think that the poet meant literally what the compound seems to mean, "military tale," "tale of war." Certainly his use of the epic formula *Hwæt* to introduce the actual *herespel* further emphasizes the heroic connotations of the compound. Epithets for God in Old English poetry frequently have an epic-military flavor, and here God has just been designated as "heaven's King," 36, and in line 39 is called "the treasure's high Keeper." The translation "adventurous song" is introduced to suggest, through its Miltonic connotations, the epic force of *herespel:* the creation is an epic subject, worthy of treatment in the loftiest flights of heroic verse.

The poet's selection of the paraphrase of Genesis I to introduce the main body of his demonstration has been anticipated by his use of *forðgesceaft,* "first creation," (3) and *sidra gesceafta,* "spacious creations" (5), as subjects for the voyager's enquiry, since the creation "in the beginning" contains in itself all subsequent creation. Augustine's commentary on Psalm 18, 1–2, may help to suggest the poet's association of "heavens" and "creation." [8] Augustine begins by making the point that the heavens represent the saints in their function of praising God:

> *The heavens show forth the glory of God.* The holy [*iusti*] Evangelists, in whom God dwells as in the heavens, proclaim the glory of our Lord Jesus

7. The reason for the statement, which introduces my study of *Creation,* that the poet's vocabulary is less interesting than that of ,*Vainglory* is precisely because the compounds in *Creation,* however significant and important they are, present no difficulty in translation because they are without ambiguity. There are seven unique compounds in the poem: *felageongne,* "far wandering," 3; *cwichrerende,* "stirring life," 5; *searoruna (gespon),* "(web) of mysteries," 15; *(gemet) moldhrerendra,* "(measure) of men stirring the dust," 27; *herespel,* "heroic message," 37; *stefnbyrd,* "direction," 45; *goldtorht,* "gold-bright, i.e., golden," 78.

8. Augustine, *St. Augustine on The Psalms,* translated by Hegbin and Corrigan, Vol. I (London, 1960), p. 177.

Christ, or perhaps the glory which the Son during his earthly life rendered to his Father.

He then introduces the concept of the original creation:

And the firmament declareth the work of His hands. It publishes the Lord's mighty deeds, this firmament which the power of the Holy Spirit has transformed into the dome of heaven, whereas under the influence of fear it was formerly mere earth.

    Day to the day uttereth the words. The Spirit reveals to the spiritual the unchangeable Wisdom of God in all His fullness, that Word which in the beginning was with God.

The paraphrase of Genesis 1.1 in the poem, lines 38–42, is close, but with differences which require explanation. The first two lines, 38–39, "Lo! in the beginning God the Father/ (the treasure's high Keeper), created heaven and earth," provide an exact translation of Genesis 1.1, "In the beginning God created heaven and earth," except for the parenthetic epithet defining God (39). *Fæder ælmihtig* for "God" does not represent a real variant, for in patristic exegesis, God of the first verse of Genesis is the first person of the Trinity, the Father, as in Ælfric's excellent précis, "The Almighty Creator showed himself through the great work which he created in the beginning. . . . Here [Genesis 1.1–2] is the Holy Trinity in these three persons: the Almighty Father, born of no other, and the great Wisdom, born of the wise Father. . . ." [9] The parenthetic epithet, "treasure's high Keeper," is probably to be explained on rhetorical grounds as developing the military-epic coloring suggested by *herespel.*

However, the next lines of the poem, 40–42, obviously diverge from the original: "the sea's vast depth, the visible creations/ which now in hosts lift high and raise/ the holy praise through the Lord's hand," [10] bear little resemblance to Genesis 1.2, *And the earth was without form, and void, and darkness was upon the face of the deep. And the Spirit of God moved upon the face of the waters.* The explanation for the poet's omissions and additions may be that he wishes to suggest the two stages of creation distinguished in patristic exegesis, which he has already suggested: the creation *in principio* (*forðgesceaft, on frymðe gescop*), and the creation of the *visibilia* (*sidra gesceafta, sweotule gesceafte*). Presumably "sea's broad ground" is intended to suggest the "face of the waters" of Genesis 1.2, but "visible creations" as summarizing the creation in the beginning would be inaccurate, for the creation *in principio* was not of the

9. Ælfric, "On the Old and New Testament," in *Heptateuch*, ed., S. Crawford, *EETS*, O.S., 160 (London, 1922), pp. 16–17.

10. The O.E. word translated by "praise" is *blæd.* The root meaning of *blæd* would appear to be "breath," or "spirit," and by extension, "honor," or "fame," so that "praise" is a legitimate inference for the meaning of *blæd* here. The resemblance of the lines to Psalm 18.1, however, does not depend on the translation of *blæd* as praise.

heaven and earth "as men now sees them." [11] Bede, enquiring why the idle emptiness of the earth but not of heaven should be mentioned in verse 2, explains that "nothing like this is to be understood of that heaven [*in principio*]; for this is the very higher heaven which, secret from all conditions of this revolving world, remains always quiet in the glory of the divine prescience. For Scripture tells in sequel how and when our heaven was made, in which are placed the windows [*luminaria*] necessary to this world." Later he explains that they were made, "*afterwards* since before any day of this time God created heaven and earth and sea, that is, that higher and spiritual world with its inhabitants, according to what is written, Ecclus, 18.1, *who lives in eternity* created all together." [12] Saint Ambrose, in a similar vein explains that the spiritual heaven is the model for the heavens that man sees as "the highest of visible things"; it is also "the representation of things invisible, the evidence of things unseen, as in the prophecy, *The heavens declare the glory of God, and the firmament shows the works of his hands.*" [13] The commentary on Genesis 1.1 by St. Ambrose helps to explain why the poet's creation song (*herespel*) includes in lines 41–42 an echo of Psalm 18.1, containing as they do the key words, "declare," "glory," "prowess," "praise," and clearly implying the subjects, "heaven," and 'firmament." The inclusion serves to establish the theme that the visible heavens are the spiritual reflection of the eternal heaven. This is also the effect of the poet's speaking of the creation *in principio* as being of heaven, earth, and sea. Although strictly speaking only the eternal heaven was then created, the "first" creation is also the eternal actuality and model of the visible creation. Only the eternal heavens can directly reflect the eternity of the creation, but creation because of its three parts, heaven, earth, sea, serves to reflect the triune nature. As Ambrose suggests they were created for man so that he may know his Creator.[14]

One phrase in the paraphrase of Psalm 18.1 presents a problem, *in þam þream*, both because it does not appear to reflect anything in the original, and because it is difficult to be sure what the phrase means. The translation, "in hosts" (41), involves an emendation, suggested by Mackie, of *þream* to *þreatum*. If the manuscript reading is to be retained, as by Krapp and Dobbie, a translation, "in afflictions," is required. Some sense can be made of this, as defining the meaning of "Now." "Now in these afflictions" would suggest the temporal present when men in the time of their trial look toward the heavens.[15] This

11. Augustine, *Confessions*, XII, viii, 8.

12. Bede, *Hexameron*, PL, 91, 13–14, and 21.

13. Ambrose, *Hexameron*, PL, 14, 14.

14. *Ibid.* Compare the inversion in *Creation* with that in *Genesis A*, 93–103, and see *Doctrine and Poetry*, 140–141.

15. Professor D. W. Robertson, Jr., has suggested to me the possibility that St. Ambrose's *Deus creator omnibus* provides an explanation for *in þam þream* as meaning "in afflictions." The two verses by Ambrose about the Creator, as printed by F. J. E. Raby, *Christian Latin Poetry* (Oxford, 1927), p. 33, describe the Creator's role as comforter: "mentesque fessas allevet/ luctus solvat anxios." The very perceptive suggestion would be decisive in equating

PLATE 3.   The Crucifixion (Wurzburg ms., Irish, 8th c.)

Reprinted, by permission, from Paul Thoby, *Le Crucifix, des Origines au Concile de Trente* (Bellanger, 1959).

interpretation appears forced, but the only other alternative—if emendation is to be avoided—is to assume that *þream* is equivalent to *þreom*, the dative plural of *þreo*, "three." *In þam þream* would then refer simply and naturally to the three parts of creation just mentioned, and would serve to reinforce the trinitarian motif. Unfortunately *þream* as dative plural of *þreo* is not attested, and *þreom* is both infrequent and of late occurrence. It is difficult to explain why this form, in place of the usual *þrim* (*þrym*) would appear in this poem, and the emendation *þream* to *þrim* would be more violent than the emendation to *þreatum*, a correction of the most obvious kind of scribal error. Finally, the appropriateness in context of the meaning, "in hosts" is suggested in Bede's commentary on Genesis 1.1–2, (a continuation of the passage cited earlier in the explanation of the poet's creation song):

> Therefore that higher heaven, which is inaccessible to the sight of all mortals, is not created formless and void, as was the earth, which did not at all in the first creation produce blooming seeds or living souls; rather [the higher heaven] was indeed created along with its inhabitants, that is, *filled with the most blessed hosts of angels*, who in the beginning were established along with heaven and earth, and, directly, along with the office of each creature of the first beginning to repay the Founder in praise—as the same Founder gives testimony, who, speaking to his holy servant Job, says, *Where were you when I established the foundations of the earth?* [Job 38.4] And a little further on, *When the morning stars sang together, and all the sons of God rejoiced.* The morning stars are plainly the same angels who are named the sons of God in distinction to the saints, who were created after, and after their confession of divine praise, like the evening stars, have to descend through death of the flesh.[16]

"In hosts" of the poem would suggest in Bede's commentary the angels, or morning stars which are their symbolic counterparts, singing "together" (*simul*) the praise of God in eternity. The phrase, as emended, *in þreatum*, would also anticipate the mention of *dryhtnes duguþe*, "the legions of the Prince" 48, and perhaps *on heape*, "in company" 69.

At the beginning of the poem, I, i, the voyager is to ask the far-wandering seer about the first creation and the natural powers of the spacious (i.e., the visible) creations. In II, i the bringing together of the creation paraphrase and the paraphrase of Psalm 18.1 provides the biblical answers to these questions and thus serves as a link with the first paragraph of I. In addition it serves to introduce the remaining periods with their description of creation (except for paragraph v which recapitulates the theme of man's insignificance of I, iii).

---

luctus with *þream* if it were not for the fact that the context of the O.E. poem is very different from that in Ambrose. Ambrose in the first verse speaks of the Creator as clothing the day with light and the night with the grace of sleep. It is from this view of the Creator that Ambrose develops the concept of God as comforter. Such a sequence of ideas does not appear in *Creation*.

16. Bede, *PL*, 91, 13–14. In plate 3 the arch of heaven is pictured.

Part II, paragraph ii describes God's ordering of creation in Boethian terms as a harmony of contraries. This theme is also developed in II, vi, a paragraph which, repeating the introductory line of ii, is clearly intended to balance ii, and to frame paragraphs iii and iv, describing the journey of the sun, and v with its comments on man's insignificance when compared to God. The Boethian influence on paragraph ii is shown particularly in the epithet for God, *steora*, "Steersman," 45, which appears to be a direct borrowing of a metaphor from the *Consolation of Philosophy*, "Ond he [God] is ana staþolfæst wealdend, and stiora, and steorroðer, ond helma, forðæm he riht ond ræt eallum gesceaftum swa swa god stiora anum scipe." [17] Except for this use of *stiora* as an epithet for God in the Alfredian translation of Boethius and in *Creation* there are no occurrences of the word, literal or metaphoric, in Old English poetry. Although it is impossible to determine the relationship between the two Old English translations of the Latin *gubernator*, for our purposes, the rarity of the word points unmistakeably to Boethius as the source of the poet's epithet. The context of the poet's description of creation is Boethian; the borrowing of the metaphor helps further to establish this context. The poet, however, may have had a more specific purpose in selecting this particular metaphor in that it serves to continue the thread of the symbolism of the journey: the heavens move in their course like a ship governed by a steersman and teach to the wayfarer in his journey the lesson of obedience to the Steersman.[18]

Paragraph iii contains two periods. Period 1, 47–53, describes the heavens praising God and thus follows directly from the introductory paragraph ii which describes their obedience. The period is introduced by *Swa*. Its immediate subject is the pronominal *hi*, "they," 47, which appears to have as its antecedants *eal*, "all," 43, 44, and *sweotule gesceafte*, "visible creations," 40. This single pronominal subject, with distant antecedants apparently governs a zeugmatic compound predicate with three components:

They, *hi*
- (a) declare, *berað forð*
  - —comeliness, *wlite* (acc. sing.)
  - —blessings, *duguþe* (acc. pl.)
  - —glory, *þrym* (acc. sing.)
  - —praise, *lof* (acc. sing.)
- (b) work, *fremmaþ* — word, *word* (acc. sing.)
- (c) hold, *healdaþ* — course, *gemære* (acc. sing.)

17. W. J. Sedgewick, *King Alfred's Old English Version of Boethius de Consolatione Philosophiae* (Oxford, 1899), 97. Metre 8 of Book II of the *Consolation* has specific relevance to the "creation" section of the poem. Its relevance, however, is secondary to that of Genesis and Psalm 18. Because the purport and order of the metre is not that of the poem, it cannot be used like Genesis and Psalm 18 as commentary on the poem.

18. The first element in *stefnbyrd*, 45, a unique compound, may contain a play on words, since it is a homonym, meaning "voice, time, prow"; in the latter sense this compound may have been coined by way of continuing the ship image.

However, there are difficulties. Although the remoteness of the antecedants for *hi* is not without precedent, the pronominal subject carries too little sensible significance to bear comfortably the weight of a compound predicate with three components, the first of which involves an object with four elements. It is no wonder that Grein, followed by Mackie, felt the need for a new subject for the last verb, *healdaþ*, reading *mere* not as adjective, but as noun nom. pl., "the seas hold their bounds." There is, however, no support in context for this reading, which would introduce, without apparent reason, mention of the seas. Further, *mere gemære* appears to be an example of rhetorical word play, akin to the device of polyptoton which the poet employs frequently: see *fricgan* (3), *fricgende* (14); *forþgesceaft* (3), *gesceafta* (4, 40), *gesceaft* (74); *frean* (50), *frea* (51); *leohte beorht* (59), *leoht . . . beorhtost* (64–65); *eadge* (90), *eadigra* (92), *eadgum* (97).

Although the Columbia editors are clearly right in rejecting Grein's reading and in accepting *healdaþ* as the verbal element of the third component of a compound predicate, their reading with *hi* as subject, "they . . . hold the sublime course," leaves unresolved the problem of the inadequacy of *hi* with its tenuous meaning to govern the elaborate compound predicate. They also leave a stylistic problem: of the six objects, five are singular; only one, *duguþe* is plural. The statement of the second problem leads directly to a possible solution, for *duguþe* may be either accusative or nominative plural, and it may mean either "blessings" or "legions" (in particular the heavenly hosts). If we adopt the latter meaning and take *duguþe* as nominative, *hi* may have anticipatory reference, common enough in Old English. The subject of the clause would then be *duguþe*, with *hi* being anticipatory; "they . . . the legions of the Prince," *hi . . . dryhtnes duguþe*, declare to the world the comeliness, glory and praise of God, work his word, and hold his course. The reading provides a satisfactory, balanced construction, with definite subject:

$$
\text{They: the hosts} \quad - \quad
\begin{cases}
\text{(a)} \quad \text{declare} \quad \left\{ \begin{matrix} \text{comeliness} \\ \text{glory} \end{matrix} \right\} : \text{praise} \\
\\
\text{(b)} \quad \text{work} \quad - \quad \text{word} \\
\\
\text{(c)} \quad \text{hold} \quad - \quad \text{course}
\end{cases}
$$

The period, so read, provides a variation on the theme of the heavens in their obedience declaring the glory of God. In the first clausule, 47–49, the phrase "glory of his works" (*his dæda þrym*, 49), is a portmanteau of key words of Psalm 18.1, "*The heavens declare the glory of God and the firmament shows the work of his hands,*" and "gleaming praise" (*lixende lof*, 50), clearly reflects the related verse from Job, "*The morning stars sang together, and all the sons of God rejoiced.*" The second and third clausules (50–52, 52–53) tell of the obedience which is the visible sign of the heaven's praise of God.

The only stumbling block to this reading is literalmindedness, for the explanation of the poet's apparently inexplicable shift in subject from "visible creations" to "heavenly hosts" is metapyhsical, not logical. What the literalist would see as an unexplained shift in subject, made utterly confusing by the anticipatory *hi,* a metaphor-minded audience would have seen as a natural association of ideas, cleverly suggested by *hi,* which looks back to "visible creations" lifting their praise, i.e., the heavens, and forward to "legions of the Prince." For the poet and his audience, the notion, derived from patristic exegesis, that the creations, i.e., heavens, which sing God's praise, symbolize the angels and saints, had the commonplace currency of the ordinary meaning of a word. In the beginning, God is surrounded by his eternal creations, the angels whose function it is to obey and to praise. In the creation in time, the visible creations, specifically the heavens, represent the creations of the eternal beginning; they stand for the angels (and later the saints) who praise God in obedience. *Hi,* then, has as its natural antecedant, "the visible creations praising God" (the heavens), but anticipates the subject, "legions of the Prince," which defines the meaning of the visible creations as symbols of the creation in the beginning, i.e., the angelic hosts praising God.

Once the true subject of the period under consideration is understood to be the angels, that is, the eternal reality represented by the heavens, the meaning of the interesting phrase, *in þam frumstole,* "in the first thrones" (51), is made clear. This compound also appears in the Old English *Consolation of Philosophy,* Metre 20, twice, 63 and 125, and in *Genesis* A, 963. In Metre 20, the word signifies the pristine positions of the four elements as God first ordained them; in *Genesis* A it signifies the original seats of Adam and Eve before the Fall, that is, Paradise. In *Creation,* the word seems to suggest both the original positions of the heavens in the creation in time, and in the eternal creation, the thrones of the angels before the fall of Satan. Because these thrones vacated by the angels who failed in their duty were to be filled by man if he remained obedient, mention of them in *Creation* has a special point.[19] The angels who resisted Satan retained their thrones; Adam and Eve in succumbing to him lost the thrones of Paradise and their claim on the vacated thrones of heaven; the saints, like the heavens which represent them, show the road home through the confession and praise of the Savior. Thus in their obedience the heavens reveal the journey back to the original creation, the thrones which are the end of man's pilgrimage.

Period 1 of paragraph iii, 47–53, in describing the praise of God by the heavenly hosts, returns to the theme derived from Psalm 18.1 in paragraph i. Period 2 of iii, 53–56, looks forward to paragraph iv, which tells of the journey of the sun, by describing the going forth of the *heofoncondelle,* 54, directed by the might of God who holds all creation in his bosom. "The whole of creation," *ealle gesceafta,* (56) would be heaven, earth, and seas, but, in fact only the *heofoncondelle,* and the "seas" (54), are mentioned. The translation of *heofon-*

19. See *Doctrine and Poetry,* 141–142.

condelle presents difficulties: is it the accusative singular, meaning "sun," as in *Andreas* 243? or accusative plural, meaning "sun and moon," as in *Christ* 608? or "stars," as Grein glosses it? (The only other meaning is figurative, *Exodus* 125, "pillar of fire.") The meaning "stars" is very possible, since the "hosts of the Prince" signify both angels and the stars that represent them, and this is probably the meaning to be given here to *heofoncondelle*, "candles of heaven," i.e., "stars." This meaning alone provides an explanation for the poet's mention of the waters and not the earth. As in the introductory paragraph of II, the poet again seems to be balancing the eternal creation and the creation in time. The former is suggested in period 1, of iii, which pictures the hosts of angels (or their symbolic semblance, the heavens) in obedience proclaiming God's glory in the thrones of heaven (or first sidereal positions). In period 2, lines 53–56, the creation in time but before the creation of the visible heavens is suggested by an echo of Genesis 1.6 (the second day), *"And God said, Let there be a firmament, and divided the waters which were under the firmament from the waters which were above the firmament, and it was so."* What was understood by the "firmament" is described in the Old English abridgement of Bede's *De natura rerum* as, "visible and corporeal, but yet we cannot ever see it because of its distant height. . . . It is all set with stars." [20] The poet's lines, "the candles of heaven/ his might sends forth, along with the seas," with no reference to the earth would seem to suggest this primeval aspect of the creation in time, for there was no earth then, only the firmament (with its stars), and the waters. The evocation of the second day further serves the poet's purpose of holding in suspension the two aspects of creation in that the "candles of heaven" participate in the visible creation, but the firmament in which they are set suggests the invisible heaven of eternity. Period 2 also serves a transitional function in a sequence involving universal time, from the creation *in principio* of iii, 1, through the primeval creation of iii, 2, to the temporal creation, typified by the journey of the sun, to be described in iv.

The climactic paragraph iv of III is introduced by a period, 57–59, in which the poet marks the transition to the time of man in the universal calendar of creation. He suggests this transition by designating God as "judge," and as the one "who created life for us." The epithet, "Judge," has clear relevance to man's estate, and the second designation of God makes specific mention for the first time in the poem of God's creation of human life. At the same time, the poet recapitulates the theme of the eternal creation in declaring that the "everlasting glory abides" in God, a phrase which recalls paragraph iii, which describes the angels obeying "The length of time . . . the eternal word." This brief introductory period, 1, introduces the major motif of paragraph iv, 59–75, the journey of the sun.

The sun, as the chief planet, is a perfectly natural choice to typify the

20. *Anglo-Saxon Manual of Astronomy*, in *Popular Treatises on Science Written during the Middle Ages,* ed. T. Wright (London, 1841), 1.

symbolic movement of the heavens, but it is more than possible that the poet's choice was governed by Psalm 18, for there, in verses 5 and 6, the sun is given special prominence. In the Old English translation the verses read:

> 5. *Drihten timbrede his tempel on þære sunnan; seo sunne arist swiðe ær on morgen up; swa swa brydguma of his brydbure.*
> 6. *And heo yrnð swa egeslice on hyre weg swa swa gigant yrnð on his weg; heo stið oð þæs heofenes heahnesse and þanon astihð, and swa yrnð ymbutan oð heo eft þyder cymð; ne mæg hine nan man behydan wið hire hæto.*

> (God built his temple in the sun; the sun arises very early in the morning, like a bridegroom from the bridal chamber.
> And it runs as terribly on its way as a giant runs on his way; it climbs to the height of heaven and from there descends, and so revolves until it returns again; nor may any man hide himself from its heat.) [21]

As in the Psalm, the description in the poem divides the journey of the sun into its rising at dawn, its ascent, and descent, contained respectively in periods 2, 3, and 4 which make up the body of the verse paragraph (introduced by period 1, 57–59): 2, 59–63; 3, 64–67; 4, 68–75.

Only in the description of the descent of the sun is any difficulty encountered. There the meaning of *on heape*, "in company," 69, is unclear, and the translation of *glom oþer cigð* as "the second darkness calls," 71, is given as doubtful by Bosworth-Toller, and requires support. The problem in Bosworth-Toller's questioned gloss is that *oþer* regularly precedes the noun it modifies, and that the poet had at his disposal *æfenglom*, and *nihtglom, Guthlac*, 1265, 916, as well as *mistglom, Waldere*, 47, to provide the metaphoric meaning Bosworth-Toller suggest, "the twilight of evening, the first being that of morning" (*s.v. glom*). Some better reason than the absence of an acceptable alternative gloss, or the need for the head stave to alliterate in *g* must be found for the poet's special emphasis on *glom*, the only attested uncompounded form of the word, and on *oþer*, with its unusual position following the noun. The explanation from *glom oþer* rests in the poet's balancing of the two aspects of creation, the eternal and the temporal, the second being an image of the first. In the poem, the sun begins its journey from the glory of God, (iv, 1) the eternal light of his praise (*lixende lof*, paragraph iii); in eternity, that is, the sun begins his journey at the beginning of time, the time *when darkness was upon the face of the deep*, "before" God said *Let there be light* 1.3, as Bede explains in his commentary on the verse:

> If, however, it is asked in which places by God's command light might be made where before this the abyss covered all the fullness of the earth, it is revealed, truly, that in the supernal parts of this same earth, which now the daily light of the sun is accustomed to brighten, the original light then shone forth.[22]

21. *The West-Saxon Psalms*, ed. J. Bright (Boston, 1907), 39.
22. Bede, *PL*, 91, 17. The relevance of Bede's commentary to the description in the poem is enforced by lines 59–61, "And this light brightness/ comes every morning over the

The first darkness would thus be that of "the beginning"; the second darkness, *glom oþer*, would be that of the end of time.

The same balancing of the two aspects of creation also explains *on heape*. In paragraph iii, 47–56, God is shown surrounded by the angels; his might sends forth the *heofoncondelle*, i.e., the (morning) stars representative of the angels. Paragraph iv begins (period 1, 57–59) with the mention of the abiding glory of God. The journey of the sun is introduced in the second period of paragraph iv abruptly, "And this light brightness comes every morning," 59, the "this" suggesting that the subject has been anticipated in the preceding period, which overtly is not so. The effect is to connect the sun, "this brightness," with the "glory of God," the immediate antecedant of "this," and thus to suggest that the sun represents its Creator, the source of light from which it springs. In its daily journey the sun appears in the company of the morning stars and leaves in the company of the evening stars, i.e., *on heape*, "in company," but this daily journey is representative of the journey within eternity, where the sun begins out of the eternal light, surrounded by the angels, and continues until the final, the second dusk, when the journey of time will cease, and the sun return to its source (*æspring*, 77) which is beyond all human knowing. Both *glom oþer* and *on heape* serve effectively to suggest the special significance of the journey to the second darkness. In addition, *on heape* recalls and elaborates the metaphorical chain, *in þam þreatum* (41), *dryhtnes duguþe* (48), *heofoncondelle* (54).[23]

The journey of the sun has obvious symbolic implications for the "voyager" preparing for his pilgrimage. The sun leaves the morning stars and descends "in company," i.e., among the evening stars. The symbolic meaning involved is suggested in Bede's commentary on Genesis 1.2:

> The morning stars are plainly the same angels [of Job 38] who are named the sons of God in distinction, truly, to the saints who were created later, and after their confession of divine praise, like the evening stars, through death of the flesh did descend.[24]

Allegorically, then, the sun moving from the stars of the morning and descending with the stars of the evening reflects spiritual history. The morning stars are

---

misty darkness/ traversing the waters." "Misty darkness" and "waters" seem echoic, in the context, of the verse which Bede explains. The translation of *misthleoðu* as "misty darkness" derives from L. Schücking's entirely convincing demonstration of its meaning as "Schatten-hüllen der Nacht, die über Erde und Meer liegen," in *Untersuchungen Zur Bedeutungslehre der Angelsächsischen Dichtersprache* (Heidelberg, 1915), 59. He corrects the glosses given by Grein and Bosworth-Toller, "misty hill." Schücking's gloss is accepted by F. Holthausen, *Altenglisches Etymologisches Wörterbuch* (Heidelberg, 1934), *s. v. hlip.*

23. *Glom oþer cigþ/ niht æfter cymþ* is parenthetical, and is set in dashes in the translation. The explanation of *on heape* makes unnecessary emendation to *on heahþe*, "on high," (Cosijn, also Supplement to Grein), or Bosworth Toller's translation as giving to *gewiteþ* the force of "accompany."

24. See note 16.

with God fixed in eternity, except the day-star, Lucifer, who fell into darkness; the sun makes the descent from the morning stars to the dark of the evening stars, but only so that it may rise again. Man instead of ascending to the light of the morning stars descended from God's "embrace" (56) into the "world's embrace" (75) and the "dark mist" (79), but man may follow the sun in the death of the flesh to join those "living in the land" who "may in the light find enjoyment after it journeys over the edge" (80–81); that is, may live in the imitation of the Son of God.

The sun as a symbol for Christ is pervasive; it is as inevitable and insistent as the word play forced by linguistic chance, sun-son. Thus in the Old English abridgement of Bede's *De natura rerum*, the writer interrupts his simple, straightforward description of the sun to make clear its symbolism, "Truly the sun goes between heaven and earth, at day above the earth, at night below . . . . The sun betokens our Savior Christ, as the prophet declared. . . . None of us has the light of any goodness except of Christ's gift, who is called the sun of true justice." [25] The poet enforces the inherent symbolism of the sun first by suggesting the connection of the sun with the glory of God, and of its diurnal journey with the great movement of the creation *in principio*, second by suggesting an association with Psalm 18, where it is possible the poet may have derived his idea for the central motif of the sun's journey. Cassiodorus, commenting on the pertinent verses of Psalm 18, in fact, supplies a background for some of the poet's lines.[26] As the poet describes the sun sent forth by "the might" of God who holds "in his embrace the whole of creation," so in Cassiodorus, God "embraces all widely, not from part, but entering entirely in the plenitude of his majesty." The sun, for Cassiodorus, represents Christ, and its light signifies, "that he who has the most pure eye of the heart can bear and perceive the brightness of the sacrament [i.e., Christ's incarnation]"; similarly the poet, "And all may delight in it/ to whom the true King of triumphs has willed/ to give sight of eyes to see it on earth" (65–67). The effectiveness of the poet's description of the journey of the sun is a factor of its plenitude of meanings.

Paragraph v, 76–81, is introduced by the logical connective, "therefore," and in it the littleness of man's knowledge is deduced from his ignorance of the source and destination of the sun, which for man journeys from the unknown to the unknown. The paragraph thus reiterates the theme of humility of I, iii, and in addition develops further the symbolic motif of the journey. The ascent of the sun from the darkness speaks to the voyager of the source (*æspringe*), God, where the journey has its beginning and its end. Those who enjoy the sun when it is gone from the earth can only be the stars of evening and morning who live in the eternal day of God's heaven, where according to the Old English

25. *Anglo-Saxon Manual of Astronomy*, 3–4.
26. Cassiodorus, *CCSL*, 97, p. 169.

De natura rerum, "there is no night, but eternal light without darkness." [27]

In paragraph vi, 82–97, the poet returns to the theme of the creation in its two aspects of eternity and time, all contained in the timeless will of God, a return marked by the repetition of the opening line, 43, of II, ii.[28] The paragraph contains two periods, 1, 82–89, 2, 90–97. Clausule a of the first period, 82–85, describes the creation in time, and again reflects the Boethian conception of the harmony of contraries, "day and night, deep and high, etc." [29] It also reflects patristic interpretation, as, for example, Bede's commentary on Genesis 1.14, "With comely enough order the world from materials of the unformed proceeded to harmonious form. . . . In the first day of this time he made light, which gave the remaining creatures abilities of perceiving. On the second, the firmament of heaven, that is, above the portion of this world, he made solid in the middle of the waters. On the third, in the lower portions he set apart sea and lands in their boundaries; the air in its places spread, the water having retired." [30]

In clausule b of period 1, 86–89, by a bold application of the journey motif, the poet turns from the creation in time to the creation in eternity, heaven, the goal of man's journey. "Earth," the poet says, 88–89, "may be lifted high in the power of his majesty;" that is, temporal creation will return to its beginnings. The journey home of creation suggests symbolically the goal of man's journey, and this goal is suggested in period 2 of vi, 90–97, through a description of the heavenly home as the abode of both angels and saints. The description makes significant, thematic parallels with earlier ones: the inhabitants of heaven see God face to face (93–94), as men on earth see the sun, the emblem of God (65–67); in heaven they see God "with no dark gloom" (95), for with the sun they have escaped the "dark mist" (79), into which men on earth see the sun disappear.

27. *Anglo-Saxon Manual of Astronomy*, 5, "Soðlice on þam heofenlicum eðele nis nan niht gehæfd, ac þær is singal leoht buton ælcum þystrum."

28. The repeated line is given additional force by the poet's employment of the uniquely attested verb, *teofonian*, in explaining which Bosworth-Toller refer to Boethius, and which Grein relates to *teofrian*, uniquely attested in Psalm 117, 21, *he has appointed it to be the support of the wall.* Whatever the poet's source for *teofonian*, the word is unusual, and gives the force of the unexpected to the repeated lines which introduce the picture of God's ordering of Creation.

29. The translation of line 85a, involves the emendation of the *flod wiþ flode* to *folde wiþ flode*, as required by the contrastive context; the scribal error involved would be a simple one of anticipatory metathesis. This emendation seems simpler than that suggested by Strunk (*MLN*, 18, 73) of *flode* to *foldan*.

30. Bede, *PL*, 91, 21.

Part III, Exhortation

That man must remember his duty of obedience to God is the lesson of the heavens summarized briefly at the end of the poem, 98–102. The conclusion is a response which is given the form of a deduction by the use of the introductory "Therefore," but the obedience enjoined upon man is defined metaphorically as a journey of two aspects—toward heaven and away from the world. The conclusion thus phrased is complex. As deduction it serves the function of conclusion to the premises established in I and II. As metaphor it serves to conclude the underlying journey metaphor. As response it serves to conclude the framework of dialectic which starts with the questioning enjoined upon the voyager at the beginning of the poem. The conclusion is carefully constructed, with the two aspects of man's journey developed in a pattern of contrastive repetition:

$$\text{Leave} \left\{ \text{idle desires} \right. \qquad \text{aspire/draw} \left\{ \begin{array}{l} \text{to the delight of redemption} \\ \text{to the good kingdom} \end{array} \right.$$

The theme of the poem, then, is creation as it reveals man's duty of humble and thankful obedience to the Creator. This theme, which is based on a nexus of ideas derived from the Genesis account of creation, and from Psalm 18, is developed deductively in the figure of question and response, and through the metaphor of the journey. Thus in I, i the reader is addressed as a "wayfarer" preparing to embark; he is told to enquire of a seer the meaning of the heavens which stir life, and in I, ii the response is defined as that provided by the prophet-poets, whose life of contemplation is, therefore, good. In I, iii, the "wayfarer" is again enjoined to learn, but in humility, recognizing the gulf between man's wisdom and God's, and recognizing that the end of man's search is the discovery of the road that leads to the eternal home to which man may come through obedience and by the grace of God.

Part II provides the response to the enquiry. Man can find his way by observing the nature of God's creation. II, i begins with the formula of exhortation of I, and a text, introduced by *Hwæt*. The text, anticipated in I, i, consists of a paraphrase, with modifications, of the opening of Genesis, and of Psalm 18.1, announcing creation in two aspects, eternal and temporal. The text is developed in five paragraphs, ii–vi, with ii, v, vi introduced by the connective *Forþon*, "Therefore," and with the first lines of ii and vi repeated so as to form a rhetorical frame for the paragraphs concerned with the journey of the sun. Paragraphs iii and iv declare the glory of God's creation, while paragraph v reveals man's insignificance. This contrast between God's might and man's insignificance thus reiterates a theme introduced in I. II, iii shows how all parts of creation are obedient to God, and vi, period 1, 82–89, shows that God's glory is revealed through the obedient accord of contraries in creation. Obedience to God and his glory are illustrated in the description, iii and iv, of the mysterious journey of the sun, which leaves the light man sees as darkness, brings light, and then returns to the light which man continues to see as darkness. In v the deduction is made from the mystery of the sun's journey that whatever understanding man has is due to the grace of God, not to his own power, since to understand the nature of reality man must comprehend what he does not understand. Finally, period 1 of vi in suggesting that the accord of the *visibilia* represents the eternal accord of creation in the beginning leads to period 2 in which the accord of heaven where the blessed dwell is described. This final picture of the blessed in heaven, through their obedience sharing God's glory, marks a return to the theme of II, i, the heavens praising God, an emblem of the reality pictured in vi.

This rhetorical structure of return echoes the most developed motif of the poem, the journey of the sun from the mystery of the morning stars, the angels, praising God in the beginning, and back to the mystery of the second darkness— the end of time—when only the eternity of heaven will exist, this and the place of eternal darkness, the negative inversion of heaven.

Part III, also introduced by *Therefore*, states the conclusion briefly. From the enquiry enjoined in Part I, and the responsive demonstration given in II, it follows that the voyager should journey toward the eternal home, by leaving behind in his journey those things which bind him to the earth.

Rhetorical Devices

Certain of the poet's rhetorical devices are intricate and cut across divisions of the poem. Because they serve a thematic function, it has seemed best to study them after the structure of the poem has been set forth. The most obvious of these devices is the repeated use of the introductory connective, *Therefore*, 17, 43, 76, 82, 98. This repetition establishes a framework of logical deduction marking the thematic contrast between the two understandings, God's and man's. The repetition, which appears in all the divisions of the poem, serves a unifying function.

The paragraphs introduced by *Therefore* are both repetitive and contrastive. Three of these paragraphs deal with man, specifically, the embarking wayfarer. These three paragraphs are linked by a pattern of echoic introductory clauses:

1. (17) *Forþon scyle ascian   se þe on elne leofaþ*
2. (76) *Forþon nænig fira   þaes frod leofaþ*
3. (98) *Forþon scyle mon gehycgan   þaet he meotude hyre*

This pattern points up the fact that the paragraphs form a logical chain, that they are steps, as it were, in a sorites. This logical structure may be demonstrated in a schematic paraphrase, where the premises (indicated in parentheses) consist of material given earlier in the poem, and the conclusions (italicized) of the gist of the three paragraphs introduced by the echoic introductory clause.

(1–16)   (Men who lived wisely were prophets.
The prophets made enquiry into creation.)

(17–22)   *Therefore, the man who lives wisely makes enquiry into creation.*

(23–75)   (Enquiry into creation is to be made in the knowledge of man's inadequacy to grasp its mystery).

(76–81)   *Therefore, the man who lives wisely will make enquiry into creation in the knowledge of his inadequacy to grasp its mystery.*

(1–97)   (Proper enquiry into creation reveals that obedience to God is the right way of enquiry).

(98–102)   *Therefore the man who lives wisely knows that he should be obedient to God.*

Against this sequential chain of logical deduction is balanced the two paragraphs (43–46, 82–97) which declare the consequences that follow, *forþon*, from the omniscience of God, *se þe teala cuþe*. As the first group of deductive paragraphs is sequential, this pair is anticipatory, introducing a description of creation which follows from the nature of God. In effect, the structure of enquiry and response is reflected in the contrast between the two types of deductive statements introduced by *Therefore:* the logical-sequential chain has to do with man's enquiry; the anticipatory pair provides the response to the enquiry. This anticipatory pair frame and are related to the two paragraphs, II, iii, iv, introduced by *Swa*, which also serve a demonstrative, rather than a deductive function.

Parts I and II are linked by the second rhetorical pattern, that of repetitive variation of the hortatory introduction:

> *Wilt þu . . . fricgan*   1–3
> *Leorna þas lare*   23
> *Gehyr nu þis herespel*   37

The hortatory and deductive patterns interlock. Most obviously the first deductive passage follows from the first hortatory passage; in I, i the voyager is told to enquire, with the example being given him of one who "in wisdom holds the world fully/ in his mind's grasp" (9–10). The deduction made from the hortatory paragraph i in paragraph ii is that the voyager must "fully consider" (20), in order to complete "wisely his earthly way" (22).

This last phrase about the "earthly way" of the deductive paragraph ii provides a link with the hortatory paragraph iii, where it is echoed in "from hence to the heavenly kingdom we may ascend" (34–35). The linking of the three paragraphs has the effect of interlocking the theme of contemplation of i and ii with the journey motif of ii and iii. This interlocking leads to the conclusion expressed at the end of iii that through right contemplation the route of the pilgrimage may be found.

Linkage between I and II is effected by the use of the hortatory motif of I in the introduction to II; by the use of "Therefore" to introduce I, ii and II, ii, v, vi; finally by the echo in the first line of II, ii and vi, *se þe teala cuþe* (43, 82) of a key phrase in I, ii, *þencan forþ teala* (20). More is involved in the echo than a superficial unifying rhetorical pattern. The linkage is functional to the development of the theme of the poem: man may know completely (*teala*) only to that degree permitted by God's grace; man's knowledge is complete only in his understanding of his need to be obedient to God, who alone truly knows completely, the point made in the second exhortation, I, iii. The repetition of *teala* is contrastive, measuring the gulf between God's understanding and man's. This contrast, in turn, provides the link between the three "sequential" paragraphs which are concerned with man's enquiry: I, ii; II, v; III, each brief and comprising only one period. As I, ii reveals that the life of contemplation is good if man is to complete "wisely this earthly way;" II, v shows that man's intellectual powers are limited since he cannot know the source (*æspringe*) to which the sun repairs in its journey; in III the conclusion is reached that man must keep in mind obedience to God so that he may take the right journey which leads to the source of light. The logical chain has as its conclusion that right enquiry leads to salvation:

> Right enquiry leads to humility
> Humility leads to obedience
> [∴Right enquiry leads to obedience]
> Obedience leads to salvation
> ∴Right enquiry leads to salvation

Part III serves not only as the conclusion of a sorites and response to the initial enquiry, but also as the end of the metaphoric journey sequence, which began with the image of the reader as one setting out on a journey, enjoined to enquire of the wise wanderer. The wanderer is one who understands what the prophets have told of the significance of the heavens, as in turn the heavens thus understood reveal that they symbolize those who have searched rightly, in humility, and found the path of praise and obedience. This right path is symbolized in the journey of the sun from its obedient beginning among the stars praising the Light, and its return to the Light. Here is man's journey; here is how he "draws to the good kingdom."

Diction

Finally, the poet's selection of words to support and adorn the structure of the poem may be illustrated by a brief review of his handling of two word clusters, centering on the referents "God" and "Creation," respectively, and of his handling of the image of light in the central description of the journey of the sun.

The poet refers to God twenty-five times, using twelve distinct bases, singly or in composition, and thirteen repetitions or variants. These statistics suggest a resourceful, but not strikingly unusual, handling of repetitive variation. From only one base, —*cyning*, does the poet derive any considerable store of variants (five). On the other hand, he does not range very far in finding alternative epithets for God, ignoring as he does such obvious epithets as *Wealdend*, *Ealdor*, *Hlaford*, *Brytta*, *Brega*, *Hælend*, to give only those which come first to mind. He would appear then to have selected his epithets for God with an eye to their place in the patterned structure of the poem. (It may be noted that the translation attempts carefully to reflect the poet's variant epithets for God.)

Of the twelve bases, four are used only once: *fæder* (*fæder ælmihtig*), "Father Almighty" (38); *steora*, "Steersman" (45); *agend*, (*lifes agend*), "Holder of life" (55); *dema* (*ealra demena þam gedefestan*), "Of all judges the kindest" (58). The first of these singly occurring epithets, *fæder ælmihtig*, which in the paraphrase of Genesis 2.1 in II, i replaces the simple God of the original, reflects patristic exegesis. The remaining three single epithets also appear in II. *Steora* is the only uncommon form, being found in poetry only here and in the *Metres of Boethius*. The word functions in II, ii to evoke the Boethian concept of the order and concord of creation, as well as to provide a reminder of the key metaphor of the journey. In II, iii *lifes agend*, "Holder of life," in relating God to his temporal creation, life, stands in contrast to *heofenes weard*, "Keeper of heaven" (52), which relates God to the eternal creation, heaven. The poet's selection in II, iv of the last of the singly occurring epithets, *ealra demena þam gedefestan*, completes this same chain by invoking the aspect of God at the Day of Judgment, when life ends and all returns to its eternal beginning.

There are four words and one designating clause which appear twice: *meotud*, *weard*, *þeoden*, *dryhten*, *se þe teala cuþe*. The structural function of the repeated clause as rhetorical frame and contrastive link has already received sufficient attention. The repetition of *meotud* in *meotudes mægensped*, "the Creator's majesty" (24), and *þæt he meotude hyre*, "to serve his Creator" (98), has an important structural function. It is the final epithet for God employed in the poem as it is the first metaphoric epithet employed, the only reference to God preceding it being the plain *god* in *þurh dom godes* (6). The first use of *meotud* occurs in the paragraph of direct address, I, iii, which ends with the adjuration to give thanks to the Creator for the grace which will grant ascent to heaven; the last use occurs in the conclusion when the reader is exhorted to obey the Creator and aspire to heaven. Thus the repetition of *meotud* serves to link the first thematic declaration, spoken by the *persona* of the poet (23–24), with the conclusion. The repetition of *þeoden*, "Lord" (31, 41), also serves as a linking device: in I, iii the reader is admonished to give thanks to "the great Lord," *þeodne mærum;* in II, i, the paraphrase of Psalm 18.1, the stars give their thanks "through the Lord's hand," *þurh þeodnes hond.* Similarly the repetition of *weard* (39, 52) serves to link II, i and iii, *hordes weard* (39), signifying God in the beginning, anticipates *heofenes weard,* "heaven's Keeper (52), which has the same significance as part of a chain of metaphors which define God as Creator of eternity and of time. The repetition of *dryhten,* "Prince" (58, 73), provides a frame of reference for the central description of II, iii and iv; at the beginning of the description (48) "the legions of the Prince" are described as obedient to him; at the end (73) the sun is described as obediently keeping the "unalterable decree/ of the holy Prince."

Two words are each repeated three times in the poem; the metaphoric *frea,* "Master" (29, 50, 51); and the plain *god* (6, 30, 74). *Frea* (I, iii 29), signifies God's omnipotence in the context of man's inability to perceive anything beyond what the Master permits. In II, iii the poet repeats the word in ensuing lines (50, 51) employing polyptoton. Here too in context the epithet signifies God's omnipotence: the heavenly hosts "steadfastly work the Master's eternal word/ in the first thrones which the Master fashioned," *frean ece word . . . þe him frea sette.* The plain God appears always in the possessive, governing a variant of the base meaning decree or design: *dom godes,* "the destiny of God" (6); *godes agen bibod,* "God's very law" (30); *gesceaft godes,* "God's plan" (74). The repetition of *godes* as part of a phrase signifying "God's design" under-scores the motif of the providential ordering of God's creation, which finds its central illustration in the symbolic description of the journey of the sun. In addition, the repetition of *godes,* and the repetition of *frea* are interlaced in the most extended pattern of repeated epithets for God, the variants on the base, *cyning,* "King."

This base is found five times in the poem: *eca cyning,* "eternal king" (32); *heofoncyninges,* "King of heaven" (36); *sigora soðcyning,* "true King of triumphs" (67); *hyra sylfra cyning,* "their very King" (93); *wuldres cyning,* "King of Glory" (95). Although in each variant the metaphoric epithet signifies God as the King of heaven, the chain of linked epithets forms part of an inter-locking design. In order to demonstrate this design it is necessary to analyze in context the elaborate rhetorical structure of the passages where the variants on *cyning* appear.

As noted, the only reference to God in the first two paragraphs of the poem (I, i and ii) is in the phrase, "God's decree" (6). Since the structural fiction of enquiry governs this portion of the poem, and the enquiry leads to God, the absence of reference is appropriate. But in I, iii the poet first gives his theme directly—a theme involving repeated reference to God, and here, in contrast to the one epithet for God in i and ii (1–22), iii (23–36) contains six. In iii, period 1, 23–26, the poet contents himself with a simple statement that he will tell of the "Creator's majesty," but in period 2, 27–36, he develops an intricate pattern of direct repetition, polyptoton, and variation, in which the epithet, *cyning*, plays a strategic role.

Period 1 is linked to period 2 by chiastic repetition, *in hreþre mæge—mæge in hreþre* (25–28); furthermore, the rhetorical question, which summarizes period 1, "Is your might sufficient?" sets the question to which period 2 provides the rhetorical response. Period 2 comprises two clausules, a, 27–30, b, 31–36. They both have the same subject reference, "man," but in grammatical variation, *he* in a, *we* in b. Both begin with a head clause upon which the rest of the clausule depends. The head clause in a is simple (27), but is completed by a complex *þæt* clause as object (28–30):

> Nis þæt monnes gemet   moldhrerendra
> þæt he mæge in hreþre   his heah geweorc
> furþor aspyrgan. . . .

The head clause of b is complex (31–33) and is completed by a complex *þæt* clause as object (34–36):

> ac we sculon þoncian   þeodne mærum
> awa to ealdre,   þæs þe us se eca cyning
> on gæste wlite   forgiefan wille
> þæt we eaðe magon   upcund rice
> forð gestigan. . . .

The objective *þæt* clauses of a and b are balanced, with polyptoton of the main verbs (*mæge-magon*) and with grammatical parallelism of objects, both being infinitive phrases with identical word order (*his heah geweorc/ furþor aspyrgan —upcunde rice/ forð gestigan*). The parallelism of structure is completed by verbal parallelism. *Heah geweorc* and *upcunde rice* have the same referent, "heaven." *Aspyrgan*, literally "to follow a track," and *gestigan*, "to ascend to," are verbs of motion toward something; in context both have metaphorical meanings, the former of an interior search, the latter of a spiritual striving. Finally, even the adverbs, *furþor—forþ*, are echoic.

Both *þæt* clauses are grammatically completed by dependent clauses (29–30, 35–36), which though grammatically secondary carry primary meaning:

> þonne him frea sylle
> to ongietanne   godes agen bibod;
> gif us on ferðe geneah
> ond we willað healdan   heofoncyninges bibod.

Each is given special emphasis by ending in the key word, *bibod*, "law," but despite this parrallelism and the prevailing balance of the two clausules, these final dependent clauses, ending in *bibod* are not parallel. The final clause of a is comparative, and is introduced by *þonne*; that of b is a conditional clause introduced by *gif*. Further, the idea of God's giving of the former clause is replaced in the latter by the idea of man's obedience to God's law.

However, the concept of God's giving, expressed by *sylle* in the *þonne* clause of a is found in the head clause of b, expressed in an auxiliary construction (33), with variation of subject:

> *þonne him frea sylle . . .*
> *þæs se eca cyning . . . forgiefan wille.*

The displacement of pattern is deliberately designed so that the two clausules end with *bibod*.

In the rhetorical structure of the period, the pattern of epithets for God plays an important role. To begin, the variation in the key phrases, *godes agen bibod—heofoncyninges bibod*, is significant. The use of the plain *god* is entirely appropriate to the subject of clausule a, the limitation of man's understanding, particularly because the unadorned epithet is given special force in context by the immediately preceding epithet for God, *frea*, "Master," the subject of *sylle*, which here as elsewhere in the poem suggests God's power and dominion. In clausule b, where the subject is God's promised reward for obedience, *heofoncyning* is equally appropriate as suggesting God's role as king of the promised heaven. This significance has been prepared for by the context of the earlier epithets for God in b, *þeodne* and *eca cyning*; the former is used in the context of thanksgiving, related here to thanksgiving for the promised reward; *eca cyning*, with its adjectival reference to eternity also suggests heaven, and in addition it is directly related to *heofoncyninges* by polyptoton (nominative—genitive). Considerable weight is given to clausule b by this close repetition of *cyning*.

This emphasis is important thematically because it is here that the goal of man's journey is first indicated, but it is also important structurally, for the poet makes further significant use of the base epithet *cyning*. Thus in the description of the rising and ascendancy of the sun, II, iv, periods 2 and 3 (59–67), the only reference to God appears at the very end (67), *sigora soðcyning*, "true King of triumphs," an elaborate compositional phrase with *cyning* as its base. The context is again God's giving, here of sight, which in its symbolic significance is to be equated with the gift of understanding elaborately described in I, iii, 2.

The final use of *cyning* is in period 2 of II, vi (93, 95), where close repetition of the base epithet is again employed. As before the context is God's giving, here of the sight of Him to the blessed in heaven:

> *Hy geseoþ symle   hyra sylfra cyning*
> *eagum on wlitaþ*

> They see their very King, and with sight of eyes
> gaze on him forever

> *Nis him wihte won   þam þe wuldres cyning*
> *geseoþ in swegle*

> With no dark gloom the King of glory
> they see in heaven

This final repetition of *cyning* serves to complete a sequence: I, iii, 2, man is given understanding by the King so that he may know his commands; II, iv, 3, man is given the sight of the sun by the King so that through its journey he may recognize his own journey home; finally, II, vi, the King grants that the obedient may join the blessed who see him face to face.

The binding force of the poet's employment of *cyning* is underscored because this is the only base epithet so developed, the only one which twice appears in close repetition, these close repetitions (I, iii, II, vi) framing the single yet centrally important use of the epithet in the description of the journey of the sun (II, iv). It is additionally significant that the only other epithets which appear more than twice, *god* and *frea*, are employed in the cross pattern of the poet's first use of *cyning*, with *frea* the only other epithet used in close repetition involving polyptoton.

In considering the second word cluster, that involving Creation, it is important to recall that the poet distinguishes two aspects of creation, the invisible and the visible. This is reflected in his use of *gesceaft* as a base upon which variants are made to emphasize the dual connotations involved:

visible $\begin{cases} \textit{forþgesceaft,} \text{ "first creation" (3)} \\ \textit{dygelra gesceafta,} \text{ "of the secret creations" (18)} \end{cases}$

invisible $\begin{cases} \textit{sidra gesceafta,} \text{ "of the spacious creations" (4)} \\ \textit{sweotule gesceafte,} \text{ "visible creations" (40)} \end{cases}$

The other two appearances of the word *gesceaft* are in II, iv, the journey of the sun; *Ealle gesceafta*, "whole of creation" (56), is, in effect, combinative, including in its meaning both the visible and invisible creations. In the phrase *in gesceaft godes*, "in God's design" (74), the poet uniquely varies the meaning of the word, it here having the connotation of God's decree itself, not the result of that decree. This final use of *gesceaft* establishes the identity of God's will and the actualization of that will.

On the other hand, the series of words beginning with and semantically related to *heah geweorc* (28) tend to have only the connotation of the invisible and eternal creation: *upcund rice* (34), *in þam frumstole* (51), *sellan rice* (102). Against this series is balanced, however, one use of *geweorc* in the plural (86), thus having reference to the visible creation, but in a context which makes clear that the visible "works" are symbolic of the invisible *heah geweorc*. "His works do not weaken," the poet says; that is, they symbolize eternity, a point boldly enforced by the poet, who continues, "They stand steadfast/ . . . in the power of his majesty/ through which heaven and earth may be lifted high" (87–89). The return of temporal things to the beginning out of time, to their *telos* in God's will, symbolizes the journey to eternity, which for man is the reason of Creation.

Finally, the poet's masterful handling of the image of light in the description of the journey of the sun may be noted briefly. That journey has its source (47–57) in the beginning, before time, in the eternal light of "gleaming praise," *lixende lof* (49), rendered by the eternal creatures in the thrones fashioned by "heaven's resplendent Keeper," *hluttor heofones weard* (52), who sends forth the candles of heaven, *heofoncondelle* (54). The description of the journey of the sun is introduced by a brief period proclaiming God's perdurable glory, *wuldor* (57). The description of the actual journey begins abruptly in the second period, *ond þis leohte beorht*, "and this light brightness" (59), with "this" connecting *leohte beorht* and *wuldor*, which is its source and the reality which it represents. When the sun departs to return to its source (*æspringe*, 77), it *gewiteð þonne mid þy wuldre*, "makes its glorious way" (68). The repetition of *wuldor* in polyptoton (*wuldor-wuldre*) provides a significant frame for the journey. A frame is also provided by the intricate inverted repetition, *leohte beorht* (59)—*leoht . . . bronda beorhtost*, 64–65:

> *leohte* (adjective modifying) *beorht* (noun, subject)
> *beorhtost* (superlative, adjectival component of phrase modifying) *leoht* (noun, object)

In the final period of II, iv, the sun is designated as *forðmære tungol*, "sublime globe" (69), *heofontorht swegl*, "heaven's bright planet" (73), *farende tungol*, "wayfaring globe" (75). The repetition of *tungol* serves to frame the final period, which tells of the descent of the sun. In the next paragraph (II, v) the journey of the sun is followed into the darkness with the declaration that men cannot know where the *goldtorht sunne*, "golden sun" (78), goes (cf. *heofontorht swegl*, 73) or who *þæs leohtes . . . brucan mote*, "in the light/ may then rejoice" (80–81, cf. *brucan mot*, 65, *leoht*, 59, 64). Here, for the first time all the various metaphors are given their actual referent, *sunne* "the sun" (78). The poet has managed a remarkable example of suspended construction.

In contrast to his very sparing use of variant epithets for God, the poet rings the changes on the metaphors for sun, the bearer of light. Through his elaborate development of the image of light the poet gives his description of the journey of the sun a rhetorical prominence which its central position demands. He invests the journey with symbolic force through elaborate description, which suggests the mystery of the sun's journey, from its beginning to its end. This sense of mystery is heightened by the poet's device of suspending actual identification of the referent of the metaphoric excursus until the sun has actually departed into darkness, its diurnal journey complete, its mystery noted.

II. the dream of the rood

gesyhþ rodes

I

 i Hwæt! Ic swefna cyst secgan wylle
 hwæt me gemætte to midre nihte
 syðþan reordberend reste wunedon.

 ii Þuhte me þæt ic gesawe syllicre treow
5 on lyft lædan leohte bewunden
 beama beorhtost; eall þæt beacen wæs
 begoten mid golde; gimmas stodon
fægere æt foldan sceatum, swylce þær fife wæron
uppe on þam eaxlegespanne. Beheoldon þær engeldryhte
10 fægere þurh forðgesceaft —ne wæs ðær huru fracodes gealga;
 ac hine þær beheoldon halige gastas
 men ofer moldan ond eall þeos mære gesceaft.
 Syllic wæs se sigebeam, ond ic synnum fah
 forwunded mid wommum.

 iii   Geseah ic wuldres treow
15 wædum geweorðode wynnum scinan
 gegyred mid golde, gimmas hæfdon
 bewrigene weorðlice wealdes treow.
 Hwæðre ic þurh þæt gold ongytan meahte
 earmra ærgewin þæt hit ærest ongan
20 swætan on þa swiðran healfe. Eall ic wæs mid sorgum gedrefed,
forht ic wæs for þære fægran gesyhðe.

 iv   Geseah ic þæt fuse beacen
wendan wædum ond bleom; hwilum hit wæs mid wætan bestemed
beswyled mid swates gange, hwilum mid since gegyrwed.

I

i Give heed! I will reveal   the extraordinary vision
which came to me   at midmost night
when speaking men   remained asleep.

ii   It seemed to me I saw   the seemliest of trees
lifted in the sky   enveloped in light
the brightest of beams;   all of the beacon
was covered with gold;   jewels gleamed
fair at the corners of earth,   and there were five more jewels
on high at the center crossing.   Created fair in the beginning
the angelic host gazed upon it   —but not upon a gallows vile;
these too gazed upon it   the godly saints
men in the world   and all creation's wonder.
The victory tree was lovely, but I was stained with villainies
wounded by sins.

iii   I saw heaven's tree
robed in purple   joyfully radiant
sheathed in gold,   shining jewels
worthily covered   the woodland tree.
Yet through the golden gleam   I glimpsed the ancient
malice of foes   when the cross first
began to bleed from the right side.   I was utterly overwhelmed with
        sorrow,
I was afraid because of the fair sight.

iv   I saw the journey-ready beacon
shift in robes and colors;   now it was reddened with wet
drenched with the shedding of blood,   now it was sheathed with
treasure.

II

   i Hwæðre ic þær licgende   lange hwile
25   beheold hreowcearig   hælendes treow,
       oððæt ic gehyrde   þæt hit hleoðrode
       ongan þa word sprecan   wudu selesta:

   ii "Þæt wæs geara iu   —ic þæt gyta geman—
       þæt ic wæs aheawen   holtes on ende
30   astyred of stefne minum.   Genaman me ðær strange feondas,
       geworhton him þær to wæfersyne,   heton me heora wergas hebban;
       bæron me ðær beornas on eaxlum   oððæt hie me on beorg asetton
       gefæstnodon me þær feondas genoge.

   iii   Geseah ic þa frean mancynnes
       efstan elne mycle   þæt he me wolde on gestigan;
35   þær ic þa ne dorste   ofer dryhtnes word
       bugan oððe berstan   þa ic bifian geseah
       eorðan sceatas;   ealle ic mihte
       feondas gefyllan   —hwæðre ic fæste stod.
       Ongyrede hine þa geong hæleð   —þæt wæs god ælmihtig—
40   strang ond stiðmod   gestah he on gealgan heanne
       modig on manigra gesyhðe   þa he wolde mancyn lysan.
       Bifode ic þa me se beorn ymbclypte,   ne dorste ic hwæðre bugan to eorðan
       feallan to foldan sceatum   —ac ic sceolde fæste standan;
       rod wæs ic aræred,   ahof ic ricne cyning
45   heofona hlaford   —hyldan me ne dorste.

   iv Þurhdrifan hi me mid deorcan næglum,   on me syndon þa dolg gesiene
       opene inwidhlemmas   —ne dorste ic hira nænigum sceððan.
       Bysmeredon hie unc butu ætgædere;   Eall ic wæs mid blode bestemed
       begoten of þæs guman sidan   siððan he hæfde his gast onsended.
50   Feala ic on þam beorge   gebiden hæbbe
       wraðra wyrda;   geseah ic weruda god
       þearle þenian.   Þystro hæfdon
       bewrigen mid wolcnum   wealdendes hræw
       scirne sciman,   sceadu forðeode

II

i Yet lying there   for a long time
25 I gazed in sorrow   at the Savior's tree,
until I heard   this highest rood
begin in speech   to speak these words:

ii "It was many years ago   —I yet remember—
that I was hewn down   in a corner of the holt
30 torn away from my roots.   Then rough enemies took me afar,
made me an object of terror, and commanded me to hang their felons;
these men, these many foes   bore me on their shoulders to a mount
where they set me and made me fast.

iii   I saw mankind's Protector
most manfully hasten   to ascend me;
35 through the will of the Lord   I was stayed in my wish
to crack and bow   when I saw that the boundaries
of earth were trembling;   truly I had the might
to fell these foes   —yet I stood fast.
The young hero prepared himself   —he who was God almighty—
40 great and gallant he ascended   the gallows' abject height
magnanimous in the sight of many   when mankind he wished to free.
I trembled when the Son clasped me,   yet I dared not cling to the
          ground
or fall to the boundaries of earth   —for I had need to stand fast;
a cross I was erected,   I raised the King
45 of the heavens above   —I dared not bow.

iv They pierced me with dark nails,   the wounds are visible on me
the gaping blows of hate   —I dared harm none of them.
Both of us two they besmirched;   I was all besmeared with the blood
which poured from the side of the Man   after he had surrendered his
          soul.
50 There on the mount   I endured many
hateful misfortunes;   I saw the God of hosts
sharply suffer.   The shadows had
covered with clouds   the corpse of the Ruler
the clear splendor,   black under clouds

55   wann under wolcnum;   weop eal gesceaft
           cwiðdon cyninges fyll   —Crist wæs on rode.

           v Hwæðre þær fuse   feorran cwoman
           to þam æðelinge.   Ic þæt eall beheold,
       sare ic wæs mid sorgum gedrefed, hnag ic hwæðre þam secgum to
               handa
60   eaðmod elne mycle.   Genamon hie þær ælmihtigne god,
           ahofon hine of ðam hefian wite;   forleton me þa hilderincas
           standan steame bedrifenne.   Eall ic wæs mid strælum forwundod.

           vi Aledon hie ðær limwerigne   gestodon him æt his lices heafdum
           beheoldon hie ðær heofenes dryhten.   Ond he hine ðær hwile reste
65   meðe æfter ðam miclan gewinne.   Ongunnon him þa moldern wyrcan
           beornas on banan gesyhðe,   curfon hie ðæt of beorhtan stane,
           gesetton hie ðæron sigora wealdend;   ongunnon him þa sorhleoð
               galan
           earme on þa æfentide   þa hie woldon eft siðian
           meðe fram þam mæran þeodne.   Reste he ðær mæte weorode.

70   vii Hwæðere we ðær greotende   gode hwile
           stodon on staðole   syððan stefn up gewat
           hilderinca.   Hræw colode
           fæger feorgbold.   Þa us man fyllan ongan
           ealle to eorðan   —þæt wæs egeslic wyrd—
75   bedealf us man on deopan seaþe.   Hwæðre me þær dryhtnes þegnas
               freondas gefrunon,
           gyredon me   golde ond seolfre.

III

           i Nu ðu miht gehyran   hæleð min se leofa
           þæt ic bealuwara weorc   gebiden hæbbe
80   sarra sorga;   is nu sæl cumen
           þæt me weorðiað   wide ond side
           menn ofer moldan   ond eall þeos mære gesceaft
           gebiddaþ him to þyssum beacne.   On me bearn godes
           þrowode hwile;   forþan ic þrymfæst nu
85   hlifige under heofenum,   ond ic hælan mæg
           æghwylcne anra   þara þe him bið egesa to me.
           Iu ic wæs geworden   wita heardost

55   the darkness spread;   all things weeping spoke
               their Creator's death   —Christ was on the cross.

              v   Yet the ready men   rallied from afar
              to the King's son.   I saw all that;
       I was bitterly oppressed with sorrows,   yet I bowed to the hands of the
               men
60   humbly, very bravely.   They laid hold of the almighty God,
        there lifted him from heavy torment;   the men of battle then left me
        to stand mired in blood.   I was mortally wounded with arrows.

             vi   They laid him down weary to the bone   stood at his body's head
        gazed at the Ruler of heaven.   And there he rested himself awhile
65   tired after the great conflict.   They began to make a tomb for him then
        the men in the sight of the murderers,   hewed it from the marble stone,
        therein did set the Ruler of victories;   they began to sing the mournful
               dirge
        bereaved in the evening time   when tired they thought
        to depart from the great Lord.   There he rested with a little company.

70   vii   Yet a length of time   in lamentation
              we rested there in place   after the cry was raised
              of the bold in battle.   The body grew cold
              the fair corpse.   Then they felled us
              all to the ground   —a grim misfortune—
75   they entombed us in a deep pit.   Yet the retainers of the Lord
              his friends heard tell of me,
              they set upon me   both gold and silver.

III

             i   Now you have learned   my beloved
              that I have suffered   grievous sorrows
80   the work of the sinful;   the season now has come
        when far and wide   men in the world
        make known my worth,   and all creation's wonder
        makes supplication to this sign.   The Son of God on me
        suffered for a time;   therefore I tower now
85   triumphant under the heavens,   and I may heal
        each man who lives   in awe of me.
        I was for a time   the most terrible

leodum laðost   ærþan ic him lifes weg
rihtne gerymde   reordberendum.
90   Hwæt me þa geweorðode   wuldres ealdor
ofer holmwudu   heofonrices weard,
swylce swa he his modor eac   Marian sylfe
ælmihtig god   for ealle menn
geweorðode   ofer eall wifa cynn.

95   ii   Nu ic þe hate   hæleð min se leofa
þæt ðu þas gesyhðe   secge mannum,
onwreoh wordum   þæt hit is wuldres beam
se ðe ælmihtig god   on þrowode
for mancynnes   manegum synnum
100   and Adomes   ealdgewyrhtum.
Deað he þær byrigde,   hwæðere eft dryhten aras
mid his miclan mihte   mannum to helpe;
he ða on heofenas astag,   hider eft fundaþ
on þysne middangeard   mancynn secan
105   on domdæge   dryhten sylfa;
ælmihtig god   ond his englas mid;
þæt he þonne wile deman   se ah domes geweald
anra gehwylcum   swa he him ærur her
on þyssum lænum   life geearnaþ.
110   Ne mæg þær ænig   unforht wesan
for þam worde   þe se wealdend cwyð,
frineð he for þære mænige   hwær se man sie
se ðe for dryhtnes naman   deaðes wolde
biteres onbyrigan   swa he ær on ðam beame dyde;
115   ac hie þonne forhtiað   ond fea þencaþ
hwæt hie to Criste   cweðan onginnen;
ne þearf ðær þonne ænig   unforht wesan
þe him ær in breostum bereð   beacna selest;
ac ðurh ða rode sceal   rice gesecan
120   of eorðwege   æghwylc sawl
seo þe mid wealdende   wunian þenceð."

IV

i   Gebæd ic me þa to þan beame   bliðe mode
elne mycle   þær ic ana wæs

and loathsome of tortures   until life's right way
I made manifest   to speaking men.
90 Hear how above any holm-tree   the Guardian of heaven
the Lord of glory   lifted me in worth,
just as almighty God   for the good of men
did also make his mother   Mary herself
to be worshipped   above all womankind

95 ii Now I command you   my beloved
to make known this vision,   reveal to others
with contrivance of words   that it is a tree of glory
on which almighty God   miserably suffered
for the sake of mankind's   manifold sins
100 and for the deeds of old   then done by Adam.
Death he there savored,   yet the Saviour arose
through his great might   in succor of men;
to his kingdom he ascended,   from whence he will come
on the Last Day   the Lord himself
105 he with his angels   humankind to seek
on this middle-earth   almighty God;
he will judge then   who has power to judge
the measure of merit   each man has earned
by the way he lived   life's fleeting moment.
110 Then none will be found   free of all fear
as he awaits   the word of the Master,
who will ask of the many   where the man may be
who in the name of the Lord   elected to taste
as Christ did on the gallows   the gall of death;
115 but they are fearful,   and few have in mind
what they may say   to the Saviour;
only he will feel   free of all fear
who bears in his soul   the best of signs;
for through the rood   he must reach the kingdom
120 from the paths of the world   each wayfaring soul
who with the Master   hopes to remain."

IV

i   Then I prayed to the tree   most pressingly
in delight of soul   alone where I was

         mæte werede;   wæs modsefa
125   afysed on forðwege,   feala ealra gebad
         langunghwila.   Is me nu lifes hyht
         þæt ic þone sigebeam   secan mote;
         ana oftor   þonne ealle men
         well weorþian   me is willa to ðam
130   mycel on mode,   ond min mundbyrd is
         geriht to þære rode.   Nah ic ricra feala
         freonda on foldan;   ac hie forð heonon
gewiton of worulde dreamum,   sohton him wuldres cyning,
         lifiaþ nu on heofenum   mid heahfædere
135   wuniaþ on wuldre.   Ond ic wene me
         daga gehwylce   hwænne me dryhtnes rod
         þe ic her on eorðan   ær sceawode
         on þysson lænan   life gefetige
         ond me þonne gebringe   þær is blis mycel
140   dream on heofonum   þær is dryhtnes folc
         geseted to symle   þær is singal blis,
         ond he þonne asette   þær ic syððan mot
         wunian on wuldre   well mid þam halgum
         dreames brucan.

         ii   Si me dryhten freond
145   se ðe her on eorþan   ær þrowode
         on þam gealgtreowe   for guman synnum.
         He us onlysde   ond us lif forgeaf
         heofonlice ham   —hiht wæs geniwad
         mid bledum ond mid blisse   þam þe þær bryne þolodan.
150   Se sunu wæs sigorfæst   on þam siðfate
         mihtig ond spedig   þa he mid manigeo com
         gasta weorode   on godes rice
         anwealda ælmihtig   englum to blisse
         ond eallum ðam halgum   þam þe on heofonum ær
155   wunedon on wuldre   þa heora wealdend cwom
         ælmihtig god   þær his eðel wæs.

with a little company;   for the call to pilgrimage
125   my mind was prepared,   I awaited full many
times of languishing.   Now my hope of life
rests in the voyage   to the tree of victory;
alone now well   to worship it
above any man   much is this desire
130   set in my heart,   and my hope of protection
is placed in the cross.   I have on earth no plenty
of goodly friends;   for they have gone
away from the gladness of the world,   have sought the King of glory,
dwell in heaven   with the Father on high,
135   live now in glory.   And I look to the time
every long day   when the cross of the Lord
which here on earth   once I beheld
may bear me aloft   from life's fleeting moment
and fetch me thence   to the fullness of bliss
140   gladness in heaven   where the host of the Lord
is appointed to the feast   in perpetual bliss,
and where in glory   I may enjoy gladness
well with the saints   —there may he set me
to live thenceforward.

ii   May the Lord be my friend
145   who suffered once   for the sins of men
here upon earth   on the hangman's tree.
He released us   and gave us life
a heavenly home   —hope was renewed
with bounties and bliss   for those who suffered the burning.
150   The Son in his venture   was crowned with victory
mighty and conquering   when he came with the multitude
the company of souls   into God's kingdom
the almighty Sovereign   to the solace of the angels
and of all the saints   who for some time in heaven
155   had rested in glory   when the almighty Ruler
their lord returned   to his native land.

RUTHWELL

Fragment
from the
churchyard

FIGURE 2.

Reprinted, by permission, from W. G. Collingwood, *Northumbrian Crosses of the Pre-Norman Age* (Faber & Faber Ltd.).

the basic design of the *Dream of the Rood* is clear. It consists of four scenes: I, 1–23, the vision; II, 24–77, the narrative of the Cross; III, 78–121, the peroration and exhortation of the Cross; IV, 122–156, the dreamer's prayer to Cross and Christ. However, this relatively simple frame supports an elaborate rhetorical structure in which a series of striking antitheses is developed. The antitheses derive basically from the juxtaposition, the *communicatio idiomatum*,[1] of the two aspects of Christ as God and man. In the Crucifixion, Christ suffered as man, but without diminishing his godhead. His passion is universal and particular, and the ignominy of his shameful death is the glory of his triumph over death. Without sin he died for sinners. The Cross, in turn, is the symbol of the mystery of the Redemption, the triumph of mortification.

In the second paragraph of I, the vision, the cross of universal triumph is described. Early representations of the cross suggest what the poet has in mind, for the emphasis there is entirely on Christ as God triumphant, not on Christ as suffering man. The Crucifixion as a subject in early plastic and pictorial art had none of its later prominence, and the representation of the figure of the Savior on the cross is both late and infrequent. When the figure does appear it is impassively heroic.[2] When describing the cross as "lifted in the sky," and extending to "the corners of the earth," the poet has in mind the universal and figurative cross of tradition, which visualized the cross as extending from the heavens above to the infernal regions below, and from the furthest East to the furthest West.[3]

1. See R. Woolf, "Doctrinal Influences on *The Dream of the Rood*," *M.Æ.*, 27 (1958), pp. 137–153; also S. Greenfield, *A Critical History of Old English Literature* (New York, 1965), pp. 136–140.

Robert B. Burlin's "The Ruthwell Cross, *The Dream of the Rood* and the Vita Contemplativa, *S.P.*, 65 (1968), 23–43, and Neil D. Isaacs' *Structural Principles in Old English Poetry* (Knoxville, 1968) came to my attention only after this book was set in type; I am sorry I did not see them before because they are interesting and valuable studies.

2. Paul Thoby, *Le Crucifix* (Nantes, 1959), pp. 34–35. See plate 3, following p. 42.

3. See Cassiodorus *Expositio Psalmi*, 21.17, *CCSL*, 97, 198–199; also see Alcuin, cited by R. Füglister, *Das lebende Kreuz* (Einsiedeln, 1964), p. 178, "Ipsa crux magnum in se mysterium continet; cuius positio talis est, ut superior pars coelos petat, inferior terrae inhaereat fixa, infernorum ima contigat, latitudo autem eius partes mundi appetat." See a description by an earlier Latin Christian poet Sedulius who might have had an influence on the *Dream of the Rood*; *Carmen Paschale*, V, 182–195, *PL*, 19, 724:

> Protinus in patuli suspensus culmine ligni,
> Relligione pia mutans discriminis iram,
> Pax crucis ipse fuit, violentaque robora membris
> Illustrans propriis, poenam vestivit honore,

This triumphant cross, the hope of man's salvation and the object of the adoration of the entire universe, is also the cross of suffering; its jewels are the transfigurations of nails and wounds. Seeing this essential aspect of the cross, the dreamer is led to the story of the Passion, as related in prosopopoeia by the cross itself (II). The Passion explains the mystery of the interweaving of radiance and suffering, *communicatio idiomatum.*

Thus the narrative of the Passion by the Cross develops the inevitable and interlocked antithesis implicit in the vision of the universal cross, for the glory and victory of the cross is derived from the ignominy of its function, as Christ's triumph derives from his suffering. The Crucifixion is pictured as a battle and both Christ and the Cross as warriors whose deaths are victories, and whose burials are preludes to the triumph of their Resurrections. In paragraph i of scene III, the peroration of the Cross, the theme of triumph through suffering is explicitly developed. In paragraph ii, the adjuration, the Cross bids the dreamer make known that the cross of suffering has been transfigured into the cross of victory, and has become the means by which man may also be transfigured. In IV, i, the poet addresses the cross, and in ii, he prays to Christ for salvation.

The thematic development of the poem is clear in outline, but what distinguishes this development is the elaborate artifice of echo and re-echo, of the pattern of incremental repetition within the ordering of the verse paragraph. The dream is like an illuminated page from the Book of Kells, recounting the Crucifixion. (See plate 4, following p. 106.)

Scene I: The Vision

Scene I, the vision, is introduced by a brief, simple paragraph (1–3) in which the poet declares that he will speak of a dream, which came to him at midnight when men are asleep. To designate the sleeping men, the epithet, *reordberend*, is employed (and repeated in another context in the peroration of the Cross, line 89). In the context of the introduction the epithet has homiletic

---

Supliciumque dedit signum magis esse salutis,
Ipsaque sanctificans in se tormenta beavit.
Neve quis ignoret, speciem crucis esse colendam,
Quae Dominum portavit ovans, ratione potenti
Quattuor inde plagas quadrati colligit orbis.
Splendidus auctoris de vertice fulget Eous,
Occiduo sacrae lambuntur sidere plantae,
Arcton dextra tenet, medium laeva erigit axem,
Cunctaque de membris vivit natura creantis,
Et cruce complexum Christus regit undique mundum.

Also see plates 2 and 3 (following pp. 10 and 42); in plate 3 the arch, as Thoby points out, p. 32, is symbolic of the "voûte céleste et de l'orbe des astres, oeuvres da la Divinité." For *on lyft lædan*, see Schücking, *op. cit.*, pp. 56–57.

overtones ("Let them who have ears, hear"); the poet will make use of his power of speech to relate a dream which made fruitful his slumber to men with power of speech who were slumbering when the dream occurred. The poet's use of *reordberend* serves also to create the effect of synesthesia; the poet will *speak* of a *vision* which came to him while men who *speak* were asleep. This suggestion of synesthesia provides a contrastive transition. In the introductory paragraph the emphasis is on speech; in the body of the scene it is on sight. Again in the transition from scene I, the vision, to scene II, as will be seen, the poet employs synesthesia to mark the transition from the vision of the Cross to the speech of the Cross.

The body of scene I, the vision, is developed in three paragraphs: ii, 4–14; iii, 14–21; iv, 21–23. These are marked by a pattern of introductory repetition of the verb of seeing in the first person, each verb having as object a different epithet for cross. The repetitive pattern is varied by polypoton; the second and third verbs governing independent clauses, the first governing a dependent clause, the object of the impersonal, *þuhte me:*

> 2) *Þuhte me þæt ic gesawe   syllicre treow*   (4)
> 3) *Geseah ic wuldres treowe*   (14)
> 4) *Geseah ic þæt fuse beacen*   (21)

Within this frame of introductory clauses the description is developed by a series of parallels and antitheses. Paragraph ii begins with a description of the dreamer gazing at the Cross (period 1, 4–9); against this is balanced a description (period 2, 9–12) of the entire creation gazing at it (*beheoldon*, 9); the paragraph is concluded (period 3, 13–14) with a statement contrasting the resplendence of the Cross with the sin-stained wretchedness of the dreamer. In paragraph iii the antithesis between the Cross triumphant and the Cross suffering is developed in period 1 and 2, 14–17, 18–20. In period 3, 20–21, against the aspectual antithesis is again balanced the wretchedness of the dreamer, oppressed by sin and terrified at the glory of his vision. Finally in paragraph iv, the antithesis between the two aspects of the Cross is briefly summarized by incremental repetition of key phrases of paragraphs ii and iii. Apart from the introductory framework the vision scene is held together by an elaborate verbal and phrasal pattern of repetition, too complex to be summarized.

Paragraph ii, the beacon: Paragraph ii has as its center, period 2 (9–12), a description of the angels, saints, men, all creation gazing at the Cross. The period is in the third person plural with the verb, *beheoldon*, repeated in lines 9 and 11. This description is framed by periods 1 and 3, both in the first person singular: *ic gesawe*, 4; *ic [wæs] synnum fah*, 13. The rhetorical effect of this framing pattern is to place the universal vision within the dreamer's particular vision. Period 1 presents the primary vision of the dreamer. As in each of the other periods of paragraph ii period 1 consists of two balanced clausules. Clausule a, 4–6, gives in the first person, the gist of what the dreamer saw. Clausule b, 6–9, in the third person, describes briefly the resplendent Cross of the vision. In clausule a two variants are used to designate the Cross; in b a third variant appears. A progression is involved from the inanimate, generalized *treow*, 4, to the functional, specific *beam*, 6, to the metaphoric *beacen*, 6, of the b clausule. The variant in the b clausule is central to the description of the cross as a vast heavenly luminary, a kind of sun: first the tree (*treow*) is said to appear in the sky (*on lyft*); second, the rood (*beam*) is described as "enveloped in light," *leohte bewunden*; it follows that the cross is metaphorically a "beacon," a guiding light.[4]

However, man usually does not see this heavenly cross, but rather the jewel-bedecked cross of church ceremonial, or of the mosaics, wall-paintings, and illuminated manuscripts. To suggest this cross of man's usual view the second clausule, except for the word *beacen*, concentrates on the fact that the radiance of the cross arises from its rich ornamentation; thus in clausule b, as against a, the cross is described in terms of the gold which covers it and of the jewels at its extremities and at its center. By the juxtaposition of clausules a and b, two aspects of the cross are suggested. The cross has a transcendent reality; it also has a representational reality as a man-made object of veneration. However, since the man-made bejeweled cross is not worshipped for itself but for its universal and spiritual significance as the means to Redemption, the representational aspect of the cross itself implies its metaphoric value as a heavenly luminary, a beacon symbolizing the hope of Redemption, of eternal victory. In this aspect it participates in the providential design of Creation. To suggest the symbolic universal aspect the representational ornamented cross of clausule b is described as coextensive with the created universe, its jeweled ends extending to the corners of the earth, *foldan sceatum*, 8. The two clausules of period 1 thus present two aspects of the cross, the ornamental representation and the universal reality as the beacon of the Redemption. A further symbolic duality is suggested in clausule b by the five jewels at the crossing, which represent the five wounds of Christ, and by the four jewels at the extensions which represent the universality of the cross, its participation in the quadripartite creation, with its four dimensions, four directions, four seasons and four elements.[5] In short, the ornamental cross suggested in b is representative both of universal reality, and of the mysterious duality of the Passion where anguish and triumph are united as means to end.

4. See Bosworth-Toller and supplement, *s.v. beam, sun-beam, sunnebeam*. The translation of *leohte bewunden / beama beorhtost*, 5–6, "enveloped in light/ the brightest of beams" tries to suggest the possibility, in context, of a play on the central meaning of *beam*, "tree," "pillar," and the derivative, compositional meaning, attested in prose, "ray of light."

5. The significance of four is standard. See Cassiodorus and Sedulius cited above note 3, and see Ælfric, "Palm Sunday. On the Lord's Passion" in *The Homilies of the Anglo-Saxon Church*, ed. Thorpe (London, 1846) II, pp. 254–256. "Drihten wæs gefæstnod mid feower nægelum, to westdæle awend; and his [s]ynstra heold ðone scynendan suð-dæl, and his swiðra norð-dæl, east-dæl his hnol; and he ealle alysde middaneardes hwemmas swa hangiende."

Period 1, which describes the dreamer's view of the cross, balances period 2 (9–12), which describes the viewing of the cross by "the angelic host," "the godly saints," "men in the world," "all creation's wonder." [6] In this period the emphasis shifts from the cross to its worshippers. As the universal cross is described in 1, line 8, as *fægere æt foldan sceatum*, the angelic host is described in 2, line 10, as *fægere þurh forðgesceaft*. The echo underlines a deeper resemblance; as the description of the cross in 1 suggests its redemptive aspect, so the description of those gazing on the cross in 2 is worded to suggest the redemptive path. The angels are described as created in the beginning, and thus identified with the spiritual heaven, as are by definition the "godly saints." These have attained the goal toward which "men in the world" must aspire by following the cross upon which they gaze. "All creation's wonder," as the fourth group, completes a quadripartite universality, and anticipates the responsive participation of nature in Christ's passion, described in Part II.

Strikingly the only reference to the cross in period 2 is negative; it is not "a gallows vile." This negative description prepares for the introduction in the next paragraph, iii, of the specific description of the suffering of the cross perceived through the jeweled gleam (18–20).

The final period of ii, 3, 13–14, marks the contrast between the cross and the dreamer. Returning to the first person viewpoint of 1, that of the dreamer, period 3 serves, with 1, to frame the third person vision of the universal adoration. Periods 1 and 3 are linked rhetorically by chiastic reversal. In both periods third person clausules describing the beauty of the cross are balanced against first person clausules, but in period 1, the third person is found in the b clausule, in period 3 it is found in a. Periods 1 and 3 are also linked by the repetition, *syllic*, 13, of the first adjective used to describe the cross in 1, *syllicre*, 4. *Sigebeam* in 3, line 13, is an incremental variant of the epithets for the cross in 1; the second element of the compound, *beam*, echoes in polyptoton *beama*, 6, and the first element with its meaning of "victory" in effect explains why the cross is the "seemliest," 4, why it is "the brightest of beams," 6, why it is a "beacon." The negative designation of the cross in 2 is picked up in period 3, where to mark the contrast between Cross and dreamer, clausule a describes the resplendence of the cross, clausule b, inversely, the vileness of the dreamer stained with sin.

Paragraph iii, suffering and triumph: Paragraph iii consists of three brief periods: 1, 14–17; 2, 18–20; 3, 20–21. The first two periods present the cross in its antithetical aspects: period 1 describes its glory, thus continuing the em-

6. The translation assumes an emendation of the MS *engel dryhtnes ealle*, which cannot be defended, to *engeldryhte*; many solutions have been suggested; the simplest seems to me to be suggested by Dickens and Ross, *The Dream of the Rood* (New York, 1966), p. 21; it is possible that the *ealle* should be retained with plural meaning, in opposition to *dryhte*, or governing *dryhtes*, genitive singular, "all of the angelic host."

phasis of paragraph ii; 2 describes its suffering, an aspect only implied in ii through mention of the five jewels, and through the negative designation of the cross as not a vile gallows. Period 3 is related to period 3 of ii, returning to the dreamer, and adding to the description there of his vileness a description of his grief.

Period 1 of paragraph iii opens with the structural formula, *Geseah ic*, the object of which, *wuldres treow*, 14, is echoed in the alliterating variant, *wealdes treow*, 17, which concludes the period. The latter phrase may incorporate two possible meanings of *weald*, "power" and "highland covered with wood." [7] In its latter meaning *wealdes* would anticipate *holtes* of line 29, at the beginning of the narrative of the cross; in the former meaning it echoes *wuldres*. The two meanings would reflect the antithesis between the lowly specific and glorious universal aspects of the cross, and thus provide a transition to the next period of paragraph iii, 2, 18–20, where the antithesis is developed. The repetition of *treow* frames within period 1 a series of phrases which are variants of phrases in the preceding paragraph describing the radiance of the cross. Thus *gegyred mid golde*, 16, is a variant of *begoten mid golde*, 7; *gimmas hæfdon bewrigen*, 16–17, is a slightly more complex variant of *gimmas stodon*, 7; finally *wædum geweorðod wynnum scinan*, 15, is an intricate development of the concept of adornment in *leohte bewunden*, 5. In addition, *wædum geweorðod wynnum scinan/ gegyred mid golde*, 15–16, stands in word-play contrast to *synnum fah/ forwunded mid wommum*, 13–14, enforcing the antithesis between the wretchedness of the dreamer and the radiance of the cross made in ii, 3.

The two dative plurals *wædum, wynnum*, 15, have caused difficulty. Dickins and Ross find the meaning of *wædum* "not at all clear," but tentatively approve Cook's notion that "some kind of streamer" is suggested. They mention Patch's citation of Fortunatus' "arbor . . . ornata regis purpura" as indicating that the processional cross was embellished with the royal purple. At the same time they observe that Walpole, *Early Latin Hymns*, cites "parallels to show that the purple is that of the blood which consecrated the tree . . . not the hangings of the processional cross." The uncertainty about the word results from seeking too literal a referent for the cross adorned with *wædum*. It is not simply the processional cross, but the cross of the first scene with its dual aspects, specific and universal, which supplies the referent. The parallel with the line from Fortunatus when properly interpreted according to Walpole's reading is, in fact, most apt; the adornment of the cross of glory derives from the royal blood which stained it in the Passion. The poet's use of *wædum* is exactly appropriate to his intention of revealing both the cross triumphant and the cross suffering;

7. See Bosworth-Toller *s.v. weald*. This explanation has the advantage of supporting the MS reading as against the *wealdend* suggested by Dietrich and accepted as "certain on grounds of metre and sense alike" by Dickens and Ross, p. 23. If the emendation is certain, then *Wealdendes treow* stands in echoic relation to *Hælendes treow*, 25, in the introduction to the narration of the Cross.

its robes are the blood of Christ, transformed into rich raiments. The translation "robed in purple" attempts to approximate this double meaning. The connotations of *wædum* are also developed by its position in an echoic pattern: on the one hand, *wædum geweorðod*, as a variant of *leohte bewunden* suggests the triumphal aspect of the cross; on the other hand, standing in echoic contrast to *forwunded mid wommum* (14), it suggests the ignominious aspect of the cross. The explanation for *wynnum* also rests in its contrastive echoing of *wommum*. It is not necessary to seek a generalized equivalent, "pleasantly, beautifully"; in its literal meaning "with joys," i.e., "joyfully," *wynnum* is an example of metonymy, the joy being the effect of which the cross is the cause.

Period 2 of iii is contrastive. It is introduced by *Hwæðre*, "yet," and describes how the dreamer perceives through the gold a sign of strife, the bleeding of the cross. The strife is designated by a hapax legomenon, *ærgewin*, 19. Special emphasis is given to the word by the immediate echo of the first part of the compound in *ærest*, the key stave of the second half of line 18. Not only is the unique word given emphasis by the unusual use of initial rhyme, but this device in 18 is also supported by an echoic pattern: *ongytan—ongan* of 17, *swætan—swiðran* of 19. Additional attention is directed to *ærgewin* by the difficulty in determining the syntax of *earmra*, the first word in the phrase *earmra ærgewin*. There are two possibilities.[8] Either *earmra* is the genitive plural of *earm*, or it is the nominative singular of the adjective in the comparative. If the latter, its agreement would be with the nominative singular, *ic*, not with the accusative *ærgewin*, and would represent a further example of the absolute use of the comparative as in *syllicre*, line 4; it would be translated, "I, most wretched." On the other hand, the relation of the adjective to *ærgewin* seems clear, but this reading would involve an emendation to *earmran*. A preferable alternative would be to read *earmra* as an adjective in the genitive plural, "the former agony of the wretched ones." The difficulty is that the plural reference would not then relate to Christ's agony which is the usual meaning given to *ærgewin*. However, if *ærgewin* is glossed as "former hostility," the reference of *earmra* would be to the Jews and Roman soliders. Both glosses are unforced; "hostility" is a normal meaning of *gewin*, and *earm* is frequently used with reference to the sinful and evil. What the dreamer perceives is the cause of Christ's agony, the "ancient malice of foes." It is this which produces the result described in the ensuing *þæt* clause, "when the cross first (*ærest*) began to bleed from the right side"; that is, when in the final act of the Passion, Christ's right side was pierced with the spear. The ambiguity of *ærgewin* is reflected in the adverb *ærest* with which it is connected by initial rhyme. The adverb has a twofold reference; to the time in the vision when the dreamer first perceived the blood, and historically to the time of the *ærgewin* when at the end of the Pas-

8. Unless the manuscript reading is emended, as in Karl Bouterwerk, *Cædmon's des Angelsachsen biblische Dichtungen* (Gütersloh, 1854), p. clxviii.

sion Christ's blood streamed from his side. Finally, if *earmra* has reference to the enemies of Christ, as seems demanded, the word would anticipate *strange feondas*, line 30, the enemies of the cross in the ensuing narrative.

The third period of paragraph iii consists of two balanced half-line clausules. Clausule a, *eall ic wæs mid sorgum gedrefed*, 20, forms a contrastive pattern with *eall þæt beacen wæs/ begoten mid golde*, 6–7 in the description of the cross in paragraph ii. Clausule a thus reflects the thematic contrast between the dreamer's wretchedness and the resplendence of the cross. A further intertwining of motifs is involved. The dreamer in paragraph ii has indicated his sense of sin (*synnum fah*). In sinning he wounds Christ and thus he shares in the evil wretchedness of the *earmra* who crucified Christ, but his sorrow for the suffering revealed by the cross may teach him that the escape from his wretchedness lies in renouncing the ways of the evil and in following the way of the cross. Clausule a is balanced by b, *Forht ic wæs for þære fægran gesyhðe*, 21, which describes the terror aroused in the dreamer by his vision of the beautiful cross. Clearly the cause of the dreamer's fear cannot be the beauty of the cross; rather the beauty of the cross causes the dreamer to recognize sharply his own sinful state, and his involvement in the suffering which is intertwined with the radiance of the cross. The metonymy gives a paradoxical turn to the clausule, and reflects the paradoxical nature of the vision.

Paragraph iv, recapitulation: The final paragraph, iv, 21–23, serves both as summary conclusion to the vision and as transition to the narrative of the Cross. It is introduced, as noted, by the third repetition of the formula *Geseah ic* with variation of the immediate objective phrase; *fuse beacen*, 21, as against the earlier *syllicre treow*, line 7 of i, and *wuldres treo*, line 14 of ii. *Beacen* replaces *treow*, and *fuse* replaces the honorific words, *syllicre* and *wuldres*. *Beacen* is, of course, a repetition of the epithet found in paragraph ii, line 6, where the motif of the adornment of the cross was introduced. As *beacen*, 6, is the last of the three variants designating the cross in the first two paragraphs introduced by *Geseah*, so it is the final epithet employed in the entire introductory sequence of three. It is, of course, the key word in the scene, crystallizing the images of radiance.

The variant adjective *fuse* presents a difficult problem because it apparently does not complete the chain of words glorifying the cross, *syllicre*, *wuldres*. Dickins and Ross, however, suggest that by semantic extension "eager>brilliant," the latter meaning applies here. This may be so, and would give the word its expected meaning. On the other hand, a central connotation for *fus* is "readiness for journey." In the specific context of the word here as modifying *beacen*, its connotation may be connected with "the journey of the Sun," as in *Beowulf* 1966 and *Genesis* 154. *Fus* has also, as we have seen, a connotation connected with "the journey of death." [9] What we have then is an adjective of ambiguous

9. See Chapter I, B, note 2, p. 35.

meaning, and the ambiguity is the clue to its connotations. In the context of the earlier attributions of glory (*syllicre, wuldres*), *fus* may carry a contextually extended meaning of "glorious," as suggested by Dickens and Ross; in the context of the dreamer's terror at the blood caused by the "ancient malice of the foes," *fus* would suggest connotations of death. This level of connotation would relate the term directly to the ensuing narrative of the Crucifixion. Thus the ambiguity of *fus* serves both to recapitulate and to anticipate.

To complete the introductory *geseah* pattern, the *fuse beacen* is described in an infinitive phrase, *wendan wædum ond bleom*, parallel to the infinitive phrases in paragraphs ii and iii, *on lyft lædan*, 5, and *wynnum scinan*, 15. Further, *wædum*, repeats a key word in the description of the cross in paragraph iii, line 15, suggesting the ambivalent purple of blood and glory. In paragraph iv to this word is added *bleom*, "colors," that is, in context, the colors of glory and blood. The brief paragraph is completed by a compound clausule the two elements of which are introduced by *hwilum*; this clausule is set in opposition to the introductory *geseah* clausule, and describes vividly the nature of the shifting robes and colors.

Scene II: The Narrative of the Cross

The story of the cross is introduced by a brief paragraph, lines 24–27, which makes the transition from the dreamer's vision of the cross to his vision of the narrative of the cross, the dreamer being described as *looking* at the cross until he *hears* it speak. This oxymoron ("seen speech") develops the device of synesthesia which the poet has employed by suggestion in the first paragraph of I. The transitional paragraph is introduced by *Hwæðre*, the conjunction which is used in I, iii, line 18, to introduce the dreamer's perception of evidences of suffering on the cross. The first designation for the cross to be found in II, i, *hælendes treow*, 25, suggests a further shift of emphasis; hitherto the cross has been defined in terms of its attributes (*syllicre, wuldres, wealdes*, etc.), now it is defined in terms of the sufferer and Saviour.[10] The result is to suggest an animate relation for the cross, appropriate to its ensuing speech (prosopopoeia). However, to designate the cross in the act of speaking the poet uses *wudu selesta*, "most worthy of trees," 27, a designation which leads directly to the first paragraph (II, ii) of the narrative, which begins with the cross in its original state as a tree in the woods.

The narrative of the cross, II, lines 28–77, is told in a series of six brief paragraphs, ii–vii, carefully distinguished by their rhetorical structures and interlaced within the narrative by an overall design of phrasal repetition and variation which have relation also to key phrases from Scene I. Like the descrip-

10. If the emendation *wealdes, wealdendes*, line 17, is accepted the shift is from the generalized concept, the tree of creation, to the specific tree of the Passion, but see note 7.

tive Scene I, the narrative Scene II is governed chiefly by the first person, the "I" being the cross, not the dreamer whose function as reporter remains only by implication until the final scene. The "I" narrative of the cross (II) like the "I" narrative of the dreamer (I) is marked by repeated use of *Geseah* and by verbs which reflect the feelings of the narrator. Also as in I, balanced against the first person are passages in the third person plural ("enemies of Christ," paragraphs ii, iv; "the followers of Christ," v, vi), and in the third person singular ("Christ," iii, iv, vi; "creation," iv; "the enemy," vi). The interlocking of grammatical design between I and II is not fortuitous because the tale of the cross inversely reflects the vision. As in I the dreamer perceived first the glory of the cross and then its suffering; in II the cross begins with a tale of ignominy and ends on the note of triumphant Resurrection. In effect, II explains the dreamer's sympathetic perception in I of the suffering caused by ancient malice, and why, like all creation, he stands in awe of the cross.

Although paragraphs ii–vii are elaborately constructed, they follow a fairly straight and uncomplicated narrative line.

ii)	28–33	The Preparation of the Cross
iii)	33–45	The Ascent of the Cross
iv)	46–56	The Crucifixion
v)	57–62	The Descent
vi)	63–69	The Entombment
vii)	70–77	The Entombment and Resurrection of the Cross

Striking in the narrative are the conceptions of the cross as a tree, of Christ as a triumphant warrior, and of the responsiveness of creation. All these motifs have close analogies in early pictorial representations of the Crucifixion. The conception of the warrior-like participation of the cross in the Passion, on the other hand, has no such analogy, but follows from the poet's use of prosopopoeia. The obvious rhetorical function of the device is to give a sense of immediacy, of participation in the traditional story. Beyond rhetorical effect, the use of the device is justified as a bold but natural metaphoric extension. Itself an inanimate object, the cross reflects the animate suffering of the Passion. It is an easy step to perceive the cross as actively participating in the Passion of which it is representative.

Paragraph ii, the preparation of the Cross: The straightforward narrative of the paragraph is developed in two balanced periods, 1, 28–30, in the oblique first person singular, 2, 30–33, in the third person plural. The referent for the "I" of period 1 is the cross which tells how it remembers being hewn down where it stood "in a corner of the holt." [11] The subject of 2 is *feondas*, the "enemies" who: a^1) carried the cross away (*genaman*), a^2) made it into a spec-

11. *Holt* has an early primary meaning of "wooded hill" which may be the meaning here; cf. *wealdes treow*, 18, and *holmwudu*, 91.

tacle (*geworhton . . . to wæfersyne*), and a³) commanded it to hang felons (*heton me heora wergas hebban*), b) bore it on their shoulders and placed it on a mount (*bæron . . . asetton . . . gefæstnodon*).

In its narrative of events prior to the Crucifixion, the Cross relates, in effect, the beginnings of the "ancient malice of foes" (*earma ærgewin*, 19). Its emphasis is upon the transformation of a natural, living thing into an ignominious object of death by the "enemies" both of Christ and the cross. The cross which is made into an inglorious instrument of death is called a spectacle, *wæfersyne*, recalling that the glorious cross of the vision (I) is also a spectacle, *beacen*, 6 and 21; although it is "death-ready," *fuse*, 21, it is specifically not an instrument of death, *ne wæs . . . gealga*, 10. The contrast and comparison suggest that in the cross is represented the mysterious conjunction of the antitheses, life and death, glory and ignominy.

II ii incorporates a variant from the Gospel in that the "enemy," not Christ, carry the cross on *their* shoulders (*eaxlum*) and place it on the mount where it awaits Christ's ascent. This variation, which has precedents, is not a reflection of a heterodox version of the gospel narrative, but of the poet's use of prosopopoeia and of his focusing on the act of crucifixion as victory in death.[12] The result for the poem is to end the first paragraph of the actual narration (II, ii) with the act of fixing the cross on Golgotha, the beginning of the onset of the enemy. The cross becomes, as it were, the enemy's war-banner, *wæfersyn*, the visible symbol of their act of defilement of nature.

Paragraph iii, the ascent: The next paragraph, iii, has as its central action Christ's ascent of the cross, which is narrated in period 2, 39–41, with third person singular subject, Christ. This period is framed by period 1, 33–38 and period 3, 41–45, both in the first person singular telling what the cross saw and what it felt. Period 1 twice employs the *geseah* formula of I, *Geseah ic*, 33; *ic geseah*, 36. It contains three first person clausules. In a, 33–34; the cross speaks of his seeing the Savior approach. In b, 35–37, the cross tells of its dilemma. As a tree, part of creation, which trembles in awe before the Lord, it is impelled to bow. However, this instinctive desire is checked by the more impelling requirement of obedience enjoined upon it, for in God's providential design the cross must play its part by supporting the Lord in his suffering. The cross amplifies the nature of its dilemma in c, 37–38, where it gives a further dimension to its inner conflict. The cross is more than a tree. It is a man-made object, designed to deal the most ignominious of deaths. Thus it shares the human wish to react manfully, exact vengeance. By falling prostrate the cross would not only follow its natural instinct of reverence, but by crushing its foes in the act of

---

12. The same kind of omission by reason of peculiar emphasis may be illustrated in Ælfric's sermon on the Passion (*Homilies of the Anglo-Saxon Church*, ed. B. Thorpe, (London, 1846) II, p. 254) "Hwæt ða cempan hine gelæddon to ðære cwealm-stowe, þær man cwealde sceaðan, and him budon drincan gebitrodne win-drenc. . . ."

reverence it would also satisfy the human craving for battle. On the other hand, it shares even more compellingly in Christ's redemptive love, and must repay good for evil. Thus the cross cannot fell its enemies; it must stand fast (37–38). This striking presentation of the psychology of the cross follows naturally from the poet's use of prosopopoeia with its concomitant personification of the cross. Endowed with human feelings and perceptions, the cross transcends not only its nature as a tree but also its man-ordered function as an instrument of death; and is equated with man's destiny and God's providential design. The attribution of human feelings to the cross makes possible the extraordinary effectiveness and impact of the poet's narration of the Passion.

Period 2 of iii, 39–41, has two clausules, both in the third person singular with Christ as subject. The first, 39–40, introduces the action of ascent by a very striking military metaphor, *ongyrede hine þa geong hæleð*, "the young hero prepared himself." The verbal compound *ongyrede* is not found elsewhere in poetry. The prefix *on-* having most naturally here the significance of "off," the literal meaning of *ongyrede* would be "stripped." But the root *gyrwan* has the common meaning "prepare" and the prefix *on-* is not necessarily to be equated with "un-," but may have the significance of "beginning," as in *on-bærnan*, "to begin to burn." In the context of the subject *hæleð*, "warrior," the apparent meaning of the verb with its literal referent in the Gospel narrative, "stripped," takes on the contextual meaning of "stripped for action," i.e., "prepared himself."

The military action for which Christ prepared himself was to ascend the cross. The verb, *gestah*, used to describe Christ's ascent, repeats in polyptoton the infinitive *gestigan* of the a clausule of period 1, line 34, and marks the completion of the action there begun; that is, in clausule a Christ is described as desiring to ascend the cross (*wolde . . . gestigan*); in clausule b of period 2 his reasons are given—he wished to free mankind, *gestah . . . þa he wolde mancyn lysan*. The second clausule of 2 also contains the only specific designation of the cross in the paragraph, *gealgan*. This echoes the single designation of the cross in I, ii, 2 by the negative, *ne wæs . . . gealga*, 10. The repetition is enforced by the parallelism of structure—both appear in periods in the third person, framed by periods in the first person. The repetition also serves a thematic purpose. As the function of the negative designation of the cross in I, ii, 2 was to suggest the ignominy underlying the triumph of the cross seen in the vision, so in II, iii, 2, the designation of the cross as "gallows" places the onset of triumphant battle in counterpoint to the ignominy of the Crucifixion. This counterpoint is further enforced by the potential of word-play in the adjective *heanne* modifying *gealgan*, 40, which may be either the accusative of *heah*, "high," or of *hean*, "mean, abject." (The translation "gallow's abject height" suggests the form of the word-play.) Finally, the phrase which describes the ascent as occurring in the sight of many (*on manigra gesyhðe*, 41) not only reflects I, ii, 2, which describes the multitude gazing at the triumphant cross which is not a gallows, but also reflects the designation of the cross in the preceding paragraph, as a "spectacle," (*wæfersyn* II, ii, line 31). This suggests the ignominious aspect of the cross, which from a tree of nature had been transformed by the enemy into an object to be gazed upon in terror.

The action of the ascent, given in the third person narrative of period 2, has its prelude in period 1 where the Cross describes its feelings as it awaits the Savior and perceives the trembling of creation. The action of 2 is completed in 3 where the Cross describes itself as trembling in the embrace of the Savior. The device of framing the action of the ascent by a prelude and conclusion is supported by the rhetorical balance of the two first person periods, 1, 33–38, and 3, 42–45:

	Period 1	Period 3
(Verbal polyptoton)	*bifian,* 36	*bifode,* 42
(phrasal repetition)	*ic þa ne dorste . . . bugan,* 35–36	*ne dorste ic hwæðre bugan,* 42 . . . *hyldan me ne dorste,* 45
(phrasal repetition with polyptoton)	*hwæðre ic fæste stod,* 38	*ac ic sceolde fæste standan,* 43
(polyptoton and variation)	*eorðan sceatas,* 37	*to eorðan . . . to foldan sceatum,* 42–3

The image of the embrace developed in period 3 is striking. In period 1 the cross declares that it did not bow when it saw the boundaries of earth tremble. In period 3 it declares that it trembled but still did not dare bow. Thus the trembling of the universe as the Savior approaches the cross is completed in the trembling of the cross when the act of ascent is accomplished. The cross shares in the awe of the universe, but in a special way, because the trembling of the cross is occasioned by the embrace, *Bifode ic þa me se beorn ymbclypte,* 42. The sharing of creation is universal; the role of the cross involves an immediate and particular sharing, especially in the context of the poet's use of the verb "embraced," *ymbclypte,* where an analogue to the trembling in the passion of love may be suggested. Governed by the Savior's law, the cross dared not participate in the outward adoration of creation, but participating in the great act of God's love, it trembled in the Lord's embrace. As the universe trembled in the awesome disruption of Nature occasioned by God's death, the Cross trembled in sharing directly in the sacrificial act. Although this bold concept is not original with the poet,[13] his elaborate development of the feelings of the

13. See, for example, Patch's citation of the York Breviary, "Liturgical Influence in the Dream of the Rood," *PMLA*, 24 (1919), p. 253.

cross as it shares the Passion is clearly intended to arouse in the reader a feeling of empathy, of shared and felt experience.

The striking central metaphoric pattern of the embrace is developed with particular skill in the poet's handling of the polyptoton in periods 1 and 3: *gestigan—gestah; bifian—bifode.* The filling out of this pattern of ascent and trembling suggests how in Christ the polarities of warrior and lover are combined. In a single impact it provides an immediate sense of the horror of the Crucifixion in its particularity and of the Providential design of its universality. Through implication and through the shaping of the action the upheaval of Nature is made to reflect its cause, the combination of opposites, as God the eternal and universal suffers the mortality of men, and saves mankind by becoming its victim. As has been noted, in period 1 Christ approaches the cross wishing to ascend it; in 2 his wish is explained—he wished to free mankind; and in 3 Christ's wish is fulfilled in his embrace of the Cross. The primary antithesis is brilliantly suggested in the riddle-like final compound clausule of period 3, 44–45, *Rod wæs ic aræred, ahof ic ricne cyning/ heofona hlaford —hyldan me ne dorste.* "A cross I was erected, I raised the King/ of the heavens above—I dared not bow." The antithesis—the cross erected in ignominy raised the King of heaven—reflects the preceding action, the raising of the cross in paragraph ii, and the ascent of Christ in paragraph iii. Similarly, the epithets of divine power in the final clausule, *ricne cyning, heofona hlaford,* reflect the parenthetical clausule, *þæt wæs god ælmihtig,* 39, of period 2, and reinforce the contrast between this clausule and the subjects of the a clausules of 2 and 3, *geong hæleð,* "young warrior," 39, *beorn,* "son," 42, both suggestive of Christ's humanity.

Paragraph iv, the crucifixion: In paragraphs ii and iii the narrative action is chiefly advanced in the third person periods. In ii the enemy (third person plural) brought the Cross to Calvary; in iii the Savior (third person singular) ascended the Cross. Similarly, in paragraph iv, they, the enemy (third person plural) pierced the Cross with nails and reviled both Cross and Christ. Conversely the first person periods in the three paragraphs serve to convey the narrative through the medium of the feelings and perceptions of the cross. The effect is to superimpose upon the linear narrative an oblique "I" narrative which engages the empathy of the reader. The "I" narrative places the action in time, in place, and in the inner dimension of something recalled in fresh remembrance. In paragraph ii upon the narrative of the hewing, the fashioning, and the placing of the Cross was imposed a personal sense of violence done, "I yet remember," and intimations of the Passion to come. In paragraph iii the action of the Ascent was framed by the "I" narrative to give a sense both of a personal and of a universal participation in the anguish of the moment.

In the four periods of paragraph iv the first person and third person constructions are balanced and interlaced. Period 1, 46–47, contains three brief clausules. The third person plural indicative of the first half-line clausule, *þurhdrifan hi me mid deorcan næglum*, 46, is balanced by the third person plural passive in the second clausule, *on me syndon gesiene*, the subjects of this clausule being two inanimate nouns, *dolg* and *inwidhlemmas*. These first balanced clausules stand in logical relation to each other—the "wounds" of the second clausule are the result of the nailing in the first. Two somewhat unusual phrases, *deorcan næglum* and *opene inwidhlemmas*, are given special emphasis through position. As Dickins and Ross point out about the first, "the word *dark* is not recorded elsewhere in English with a similar sense." They note also that "*inwidhlemm* occurs only here," and that "*hlemm* usually means literally 'sound of a blow' . . . but it is here used of the actual wounds caused by a blow." The poet uses these unique forms to establish an implied contrast. The nails are called "dark" not only because they cause the wounds, but also because they will, in turn, be transfigured into the bright jewels of the cross triumphant. Similarly the wounds, *dolg*, and by metonymy, *inwidhlemmas*, were what the dreamer in his vision perceived through the gold. The sounds of the blow, *hlemmas*, exist in the particular time of the Crucifixion, but produce the enduring glory of the wounds triumphant. In contrast to the pair of balanced clausules a and b the third simple clausule is in the first person, with the cross as subject, *ne dorste ic hira ænigum sceððan*, "I dared harm none of them," 47. The clausule is parenthetical and echoes earlier simple clausules, which form a distinct rhetorical pattern in paragraph iii. Clausule 1c of iv, and 1b, 3a², 3b³ of iii have *ne dorste* as their main verb, and all present the dilemma of the Cross:

iii, 1 b, *þær ic þa ne dorste . . . / bugan oððe berstan*, 35–36
iii, 3 a², *ne dorste ic hwædre bugan to eorðan*, 42
iii, 3 b³, *hyldan me ne dorste*, 45
iv, 1 c, *ne dorste ic hira ænigum sceððan*, 47

This pattern, linking iii and iv, is supported by the related pattern in iii of oppositional clausules which state positively how the dilemma of the cross was resolved—it stood fast:

iii, 1 c², *hwæðre ic fæste stod*, 38
iii, 3 a³, *ac ic sceolde fæste standan*, 43

Clausules a and b of iv, 1, as noted, are related by cause and effect. Periods 1 and 2 of iv stand in the same relation. The besmirching and bleeding (2) are caused by the action of the nailing (1). Further, the two clausules of period 2 reflect the third person, first person structure of 1, with the third person in clausule 2a, *Bysmeredon hie unc butu ætgædere*, balancing the first person of 2b, *Eall ic wæs mid blode bestemed* 48. Further, the two clausules have a cause and effect relationship—the besmirching is the cause of the cross' being smeared with blood. The union of Christ and the cross celebrated in paragraph iii in the image of the embrace is consecrated in iv, 2 in the annointing of the cross with the blood. This sacramental union is suggested in paragraph iv, through the single use in the poem of the dual number *unc*, 48, the object of *bysmeredon*. Again the use of the dual marks the cause and effect relationship. The nailing unites the two physically, as in intention they were united in the embrace. The wounds of Christ in the nailing now become the wounds of the cross, and Christ's blood becomes part of the cross. The causal relation between 2a and 2b is underscored by the word play inherent in the root of *by-smer-ian*; *-smer-* in composition produces either *smerian*, "revile," or *smerwan*, "smear;" the result of the reviling of Christ by the enemy is the smearing of the cross with his blood. In this holy blood, *sancta sanguina*, the cross is consecrated.[14] To suggest the linked aspects of suffering and triumph, the poet places the result clausule of 2, *Eall ic wæs mid blode bestemed/ begoten of þæs guman sidan*, 48–49, so that it is echoic of two earlier lines, *eall þæt beacen wæs/begoten mid golde*, 6–7, and *hwilum hit wæs mid wætan bestemed/ beswyled mid swates gange*, 22–23. Particularly interesting is the repetition of *begoten*. The compound with *be-*, 49, is found only in *Elene* and *Dream*, 7, where its meaning is "cover, spread," and refers to the adornment of the cross triumphant. This meaning would appear to be a metaphoric extension of the literal meaning of the word found in line 49, "poured out." In the context of their repetitions in the poem, the literal meaning "poured out" provides the cause for the earlier metaphoric extension; because Christ's blood "poured out" onto the cross, the cross is "covered" with gold. A link with the vision of the cross (I) is suggested in the pouring of the blood "from the side of the man," which echoes the dreamer's first glimpse of the cross suffering as it began "to bleed from the right side," 20. Both suggest the final act of the Crucifixion, the piercing of the side with the spear of Longinus. Finally, only one epithet for the Savior appears in the first two periods of paragraph iv, *guman*, "man." The effect is to emphasize the humanity of Christ, his death as man.

The final two periods of the paragraph, 3, 50–52, and 4, 52–56 return to the motif of creation sharing in the great upheaval of Nature during the Crucifixion, a motif found regularly in many representations of the Cruxifixion where the sun and moon are shown covering their faces and weeping.[15] As a living tree, the cross shares in the involvement of Nature, another motif frequently found in early pictures of the cross which suggest its origin as a tree.[16] However, this tree has been made a cross with a special destiny above Nature. As Ælfric was to put it in a sermon on the invention of the cross, *"and seo rod is gemynd his [Christ's] mæran þrowunge, halig ðurh hine, ðeah ðe heo on holte weox."*[17]

14. See for several relevant citations Patch, *op. cit.*, p. 250.
15. Paul Thoby, *op. cit.*, nos. 20, 29 *bis*, as two examples. See figure 1, page 27.
16. Paul Thoby, *op. cit.*, nos. 29 *bis*, 31, for example. See figure 1, page 27.
17. Ælfric, *op. cit.*, II, p. 306.

FIGURE 3.

Reprinted, by permission, from W. G. Collingwood, *Northumbrian Crosses of the Pre-Norman Age* (Faber & Faber Ltd.).

Rhetorically periods 3 and 4 continue the balance between the first and third persons of 1 and 2. Period 3 consists of two clausules both in the first person: 1) "I endured many hateful misfortunes" (50–51); 2) "I saw the God of hosts sharply suffer" (50–52). They are retrospective in content and repeat earlier first person periods which 1) give the feelings of the cross, 2) tell what the cross saw (compare lines 33, 36, also 4, 14, 21). In period 4 there are three clausules, two compound (a and b) and one simple (c); a, 52–55, b, 55–56, c, 56. The compound clausules comprise simple clausules in the third person singular and plural: a^1, plural; a^2, singular; b^1, singular; b^2, plural. (It proved impossible in the translation to imitate the shift in number of clausule b, which has been rendered as a simple clausule.) Clausule c is in the singular. Clausule a describes the darkness, and b the weeping of creation.[18]

The poet uses these traditional motifs thematically in such a way as to enforce the already established design of contrast between darkness and radiance, ignominy and triumph. For example, in clausule a the shadows are described as covering the corpse of the Ruler. The object, *hræw*, "corpse," with connotations of the slain left on the battle-field, has as its appositive modifier the oxymoron *scirne sciman*, "clear splendor," 53–54. The startling inappropriateness of the

18. See above note 15, and compare the possibly derivative narrative of the Crucifixion in the OS *Heliand*, V, 5623–5635, ed. M. Heyne (Paderborn, 3rd edition, 1883) pp. 113–114.

Thuo warð thar an middian dag   mahtig tekan
wundarlik giwaraht oƀar thesa werold alla,
thuo man thena godes suno an thena galgon huof,
Krist an that kruci: thuo warð it kuð oƀar al,
hwo thiu sunna warð gisworkan, ni mahta swigli lioht
skoni giskinan, ak sia skado farfeng
thim endi thiustri, endi so githrismod wedar,
allaro dago drouƀost, dunkar swiðo
oƀar thesa widan weruld, so lango so waldend Krist
qual an themo krucie, kuningo rikost,
ant nuon dages. Thuo thie neƀal tiskred
that giswerk warð thuo teswungan, bigan sunnan lioht
hedron an himile.

Then became there at midday a mighty sign
wondrously wrought over all this world,
when man raised the son of God on the gallowstree,
Christ on the cross: then became it known over all
how the sun became darkened, nor might the bright light
shine radiantly, but the shadows went forth
dark and dusky, and the darkened air
darkest of all days, very dark
over this wide world, as long as Lord Christ
was dying on the cross, most powerful king
at the ninth hour of the day. Then the darkness dispersed
that darkness became scattered, the light of the sun began
to brighten in heaven.

modifier gives metaphoric dimension to the description. The literal reference of the clausule is to the eclipse of the sun at the hour of the Crucifixion. In this sense the shadows cover the clear splendor of the sun not the body, but the shadows which cover the sun reflect the higher reality of a death which has covered the Son, whose radiance remains, as does the sun's, though momentarily obscured. The motif recalls the dreamer's vision (I) of the radiant cross, *beacen*, 6, which becomes momentarily obscured by the evidence of suffering, *beswyled mid swates gange*, 23. Clausule b^1 of 4, *weop eal gesceaft*, 55, also reflects the vision, standing as the inverse to the description there of the adoration of the cross by *eall þeos mære gesceaft*, 12. The abrupt shift to the plural in b^2, *cwiððon cyninges fyll*, 56, gives special emphasis to the crying out of creation (in the thunder of the earthquake?), particularly because the narrative of the cross, except perhaps for the sound of blows suggested in *inwidhlemmas*, 46, has concentrated on sight and feeling, as is true also of the vision (I).

The rhetorical bravura of the a and b clausules sets in relief the simplicity of the simple final c clausule, *Crist wæs on rode*, 56. The effect produced by the flatness of c is to produce a feeling of expectancy, of time standing still until the final act, the entombment, is complete. The entombment is also anticipated metaphorically in the description of the eclipse in a as an enshrouding and con-cealing, i.e., burial, of the body of Christ. Similarly the lamentation of the followers of Christ after the entombment is anticipated in b by the weeping and speaking out of creation.

Paragraph v, the descent: The descent from the cross is narrated in para-graph v, 57–62. It is introduced by *Hwæðre*, "yet," 57, a conjunction used earlier, 24, to mark a significant narrative shift. In effect the paragraph tells of the separation of Christ from the Cross, and in its narrative structure it stands in contrastive parallel with the preceding paragraphs which tell of their coming together. Paragraph v continues the rhetorical structure of balanced periods, with contrast between first and third persons. Periods 1 and 3, 57–58, and 60–62, have third person plural subjects, the followers of Christ being understood, in contrast to the *feondas* the third person plural subjects of paragraphs ii and iv. The subject of periods 2 and 4, 58–60, 62, is the cross speaking in the first person. These first person periods are carefully linked; *Sare ic wæs mid sorgum gedrefed*, 59, in 2 being echoed with variation in 4, *Eall ic wæs mid strælum forwundod*, 62. This design within the paragraph has a wider rhetorical function in its structural echo of a climactic clause of II, iv, the Crucifixion, *Eall ic wæs mid blode bestemed* (48). A link with the "I" narrative of the vision (I) is also provided by the echo of I, iii, *Eall ic wæs mid sorgum gedrefed* (20). In addi-tion to this pattern, other structural echoes suggest a contrastive parallel with preceding paragraphs. In v the friends are described as taking away the Savior from the cross on Calvary, an action which contrastively repeats the actions of the enemy in ii who took the tree from the wooded hill (*genaman*, 30, *genamon*, 60). The cross in v saw the friends approach; and overwhelmed with sorrows "bowed" to deliver its burden; then the friends lifted Christ from his sufferings. This series of actions stands in contrastive parallel with those of iii where the cross saw the Savior, and filled with awe nevertheless stood fast, and then lifted Christ in suffering. Each parallel action is accompanied by a verbal or structural parallel: *Geseah ic*, 33—*Ic beheold*, 58; *hwæðre ic fæste stod*, 38—*hnag ic hwæðre*, 59; *ahof ic ricne cyning*, 44—*ahofon hine of ðam hefian wite*, 61. Finally the cross, left by the friends, *standan steame bedrifenne*, "to stand mired in blood," declares, *Eall ic wæs mid strælum forwundod*, "I was mortally wounded with arrows," 62, phrases which echo iv where the enemy, *þurhdrifan hi me mid deorcan næglum*, "they pierced me with dark nails," 46, and where the cross says, *Eall ic wæs mid blode bestemed*, "I was all besmeared with the blood," 48.

The echoic pattern of paragraph v is elaborated in the details of its diction. Thus, at the beginning of the paragraph, the followers of Christ are designated by an adjectival noun, *fuse*, 57,[19] as an adjective used earlier to modify *beacen*, 21. There the connotations of the word, "ready for the journey of death," was highly appropriate in its premonitory context. Here the same connotation of readiness for journey has reflexive significance; the *fuse* are prepared to complete Christ's death in his entombment. They are later in the paragraph called "men of battle," *i.e.*, men of fortitude, prepared, to follow Christ crucified. In the verb *hnag*, 59, the contrastive echo of the earlier standing fast of the cross is underlined by an accompanying use of oxymoron: the *eaðmod*, "humble," cross *hnag*, "bowed," *elne mycel*, "very bravely," 59–60. The verb and adjective (bowed, humble) provide a set of meanings antithetical to the adverbial phrase (very bravely). The effect of the oxymoron and of the use of *elne mycel* is to remind the reader of the dilemma of the cross when Christ approached it *elne mycel*, "very bravely," 34. The cross desired in humility to bow and to fall bravely upon its Lord's enemies, but it stood fast, and with a higher fortitude of obedience, accepted its humiliating gallows role. The Lord had embraced the cross, and now the Lord will be separated from it, but the separation, too, the cross accepts humbly and with fortitude (*elne mycel*) in imitation of its master. This oxymoron is continued in the first part of the following period, *Genamon hie þær ælmihtigne God*, 60, where the syntax demands what is manifestly impossible, that men could have laid hold of almighty God. The impossibility is made possible only through the Incarnation, literally true and humanly impossible: impossible for unaided reason to understand, possible of acceptance through faith. Oxymoron is also involved in the clausule b of 3, *ahofon hine of ðam hefian wite*, 61. There is a contradiction of meaning in the verb, *ahofon*, which literally means "lifted up" (as in the statement by the cross, *ahof ic ricne cyning*, 44), whereas literally the men lifted

19. Elsewhere in this paragraph and the next, the friends are designated by even less identifying words, *secgum*, "men," 59, *hilderincas*, "warriors," 61, *beornas*, "men," 66.

Christ *down* from his suffering. The effect of the oxymoron is to suggest the mystery of Redemption; as Christ ascended the Cross to suffer for mankind, he descended so that he might arise. Christ is lifted up to his suffering and lifted up from his suffering as spiritual steps in his archetypal redemptive journey upward.

Finally, to reinforce the pattern of echo in the paragraph, the metaphoric structure of the final period, 4, *Eall ic wæs mid strælum forwundod*, provides a startling contrast between "nails," the literal referent, and "arrows," the metaphoric referent. Obviously on the level of metaphor the statement by the cross, "I was mortally wounded by arrows," serves to continue the underlying metaphor of the crucifixion as a battle, a metaphoric level maintained in the preceding period 3 by the designation of the friends as "warriors." Then, too, *stræl* has a frequent metaphoric connotation of demonic temptation, and on this level recalls *inwidhlemmas*, "wounds of hate," 47, and *earmra ærgewin*, 19. Furthermore, in the metaphor of the arrows, an analogue to the martyrdom of St. Sebastian may be intended. This martyrdom, to which Ælfric likens that of King Edmund, had great appeal and was frequently pictured, and is itself an analogue of the Crucifixion, which it reenacts, the Saint being bound to a tree and pierced with arrows, instead of nails and spear. The analogue provides a base for the comparison in the poem between the nails and arrows. The extension of significance in the metaphor would be entirely appropriate to the poet's design of picturing the Crucifixion as an exemplar of Christian heroism.

Paragraph vi, the entombment: The sixth paragraph, 63–69, continues the prevailing scheme of syntactic balance, with the narrative developed in periods 1, 63–64, and 3, 65–69, in the third person plural, and with appositive statements concerning the dead Savior contained in 2, 64–65, and 4, 69, in the third person singular, the subject, Christ, being the object of the narrative, third plural periods. Periods 2 and 4 are placed in repetitive parallel and serve to mark the two steps of the plural narration: in 1 the laying down and gazing at the body, in 3 the making of the tomb and the lamentation before departure. In interlacing the singular, appositive (2 and 4), and plural narrative periods (1 and 3), the poet employs a single word *meðe*, "tired," with striking effectiveness. In period 2 it represents a striking litotes, used as it is to describe the dead Christ "tired after the great conflict." This litotes stands in contrast to the literal use of the word in period 3 to describe the friends "tired" after their labor, 69.

In the paragraph a contrast is developed which appears to echo an important structural element in the preceding narrative. The vision of I is marked by unbroken silence. Only at the beginning of II is the silence broken by the voice of the cross. In the narrative of the cross there is no suggestion of sound until the ascent is completed. Then in iv, sound is suggested in the metaphor, *inwidhlemmas*, 47, literally the sounds of the blows of the hammers, and with startling suddenness in the crying out of creation, line 56. Similarly, in paragraph vi, 1, the friends gaze silently at the Savior, and then in period 3 they cry out in lamentation.

This reflection in the internal narrative structure of paragraph vi of the structure of what has preceded is given emphasis by the deliberate parallel between periods 1 of vi and 2 of paragraph v. In v, 2, the cross *beheold*, 58, looked down at the men coming to deprive him of Christ; in vi, 1, the men *beheoldon*, "looked down," 64, at the body of Christ. This act of beholding reminds us also, contrastively, of the central period of the second paragraph of I, when all creation *beheoldon*, 9 and 11, "looked at" the cross lifted in the sky. The parallels between paragraphs v and vi are further developed. In v the cross gave up the body of the Savior to the men who then left the cross; in vi the men give up the body to the tomb, which they then leave. In paragraph v the cross remained on the hill, a spectacle of ignominious death (cf. *wæfersyn*, 31). In vi the friends make the tomb, *on banan gesyhðe*, "in the sight of the slayers," 66,[20] a phrase difficult to explain except as it is part of the interlocking design of paragraphs v and vi and as it relates to the previous emphasis on the act of beholding. The parallelism of cross and tomb also has anticipatory implications. The cross, which has been emptied of the Savior, stands as a spectacle awaiting the entombment and resurrection which will be described in paragraph vii; the tomb, which has been filled with the Savior, stands as a spectacle within which Christ rests until the Resurrection.

In paragraph vi, the quiet of sorrow, broken only by the cries of the friends as they prepare to depart, is emphasized and in the continuing metaphor of the battle, the grim solitude of the battle-field with the cross and tomb abandoned by the friends to the gaze of the apparently victorious enemies.[21] At the same time the interlaced emphasis upon Christ's "resting" creates an expectancy of future action which cuts through the desolation of the scene. The antithesis, which is central to the design of paragraph vi, is between the sense of finality and the sense of preparation; that is, the paragraph serves both as the final scene in the Crucifixion, and as the scene preparatory to the Resurrection. The poet enforces the antithesis between preparation and finality in the repetition, period 3, of *ongunnon*, 63 and 67. Although the verbs are apparently purely auxiliary they have inchoative force, and are to be translated "begun" because they derive such meaning from the contextual antithesis: the men *began* to perform the *final* rites.

20. I accept Wrenn's suggestion, noted by Dickens and Ross, p. 35, that banan represents a LWS genitive plural. To take it as genitive singular implies a reference to the Cross, with the consequent difficulty of having the Cross designate itself as "slayer," whereas the enemies are clearly the slayers. The poet is here making use of an authoritative tradition which placed the tomb "a stone's throw from Golgotha." See the citations in A. S. Cook, *The Old English Elena, Phoenix and Physiologus* (New Haven, 1919) p. xvi.

21. What is evoked here is the common phrase to denote defeat as in the Parker Chronicle, "ahton wælstowe gewald," year 837, and elsewhere; see also Grein, *s.v. wælstow*.

Literally, the paragraph narrates the entombment of the Savior, but cutting across this is the metaphor of battle, a battle the outcome of which has not yet been decided, whatever the desolation of Golgotha. The dead body in the sepulcher which Christ's followers gazed at mournfully was only resting in the sense that in historical time the battle was not to be completed until the Harrowing of Hell and the Resurrection had taken place. This metaphoric design explains the striking litotes employed in vi to describe the dead Christ. In period 1 he is *limwerigne*, "weary to the bone," 63, a hapax legomenon; in period 2 *he hine ðær hwile reste/meðe æfter ðam miclan gewinne*, "he rested there awhile, tired after the great conflict," 64–65; finally in period 4, after the mourners had left him, *reste he ðær mæte weorode*, "he rested with a little company," 69, that is, entirely alone. On the literal level what is described is an impossibility; the dead are not weary, nor do they rest. This literal impossibility is underscored by the contrastive repetition of *meðe*, "weary," in line 65 as applied to Christ, in 69 as applied to the friends. In its second use the adjective describes what is literally true, as in its first use it describes the impossible. By litotes, of course, Christ's weariness and resting may be taken to signify the equated state of death. Yet even as litotes the extended meaning becomes possible only when the equation, rest : death, is possible, as it is for Christ only as he is man. But Christ is man only in the mystery of the *communicatio idiomatum*, as God it is not possible to say either that he rests, or that he is dead. What remains is the metaphoric level, where the statement that Christ was weary and rested signifies simply that in human time the entombment marks a pause in the spiritual battle begun in the Crucifixion and to be ended in the Harrowing of Hell and the Resurrection.

The antithesis between the literal reality of the death of Christ and the spiritual reality of his deathlessness is further developed by the poet through oxymoron. In period 1 the friends stood gazing down at the corpse of "the Ruler of heaven," 69, and in period 3 they entombed "the Ruler of victories," (*sigora wealdend*). The apparently dead victim of battle is thus the heavenly victim whose triumph is yet to be made manifest. Both the litotes and the oxymoron suggest on the metaphorical level the antithesis between the historical and spiritual realities of the Crucifixion: as man Christ was weary and rested; that is he suffered death and was buried. As God he did not die, and his weariness and resting marked only the outward appearance of the pause before he finally overcame death.

Paragraph vii, the entombment and resurrection of the Cross: The action of paragraph vii, 70–77, the conclusion to the narrative of the Crucifixion, is structured so as to reflect the beginning of the narrative. Thus in II, ii, the enemies felled the cross on a hill, and then transformed it into a spectacle of terror; here in vii the enemies fell it on Golgotha, but the friends transfigure it by setting upon it "both gold and silver," 77.

Of the four periods comprising the paragraph 1, 70–72, is in the first person plural; 2, 72–73, is in the third person singular; 3, 73–75, is in the impersonal third person singular; 4, 75–77, is in the third person plural. This concluding paragraph is thus marked off from the others by the use of different person and number in each of the periods, and in period 1, the use of the first person plural also marks a departure from the previous first person which has been uniformly in the singular. This latter syntactic modification, although it serves rhetorically to mark off the concluding paragraph, is a simple variant of the basic pattern. The first person plural subject, the three crosses, is closely related to the first person subject of the preceding narrative, the cross. The phrasing of the opening of the first plural period 1 serves an important structural function, for *Hwæðre we ðær greotende gode hwile/ stodon on staðole*, 70–71, clearly echoes the opening lines of II, i, with its first person singular subject, the dreamer, *Hwæðre ic þær licgende lange hwile/ beheold hreowcearig*, 24–25. The first period of the concluding paragraph thus returns to the beginning of the narrative, with the "I" of the dreamer and the "I" of the cross subsumed in the first person plural of the conclusion. The dreamer and the cross are subtly linked in experience remembered. The first person plural beginning also serves to link the immediately preceding paragraph vi with vii. In vi the Savior was said, in litotes, to rest "with a little company"; here in vii the cross literally so rests in the company only of the other two crosses. Further, the lamentation of the three crosses in vii is linked to that of the friends in vi. The lament forms a continuous action, that of the crosses beginning after that of the friends had ceased, *syððan stefn up gewat*, 71. Of most importance, the first person plural serves to underscore the final ignominy of the cross and to look forward to its future triumph. The plural pronoun suggests that its fate is now bound to that of the crosses bearing the thieves. The three will be jumbled together into the pit of intended oblivion, but as the poet's audience is aware, a miracle will enable St. Helena to distinguish the true cross from its fellows, and thus to set upon it the "gold and silver," described in vi, 4.

Period 1 of vii is linked to period 4, both being introduced by *Hwæðre*, a conjunction used frequently hitherto to mark significant narrative shifts (18, 57), and internal contrasts (24, 38, 42). Period 4 has a third person plural subject, *freondas*, "friends," 76, these being so designated for the first time, in contrast to the immediate designation of the *feondas*, "enemy," in the first narrative paragraph II, ii. Hitherto the friends have been designated very generally (*fuse, beorn, hilderincas*.) By suspending the specific designation, *freondas*, till the final period of the final paragraph of the narrative, the poet succeeds in framing the narrative within the contrast, foes—friends. Since the "friends" designated in paragraph vii are not, of course, those who buried Christ, but Helena and her companions, the effect is also economically to suggest how the immediate grief of the *fuse hilderincas*, will be changed to joy in the Resurrection and in the Invention of the Cross, i.e., to suggest a temporal sequence which leads from grief over the *ærgewin* to the new joy. This circular motif in which the end of the action is a return to the beginning is suggested by the echo in vii, period 1, 70–71, of II, ii, 24–25, and by the echo in the last line of vii, 4, *gyredon me golde ond seolfre*, 77, of phrases from I, *begoten mid golde*, 7, *gegyred mid golde*, 16, and *mid since gegyrwed*, 23.

As the sorrow of the crosses narrated in vii 1, is balanced against the joyful resurrection of the cross in 4, so the description of the buried Christ of period 2 is balanced against that of the burial of the cross in 3. In period 2 the striking oxymoron of II, iv, 4, 53–54, *Wealdendes hræw/ scirne sciman*, is echoed in lines 72–73, *Hræw colode/ fæger feorgbold*, with the same antithesis between *hræw* and its appositive modifier. In period 3 the use of *ongan* in narrating the felling and entombment of the cross (*fyllan ongan*, 73) recalls the similar use of *ongan* in paragraph vi, where the taking down and entombment of Christ is narrated. The felling of the cross on Golgotha of vii, as has been noted, reflects the felling of the tree of ii. In addition, the phrasing in vii, 1, *þa us man fyllan ongan/ ealle to eorðan*, 73–74, particularly taken in connection with period 1, *Hwæðre we . . . /stodon on staðole*, 70–71, echoes paragraph iii, where the cross speaks of its standing fast although it desired to fell the enemy, *Ealle ic mihte/ feondas gefyllan—hwæðre ic fæste stod*, 37–38. The action forbidden to the cross is permitted to the enemy, a thematic irony underscored by the appositive phrase, *þæt wæs egeslic wyrd*, 74. The "grim misfortune" is really that of the enemy working out their own doom to the greater glory of the cross. Finally, the substitution in 3 of the impersonal singular *man* for the previous third person plural, *feondas* serves a clearly definable purpose. Particularly in the context of the appositive statement, "that was a grim misfortune," 74, the substitution of the impersonal *man* effectively suggests that the enemies are not after all prime movers, but rather instruments of fate. In obstinate error they consign the cross to the pit of oblivion, but in so doing work blindly, victims of a destiny, the meaning of which is revealed when in the unrolling of God's Providence the Cross is discovered and honored with gold and silver.

Scene III: The Address of the Cross

The address consists of two paragraphs. Paragraph i, the peroration, 78–94, recapitulates the narrative of the ignominious suffering of the cross which resulted in its triumph, and thus explains the vision of the triumphant cross (Scene I) in which the signs of ignominious suffering were revealed. Paragraph ii, the adjuration, 95–121, suggests the course of action which should follow from the dreamer's vision (I) and the narrative of the cross (II); thus the dreamer is commanded to make known what he has seen and heard, and to declare its significance.

Paragraph i, the Peroration: Paragraph i consists of four periods in which, through a series of antitheses, the cross recapitulates the story of its triumph after humiliation. In the first three periods, 1, 78–83, 2, 83–86, 3, 87–89, the antitheses are developed through clausular contrast. Period 4, 90–94, summarizes the antitheses in a metaphoric comparison between the honor paid to the Cross and to Mary, a comparison in which the antithesis between this glory and the lowliness of the Crucifixion and the Incarnation is implied.

Period 1 of III, i begins in direct address to the dreamer, *Nu ðu miht gehyran,* 78, which establishes the transition from the narrative of II, and provides a link to II by the echo of the beginning of II, line 26, *oððaet ic gehyrde.* The hortatory formula is completed in clausule a by a *þæt* clause as object in which the cross speaks of its suffering. The a clausule is balanced by b where an introduction in the impersonal, *is nu sæl cumen,* 80, is completed by a *þæt* clause as object in which the honoring of the cross is described. Although the juxtaposition of meaning in the two clausules is supported by a syntactic contrast between the second and first person singular of a, and the impersonal third singular and the third person plural of b, the clausules are closely linked by their structural balance, and by the repetition of *nu* (78, 80), in the introduction to each clausule. The effect of this balancing, and particularly of the repetition of the adverb of time is to establish in clausules a and b a link, a temporal relation between the antitheses of suffering and humiliation.

The cross began its narrative of suffering by placing it in the time of things remembered: it was "many years ago—I yet remember," 28. In its address it returns to the present, the now, of triumph. This "now," as relevant to the dreamer, is the "now" of his having learned that what he saw in the vision (I) as the alternation of two aspects of the cross, "now . . . drenched with shedding of blood, now sheathed with treasure," 22–23, is to be explained as a relation between past and present. The temporal explanation in III is contrived so as to be echoic of the vision: there "men in the world and all creation's wonder," 13, were seen revering the cross; here line 82, with exact repetition of the subject phrase, *men ofer moldan ond eall þeos mære gesceaft,* 12, they are said by the cross to show it reverence. Similarly, in the vision the dreamer spoke of the "ancient malice of foes," *earmra ærgewin,* 14–19, here the Cross speaks of "the work of the sinful," *bealuwara weorc,* 79.[22] The appositional clausules of period 1 thus give a temporal explanation for the dreamer's vision of the two aspects of the Cross.

Period 2 also consists of two clausules set in apposition, a, 83–84, b, 84–86. The clausules are again syntactically contrasted; a is in the third person, *bearn Godes,* 83, b in the first person, *ic,* 87. A cause-effect relation between the

22. The paralleling of *ærgewin earmra* and *bealuwara weorc* makes certain the reading of *bealuwara* as a hapax legomonon, "evil doers," as it also supports the reference of *earmra* as not being to the Cross, but to the "enemy." J. A. Burrow, "An Approach to the Dream of the Rood," *Neophilologus,* 43 (1959), pp. 123–133, argues effectively for the rhetorical unity of the poem, the hypothesis assumed and supported in this study.

appositive clausules is suggested by the use of "therefore," *forþan*, 84, to introduce b, and a relation to period 1 is suggested by the use of adverbs of time,
hwile in a, *nu* in b. In effect, period 2 explains that the temporal sequence
marked in 1 has a cause-effect relationship: because the Son of God suffered on
the Cross for a time, *hwile*, 84, (cp. line 24, 64, 70); therefore, the Cross is
now triumphant, towering in the heavens, *nu þrymfæst/ hlifige under heofenum*, 84–85, as the triumphant cross of the vision was lifted in the sky, *on lyft
lædan*, 5. This movement from earth to heaven marks the emblematic value
of the cross as a vessel of salvation which "may heal each man who lives in
awe" of it, 85–86. Here the ingeniously intertwined motifs in I of the suffering
and triumph of the Cross, and of the dreamer's awe at the sight are given their
explanation. The suffering in the Passion is the cause for the triumph, and the
awe of the dreamer reflects the attitude proper to one who glimpses in the Cross
the promise of redemption.

Period 3 returns to the simple temporal sequence of the two clausules of 1,
marked by the adverbs, *iu*, *ærþan*, 87, 88. But the temporal sequence of 3 has a
different base from that of period 1. That of 1 is based on the historical time of
the transformation of the cross; that of 3 is based on the spiritual time of the
evolution of man's view of the cross. In the a clausule of 3 the cross is seen as it
was once in time, "the most terrible and loathsome of torments," 87–88; in b it
is seen as it now appears revealing "life's right way . . . to speaking men,"
87–88. Obviously the time sequence relative to men suggests that the cross is a
token of salvation only to those who perceive that its triumphant "now" is the
true significance of its ignominious "then." Through this time sequence the
relation between the dreamer and the Cross is again explained. The dreamer,
through the vision, shares in the experience of the Passion, the function of which
is salvation; it is this that he is "to make known through contrivance of words,"
as the Cross will declare in the next paragraph.

In period 4 the conclusion to be derived from the three preceding temporal
periods is explicitly stated. The period provides the explanation of why the
Cross declared in period 1, *me weorðiað . . . menn*, 81–82; it is, the Cross
declares echoically in 4, because *me þa geweorðoðe wuldres Ealdor*, 90.[23] The
three temporal periods have shown how the Cross is now honored almost inversely to its former dishonor. The final period gives striking force to the
sequence, abasement—honor, by the startling analogy, which the Cross suggests,
between itself and the Virgin Mary; as God honored the Cross, *me þa
geweorðoðe wuldres Ealdor*, 90, God likewise honored Mary, *Marian sylfe/
ælmihtig God . . . geweorðode*, 92–94.

The force of the analogy rests in an implied contrast, a traditional one
between Mary and Eve, as in the *Carmen Paschale* of Sedulius: [24]

23. Note also the echoic linking: *geworden*, 87, *geweorðode*, 90; *gebiden*, 79,
gebiddaþ, 83.

24. Book 2, lines 30–39, *PL*, 19, 596.

Sic Evae de stirpe sacra veniente Maria
Virginis antiquae facinus nova virgo piaret:
Ut quoniam natura prior vitiata jacebat
Sub ditione necis, Christo nascente, renasci
Posset homo, et veteris maculam deponere carnis.

Thus the blessed Mary springing from the root of Eve, the new
virgin, atoned for the sin of the old virgin: so that
the former man lay in corrupted nature under the power
of death, [but] Christ being born, was able to be reborn,
and to cast off the stain of the old flesh.

The two halves of the implied analogy are clear: 1) as women in Eve first corrupted human nature, created pure, and made it subject to death, women through Mary's humble bearing of the Savior, in his Incarnation which revealed the true way of life to men, transcended their nature and were honored in her by God; 2) by nature a tree of the woods (*holtes on ende*, 29) becomes as a tree of Mount Golgotha (*beorge*, 32), a spectacle of death (*wæfersyn*, 31), but in becoming this spectacle, the tree of the hill (*holmwudu*, 92) bore the Savior humbly and transcended its nature to become, like Mary, an object of veneration through God's grace.[25] The sequence, tree of nature, tree of death, tree of life (*lignum vitae*), is directly parallel to the sequence, natural woman, woman of death, woman of life. The suggestion for the analogy, it may be noted, may have come from the play in the Vulgate on *virgo-virga*; the Virgin (*virgo*) is a branch (*virga*) of the root of Jesse. The word-play is frequently found, as in Sedulius' metaphor, in speaking of Mary as "of the root of Eve."

Paragraph ii, adjuration: The beginning of paragraph ii is linked to the beginning of paragraph i, by anaphora and repetition, *Nu . . . hæleð min se leofa*, 78, 95, and syntactic inversion, *ðu miht gehyran . . . þæt ic*, 78–79, *ic þe hate . . . þæt ðu þas gesyhðe secge*, 95–96. The repetition of *nu* at the beginning of paragraph ii, taken in connection with the immediately preceding analogy between the Cross and Mary and its implied comparison with the Crucifixion and Incarnation, links the two paragraphs in such a way as to suggest the antithesis between the eternal time, represented by the everlasting "now" of the Incarnation, and the time of man, the "now" of his understanding. Further, the transition from i, 4 to ii, 1 is subtly managed by the reference in the latter to Adam's old deeds, *Adomes ealdgewyrhtum*, 100, which picks up the implied reference to the sins of Eve in the Cross-Mary analogy of i, 4. The cross in

25. *Holmwudu*, 92, would appear by this reasoning to be a deliberate creation and should not be emended, as is usual, to *holtwuden*. *Holm* is well attested in Old Saxon with the meaning "hill," "mount," and the creation of the compound in Old English involves no difficulty, once the sense "tree of Golgotha" is understood, and the deliberate contrast to the earlier designation of the Cross as a tree of the *holt*.

the first paragraph has shown that as the true way of life it has very special relevance for mankind (*reordberendum*, 89). But the way of the cross is the way of penance and atonement, of humility and obedience, a way of life revealed both by the Cross and Mary. It is this message which the cross exhorts the dreamer in paragraph ii to tell to men (*mannum*, 96). The message is anything but unusual, but its particular emphasis has special force in what must be in some form a poem written around the beginning of the 8th Century. The Crucifixion as a subject for realistic representation was slow in developing, for even after the Edict of Milan and the Invention of the Cross, Thoby states, "si la Croix brille partout, nulle part, nous ne voyons apparaître le Crucifix; la répulsion des Chrétiens pour le *servile supplicium* semble survivre au triomphe de la Croix." He notes that the Crucifixion is depicted on a panel of the 6th-century door of Saint-Sabine in Rome, but that the panel itself is small and inconspicuous in position. "Il est remarquable, [he says,] que, dans cette porte qui comprenait au moins huit grands panneaux, l'artiste ait cru devoir n'en consacrer qu'un petit à un sujet aussi important." In resumé, he points out that "la représentation de la Crucifixion au VIIIᵉ siècle ne se répand pas encore." [26] The stone crosses, like that at Ruthwell, are, as Laurence Stone points out, "a native form of monument. . . . The Roman missionaries, with characteristic tact and adaptability, took over this insular form and made it a vehicle for their propagandist activity." On the Ruthwell Cross, which carries a portion of the poem, Stone continues, "the Crucifixion is present, but hidden away on the bottom panel of the back face of the cross." He makes the interesting suggestion that "to a primitive people brought up on traditions where might and worldly success are the main criteria of morality, the Crucifixion is a bewildering example of shame and degradation." [27]

All this suggests not only something of the originality of the poem, but gives special point to the exhortation of the cross that the dreamer must make known that it is a cross of glory (*wuldres beam*, 97) upon which Almighty God suffered (*se ðe ælmihtig God on þrowode*, 98). The poet's vision may well have been intended to advance the unpalatable doctrine that Christian life must be humble and penitential by suggesting the affinities of such a life with that of the warrior who also suffers privations that he may win triumph and glory. Thus in the *Dream of the Rood* both Christ and cross appear as soldiers engaged in a conflict which has victory as its goal. Like good soldiers they are

26. Thoby, pp. 21–34.

27. Lawrence Stone, *Sculpture in Britain, The Middle Ages* (London, 1955), pp. 10–11. See figures 2, 3, and 4 (pp. 74, 91, 105). In the Crucifixion page from the *Book of Kells*, plate 4, following p. 106, as Mr. Kjell Meling has pointed out to me, no attempt is made to picture the Crucifixion, although the cruciform Chi beginning Christ's name is placed at the center, and the whole design is cruciform. It is interesting that the illuminator pictures faces, perhaps suggesting the multitude gazing toward the Cross, or away from it. For the Ruthwell Cross see F. Saxl, "The Ruthwell Cross," *JWCI*, 6 (1943), pp. 1–18, and Meyer Schapiro, "The Religious Meaning of the Ruthwell Cross," *Art Bulletin*, 26 (1944), pp. 232–245.

absolutely obedient to a command which calls upon them not to strike but to accept in penitential humility. The cross reveals in its own story the tensions inherent in a warrior society become Christian; it wishes to engage in active battle against the enemy, but with great fortitude obeys the command to endure. The reward is the palpable reality of a place in the kingdom of heaven, a reward the cross promises in its exhortation. The appeal of the cross touches the same nerve as that which Paulinus touched in the counsellor of King Edwin who was moved to belief by the promise of a reward beyond the measure of an earthly king:

> Thus to me, oh king, this present life of man on earth seems in the measure of the time which is unknown to us, as if you were sitting with your earls and nobles in the wintertime; the fire is kindled and your hall is warm, and it rains and snows and storms without; a sparrow comes and quickly flies through the house; it comes through one door and goes out the other. Lo, in the time that it is within, it is untouched by the winter's storm, but this is a twinkling of the eye and the smallest moment, and from the winter out into the winter it soon returns. So the life of man appears as the merest moment; what comes before it and what follows after, we know not. Therefore if this teaching brings anything more truthful and suitable, it is worthy that we follow it.[28]

The Dream of the Rood would then have been intended to promote the veneration of the Cross by men for whom death in battle held a traditional place of honor. It functions to give to the difficult doctrine of penitential renunciation a vivid and immediate metaphoric value as a battle where dying to the world is crowned by victory over death in everlasting life.

Paragraph ii, the Adjuration: This idea is developed in ii. Period 1, 95–100, consists of the exhortation to the dreamer to make known the story of the cross. Period 2, 101–109, has as its subject, Christ, and echoing the Apostle's Creed tells of his Death, Ascension, and Judgment. Period 2 thus completes the story of Christ's triumph after death which is implicit in the narrative of the cross and parallel with its triumphant history after its burial. Period 3, 110–121, has as its subject man at the Day of Judgment and makes explicit the symbolic significance of the cross as signifying man's true way of life. The three periods are constructed around a series of antitheses. The sound-sight contrast of I, i; II, i, iv, vi, vii, is echoed in period 1 where the dreamer is exhorted "to make known this vision," *þas gesyhðe secge*, 96. Period 2 begins with a play on *byrigde*, 101, "tasted," "buried," which suggests a characteristic antithesis; in tasting death and in his burial, Christ buried (i.e., conquered) death. The narrative antithesis developed in period 2 is between the Savior's departure from earth and his return on the Day of Judgment. In journeying from death to life he revealed how men might follow him; on his return at the Final Day, he

28. My translation is of the Old English version of Bede's *History, T. Miller,* ed. (London, 1890).

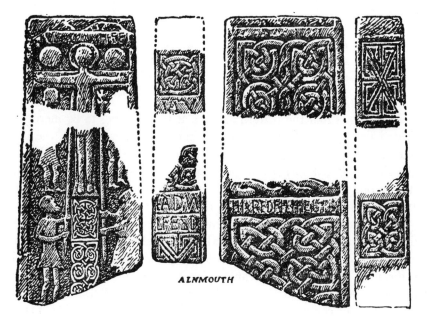

ALNMOUTH

FIGURE 4.

Reprinted, by permission, from W. G. Collingwood, *Northumbrian Crosses of the Pre-Norman Age* (Faber & Faber Ltd.).

judges those who in following him have earned heaven, and those who have not. In this journey motif there is an implicit parallel with the way of the Cross, for the Cross passed through ignominy, was buried, and after its Invention was elevated, becoming a symbol of the true way of life, the heavenly beacon which the dreamer saw in his vision. Finally, in period 2, line 106, the Lord comes with his angels, thus completing the complement of those who gazed at the cross in the dreamer's vision, men, creation, angels, only the first two having been listed in period 1, line 82, as paying honor to the Cross.

In period 3, 110–121, the Last Judgment is described. Again clausular antithesis is employed. The basic antithesis is between clausules a, 110–114, and c, 117–118. Clausule b, 115–116, is complementary to a, and d, 119–121, is complementary to c. The balance of clausules is marked rhetorically by a subtly varied repetitive pattern:

a: ne mæg þær ænig   unforht wesan   110
c: ne þearf ðær þonne ænig   unforht wesan,   117
b: ac hie þonne forhtiað   ond fea þencað,   115
d: ac . . . æghwylc sawl . . . wunian þencað,   119–121

What is striking is that the pattern appears at first reading to be merely one of repetitive balance, not antithesis. The antithesis appears through the demands of context. Thus in the *unforht* pattern (a and c) the syntactic parallel is exact, and the simple verbal variant, *mæg*, "may,"—*þærf*, "must," does not suggest that the second clause is actually the negative inversion of the first. Only in context is it clear that the prefix *un-* in the repeated predicate adjective *unforht* must be negative in its first use and intensive in its second, so that the adjectives, identical in form, are actually antithetical: "unafraid"—"very afraid." Similarly, the connectives *ac*, 115, and *ac*, 119, introducing the b and d clausules are identical in form but antithetical in meaning. In context it is clear that the first *ac* is contrastive, "but," and that the second is causative, "for." Interlacing this ambiguous pattern of contrast is the phrase in b, *ac hie þonne forhtiað*, 115, where the verb stands in polyptoton to both *unforht* phrases, but where the meaning is the inverse of the first *unforht* and complementary to the second. Further interlacing the pattern is a contrastive subject variation: a, *ne . . . ænig*, 110, *mænige*, 112, *man*, 112; b, *fea*, 115; c, *ne . . . ænig*, 117; d, *æghwylc sawl*, 120.[29]

In the contrast between the "few" and the "many" the poet may intend to remind his audience of a gospel verse, *many are called; few chosen*. The parable which contains the verse would also suggest the poet's description of the Lord's questioning and the speechlessness of his respondents, Matthew 22:71–72: "And when the king came in to see the guests, he saw there a man which

29. Note that the common reading of *fea* as an unusual and rare adverb, "a little," is not necessary if the contrastive pattern is observed; nor is the emendation of *unforht* to *anforht* necessary.

PLATE 4. Tunc crucifixerant XPI cum eo duos latrones

had not on a wedding garment: and he saith unto him, friend, how camest thou in hither not having a wedding garment? And he was speechless." Commentary on the parable also helps to explain the elaborately ambiguous rhetorical pattern. As Augustine makes clear, there is a profound and meaningful ambiguity in Christ's reference to the "few" and the "many." He explains that by the one man who was speechless, the "many," not the "few" are indicated, " 'Cast him,' He saith, 'into outer darkness.' 'Him,' that one man assuredly, of whom the Lord saith, 'for many are called but few chosen.' So then it is the few who are not cast out." [30] This ambiguity by which the one represents the many may well be reflected in the construction of period 3. The reflection in the poem of the parable also helps to explain the introduction in 3 c of the unexpected metaphor of the wearing of the cross (*in breostum bereð beacna selest*, 118). In the parable the wearing of the wedding garment is of key importance. The "few" wear it; the "many," represented by the one, do not. It is the latter who are speechless in fear. Wearing the wedding garment in the *imitatio Christi* is clearly synonymous with wearing the Cross in one's heart.

In the d clausule the metaphor of the cross as garment is replaced by the metaphor of the cross of death as the way of life, *ac ðurh ða rode sceal rice gesecan/ of eorðwege æghwylc sawl*, 119–120, echoing paragraph i of the address of the cross, *ic him lifes weg/ rihtne gerymde reordberendum*, 88–89. The metaphor derives from an analogy basic to the poem: Christ made the journey through death on the cross to the heavenly home; man by adopting the way of the cross may gain the heavenly home. The inclusion of this metaphor both at the beginning, paragraph i, and also at the conclusion of the paragraph ii of scene III is appropriate, since the metaphor relates to the most pervasive of all Christian metaphors, that of man's life as a pilgrimage. Yet the metaphor does not find its way into the address and exhortation of the cross only through weight of tradition; rather it appears as the inevitable result of a metaphoric thread which runs through the entire narrative of the cross. For the story which the cross tells is of a journey. Torn from its woods, the cross is carried to Golgotha where it participates in the Passion; it is buried, and it is resurrected; finally, as we have learned from the dreamer's vision, it ascended to the heavens, where it gleams as an emblem of man's true way of life, the pilgrimage to heaven.

Scene IV: The Dreamer's Prayer

In the concluding Scene IV the dreamer, speaking in his own person, returns to the "I" narrative of I. Paragraph i begins with the statement, "Then I prayed to the Cross," but the actual formula of prayer is reserved for the open-

30. "Sermon 40 on the New Testament," in *Nicean and Post-Nicean Fathers*, VI, 393.

ing of paragraph ii, "May the Lord be my friend," 144. In i the dreamer describes the state of mind which has resulted from his vision. In period 1, 122–126, he describes his "delight of soul," but also a concomitant sense of pilgrimage, of longing. His mind is prepared for the voyage out, and he awaits many "times of languishing," *modsefa / afysed on forðwege . . . gebad/ langunghwila*" 124–126. The pilgrimage for which he is prepared in the context of the poem is the way of the Cross. Thus in period 2, 126–131, the dreamer describes how his "hope rests in the cross"; this hope will supersede all reliance on other men. The loneliness of his vision-filled vigil, and of his renunciation of his fellow man as a source of hope and protection leads him in period 3, lines 131–135, to reflect on another kind of loneliness, that of one like the exiled wanderer whose friends have preceded him in death. In the context of his longing, these friends appear to him to have already taken the journey on which he wants to go, so that they "now live in glory," 135. It is this thought which leads him in the final period 4, 135–144, again to reflect on the journey, and on his hope that the cross will conduct him home one day "to live thence-forward," 144.

Paragraph ii begins with the prayer to Christ spoken by the dreamer, 144. The transition from Cross to Christ reflects the similar transition in III from paragraph i to ii. The transition is, of course, natural, for the cross is not itself the means of salvation, but a symbol of the way which has been opened to man through Christ. The prayer to the Lord, reflecting i, is stated obliquely; instead of developing the motif of appeal the dreamer gives a description of Christ's triumph, as it makes possible the way home for men. Christ died on the cross for men, and through his sacrifice men may now regain their heavenly home. They may follow Christ who died, arose, descended into Hell to free the saints, ascended into heaven. The conclusion of the poem, with Christ returning to his native land, suggests that if man follows Christ in the way of the cross, and turns from the world, he will find his way to the eternal reward. The dreamer has been enjoined in III to tell his dream to other men, so that his vision is not for himself alone. This is probably the reason that the prayers in IV are indirectly and obliquely phrased so as to suggest their relevance for all men.

Paragraph i, the address to the Cross: The four periods of i (1, 122–126, 2, 126–131, 3, 131–135, 4, 135–144) are developed in the first person, except for period 2 which is impersonal, its referent, however, being the first person of the dreamer, "my hope of life" 126. Period 1 contains several echoes of earlier phrases. The dreamer prayes *elne mycele*, 123, a phrase which repeats those used in the description of the Savior approaching the Cross, 34, and of the Cross surrendering its burden to the friends, 60. The verbal echo serves to link the dreamer in his address to the cross with central events of the Passion. A like purpose is served by the phrase in period 1, *ana . . . mæte werede*, 123–124, which echoes the phrase describing the Savior in his tomb, *mæte weorode*, 69. The succeeding phrase in period 1, *afysed on forðwege*, 125, suggests the dreamer's recognition, resulting from his vision, that his life is a journey in which he must be prepared to die to the world in order to live in eternity. The phrase, *afysed on forðwege*, is particularly effective because it echoes in polyptoton *fuse* of lines 21 and 57, a word used to designate both the cross and the followers of Christ. The echoism suggests the dreamer's awareness that he must live in imitation of them, following them in the journey enjoined upon men by the cross at the end of his exhortation, *Ac ðurh ða rode sceal rice secan / of eorðwege æghwylc sawl*, 119–120. The phrase thus relates to III but also serves to set the central motif of the concluding Part IV, that the way to the native land is through the way of the cross, which through death to the world brings eternal life.

Clausule b, which completes period 1, states the Augustinian concept that life is a pilgrimage to be completed, not enjoyed, "For the call to pilgrimage / my mind was prepared, I awaited full many / times of languishing." The hapax legomenon, *langunghwila*, may reflect Canticles 2.5, *in amore languesco*, "I languished in love." In his vision the dreamer has had what we would now call a mystical experience. He has been brought out of himself, has experienced the true reality, so that his hope is set on return to the contact with eternal life. From his longing for eternity springs a *taedium vitae*. The times of weariness with life, *langunghwila*, will occur when he feels most strongly the call of the native land, the sense of exile. *Langunghwila* Dickins and Ross explain as *accidia*, sloth, the spiritual sin frequently besetting the cloister. However, the likelihood is that the dreamer, with his vision freshly in mind, would not be anticipating times of sloth, but rather times of languishing, of weariness with life, a concomitant of the intensity of his longing for the native land, because, as Augustine says, "Our hearts are restless till they rest in God." Relevant to a proper definition of the poet's created compound is patristic interpretation of Canticles 2.5, *Stay me with flagons, comfort me with apples, for I languish in love*. In Alcuin's précis of traditional interpretation of the verse, it is to be understood as saying, "Console me with examples either of beginnings or endings. Show me the way to salvation, while still I languish in love of the supernal vision." [31] It is precisely such feelings which have been aroused in the dreamer by his vision.

31. Alcuin, *PL*, 100, 646. See also Bede, *PL*, 91, 1105, on the phrase, "I languish" of Canticles 2.5, which also helps to give the background of allusions which the poet may have in mind in creating the compound, "For the soul languishes in love which tastes the love of the creator set in it, is aflame in seeking the light of eternity; from this it becomes languid in love of temporal things, so that by so much as it grows cold from zeal of waning time, so it rises more ardently to contemplation." J. V. Fleming in an important article, "'The Dream of the Rood' and Anglo-Saxon Monasticism," *Traditio*, 22 (1966), pp. 43–72 (which appeared after my work on the poem was completed) argues, on pp. 62–66, for the Dickins-Ross reading of *langunghwila*. With much of his main arguments I find myself in agreement; his interpretation here, however, appears to me a misreading of the text.

Period 2, 126–131, contains three clausules with subjects in the third impersonal singular. The reference of these subjects, however, as in the other periods, is to the first person, the dreamer: a, 126–129, *Is me nu lifes hyht;* b, 129–130, *me is willa;* c, 130–131, *min mundbyrd.* The structure of the period presents difficulties, particularly in the a and b clausules. These Dickins and Ross translate, "resorting to the Cross is the joy of my life, now that I alone (by reason of my vision) am in a more favorable position for adoring it than other men." The translation is possible, but suggests a curiously un-Christian pride, with the dreamer congratulating himself for his special grace. Against such self-praise must be placed the weight of Christian theory, the humility which the Cross has just finished preaching, and also its admonition that the dreamer reveal his vision to other men. The clue to a more likely reading rests in the revelation by the Cross of its importance for men, and its position of special honor. Because of this revelation the dreamer rests his hope in the search for the Cross (a); determines to honor it especially, and above any human, that is, worldly object (b). The subject of clausule b is *willa,* 128, which is modified by *ana;* clausule b, put in straightforward order would read: *to ðam me is ana willa well weorþian* [*þone sigebeam*] *oftor þonne ealle men. Ana* causes the difficulty because it is repeated from line 123, where it modifies *ic.* There is, thus, a tendency to refer the adjective, when it is repeated in 128, to the *ic* in the preceding dependent clause of a, *þæt ic þone sigebeam secan mote.* The subject of b, however, is not in the first, but in the third person, *willa.* Similarly the subject of clausule a is *hyht,* modified by a dependent first person clause, the subject of which is modified by *ana. Willa* of b is modified by the repeated *ana,* and by *mycel on mode.* In c, *mundbyrd* is modified by *min. Ana* in b, like *min* in c, and the dependent clause in clausule a modifying *hyht,* agrees grammatically with the third person *willa,* but clearly, if obliquely, has reference to the first person subject, the dreamer, of period 1.

The shift in grammatical reference of the repeated *ana* serves both a rhetorical and a thematic purpose. It reemphasizes the motif of isolation, a motif which brings together dreamer, cross, and Christ. The dreamer in I, i, was alone while his fellow men were sleeping. In the Crucifixion the isolation of the cross from the rest of natural creation was given special emphasis. The isolation of Christ in his sepulchre was emphasized in the litotes, *mæte weorode,* 69. The dreamer's statement, *þær ic ana wæs/ mæte werede,* 123–124, at the beginning of IV recapitulates the earlier motifs of isolation. But the isolation of cross and Christ served mankind. The striking repetition of *ana* in lines 123 and 128 is a reminder that the dreamer, however alone he was in his vision, must also serve mankind by sharing his vision with his fellows, as the cross enjoined upon him. The vision which he alone had makes him realize that he must honor the Cross alone, and not any worldly thing. To honor the cross, however, is to live the Christian life of love for neighbor, to engage in the pilgrimage toward heaven like those who have gone before him. Christian loneliness is a product of the longing for eternal companionship toward which the way of the cross leads.

In period 3 the first person, *Nah ic,* of clausule a, 131–132, is balanced against the third person plural, *ac hie . . . gewiton,* of b, 132–135. Period 4, 135–144, is also in the first person, with a concluding appositive clausule in the hortative. These final two periods continue the motif of pilgrimage by picturing the journeying home of departed friends (3), and by declaring the dreamer's wish that the Cross will show him the way they have followed (4). Periods 3 and 4 are linked by repetition in polyptoton of *dream: gewiton of worulde dreamum,* 134; *me . . . gebringe þær is . . . /dream on heofonum,* 139–140; *ond he þonne asette . . . /dreames brucan,* 142–144. The effect of the repetition is to suggest the nature of man's pilgrimage away from the joys of the world (*of worulde dreamum*) to the joys of heaven (*dream on heofonum*) which joy alone is to be enjoyed (*dreames brucan*). Intertwined in this pattern is a repetition which also serves to link the periods: in 3 the dreamer's friends have sought *wuldres Cyning,* 133, and now *wuniað on wuldre,* 135; the dreamer in 4 hopes that the Cross will lead him where with the saints, *halgum,* i.e., the departed friends, he, too, may *wunian on wuldre,* 143. Period 4 is heavily marked by a series of clauses in anaphora:

þær is blis mycel	139
þær is Dryhtnes folc/geseted to symle	140–141
þær is singal blis	141
þær ic syþþan mot/ wunian on wuldre	142–143

This series in anaphora with repetition of *blis,* 139, 141, which is parallel in meaning with the repeated *dream,* gives particular emphasis to the concept that the cross reveals to man the true goal of his life's journey.

The phrasing in period 4 of the dreamer's hope that the cross will lead him to heaven reflects the longing expressed at the end of period 1, and the beginning of period 2, 124–127; *wæs modsefa / afysed on forðwege /. . . Is me nu lifes hyht / þæt ic þone sigebeam secan mote.* It also reflects the phrasing in 3 of the description of those who have preceded him on the *forðwege, sohton him wuldres Cyning,* 133; it also reflects the motif, III, ii, of Christ's coming to seek out, *mancynn secan,* 104, the blessed who will dwell with him. Finally it anticipates the similar motif expressed in the final paragraph of the poem, IV, ii, *ðurh ða rode sceal rice secan,* 119. In describing the bliss of heaven in period 4 the poet employs the figure of the feast, *þær is Dryhtnes folc / geseted to symle,* 140–141. If the poet's use in III, ii of the "many called, few chosen" theme was suggested to him by the parable of the wedding feast, his use of the figure of the feast in IV would have echoic appropriateness. It might also serve to echo the subsidiary image involved in *byrigde* of III, ii, line 101—through tasting death one tastes the eternal feast. The image of feasting may also reflect *langunghwila,* 126, for if this word is to be related to *I languish in love* of Canticles, the concept of feasting is involved there, since the verse begins,

Stay me with flagons, comfort me with apples. Thus the echoic patterns of 4 establish the underlying motifs of pilgrimage and reward. They feast with Christ who seek by way of the Cross the eternal kingdom. Christ seeks the many, but only the few who wear the robe of the Cross sit at the eternal feast.

Paragraph ii, the prayer to the Cross: The final paragraph, IV, ii, echoing period 2 of III, ii, 101–109, retells the story of Christ from the time of the Crucifixion, and like period 2 contains echoes of the Apostles Creed. The narrative line of the paragraph is simple. Period 1, 144–146, although it begins in the main clause as an apostrophe to the Lord carries its message in a dependent clause modifying *Dryhten,* described as having suffered death on the Cross. Thus the apostrophe actually begins the narrative of Christ's suffering and triumph. Period 2 contains two clausules: a, 147–148, in the third person singular, Christ being the subject, tells of his release of mankind and of his grant to them of the heavenly home; b, 148–149, stands in apposition, and in the third impersonal, the subject being *hiht,* tells of the hope which was renewed for those in Hell. Period 3, 150–156, with third person singular subject, Christ, tells of Christ's triumphal return to his kingdom.

In effect the three periods of the final paragraph reiterate the theme of spiritual pilgrimage by recounting the prototype of such pilgrimages, in 1, Christ's death, in 2, the release from death, and in 3, the ascension. Paragraph ii contains a few verbal echoes of i: *hiht,* 148 of *hyht,* 126; *blisse,* 149, 153, of *blis,* 139, 141; *wunedon on wuldre,* 155, of *wunian on wuldre,* 135, 143. These repeated words, of course, express key concepts in the poem, but essentially the final paragraph is marked by the simplicity of its rhetorical structure and diction. Characteristic of this simplicity is the simple ending with an adverbial clause of time, "when their Lord returned to his native land," *þa heora Wealdend cwom/ . . . þær his eðel wæs.* The simplicity of the ending serves magnificently as conclusion, for it marks the direction of the entire poem. The key word, *eðel,* rich in its connotations, is used for the first time here in the poem. It is, however, toward the vision of the native land of heaven that the poem has moved from the beginning. The dreamer, entering upon his vision at night, first perceived the radiance of the Cross in the heavens (I); he then heard the story of its long journey through pain and darkness into light (II); he then learned the significance of this journey as an emblem of man's true journey, "for through the rood he must reach the kingdom," 120 (III). Finally, in his prayer the dreamer translates the meaning of his vision into the actuality of man's life: he must follow the Cross in living the life of an exile, longing for the native land (IV, i); for the way of the Cross lies in the imitation of Christ, who suffered, and in release from death ascended to his native land (IV, ii).[32]

32. In plate 3, following p. 42, note the symbolic journey.

III. Judith

Judith

a: Beheafdung holofernes

I

                    . . tweode
gifena in ðys ginnan grunde.   Heo ðær ða gearwe funde
mundbyrd æt ðam mæran þeodne   þa heo ahte mæste þearfe
hyldo þæs hehstan deman   þæt he hie wið þæs hehstan brogan
5   gefriðode frymða waldend;   hyre ðæs fæder on roderum
torhtmod tiðe gefremede   þe heo ahte trumne geleafan
a to ðam ælmihtigan.

II

i   Gefrægen ic ða Holofernus
winhatan wyrcean georne   ond eallum wundrum þrymlic
girwan up swæsendo;   to ðam het se gumena baldor
10   ealle ða yldestan ðegnas.

ii   Hie ðæt ofstum miclum
ræfndon rondwiggende   comon to ðam rican þeodne
feran folces ræswan   —þæt wæs þy feorðan dogore
        þæs ðe Iudith hyne   gleaw on geðonce
        ides ælfscinu   ærest gesohte.
15   Hie ða to ðam symle   sittan eodon
wlance to wingedrince   ealle his weagesiðas
bealde byrnwiggende   —þær wæron bollan steape
boren æfter bencum gelome   swylce eac bunan ond orcas
fulle fletsittendum.   Hie þæt fæge þegon
20   rofe rondwiggende   —þeah ðæs se rica ne wende
egesful eorla dryhten.

iii   Ða wearð Holofernus
        goldwine gumena   on gytesalum;

Judith

a: the Beheading of holofernes

I

                              . . . lacked not
rewards in this spacious realm.   There she found ready
the protection of the great Lord   when she had most pressing need
the favor of the highest Judge   so that against the highest terror
5   the Ruler of creation defended her;   the glorious Father in heaven
bestowed his favor upon her   because she kept ever steady
her faith in the almighty Lord.

II

i   Then I learned that Holofernes
eagerly made invitation to carousal,   and his magnificence most richly
made preparation for banquet;   to it the lord of men ordered
10   all the worthiest nobles.

ii   Quickly the wearers of shields
hastily obeyed his command   proceeded to the mighty lord
came to the leader of folk   —that was the fourth day after
    the lady Judith   alluringly lovely
    ready in soul   first sought him out.
15   In state they proceeded   to seat themselves
    at the banquet and wine-drinking   his bane fellows
all the bold wearers of armor   —unceasingly along the benches
deep bowls were carried   pitchers and cups as well
full for the revellers in the hall.   The wearers of shields feasted
20   fearless fated for death   —but the fearsome lord of earls
in his might paid no heed to this.

iii   Then to a merry flood of wine
    Holofernes gave himself   the gold-friend of men;

hloh ond hlydde   hlynede ond dynede
þæt mihten fira bearn   feorran gehyran
25   hu se stiðmoda   styrmde and gylede
modig ond medugal   manode geneahhe
bencsittende   þæt hi gebærdon wel.

iv   Swa se inwidda   ofer ealne dæg
dryhtguman sine   drencte mid wine
30   swiðmod sinces brytta   oð þæt hie on swiman lagon;
oferdrencte his duguðe ealle,   swylce hie wæron deaðe geslegene
agotene goda gehwylces.   Swa het se gumena baldor
fylgan fletsittendum   oð þæt fira bearnum
nealæhte niht seo þystre.

III

i   Het ða niða geblonden
35   þa eadigan mægð   ofstum fetigan
to his bedreste   beagum gehlæste
hringum gehrodene.   Hie hraðe fremedon
anbyhtscealcas   swa him heora ealdor bebead
byrnwigena brego.   Bearhtme stopon
40   to ðam gysterne   þær hie Iudithe
fundon ferhðgleawe,   ond ða fromlice
lindwiggende   lædan ongunnon
þa torhtan mægð   to træfe þam hean
þær se rica hyne   reste on symbel
45   nihtes inne   nergende lað
Holofernus.   Þær wæs eallgylden
fleohnet fæger   ymbe þæs folctogan
bed ahongen   þæt se bealofulla
mihte wlitan þurh   wigena baldor
50   on æghwylcne   þe ðær inne com
hæleða bearna,   ond on hyne nænig
monna cynnes   nymðe se modiga hwæne
niðe rofra   him þe near hete
rinca to rune gegangan.   Hie ða on reste gebrohton
55   snude ða snoteran idese.

ii   Eodon ða stercedferhðe
hæleð heora hearran cyðan   þæt wæs seo halige meowle

he laughed and clamored   roared and clattered
that the sons of men   for miles could hear
25   how the stern-minded   stormed and yelled
proud and drunken,   ever prodded
the feasters on the bench   to bear themselves stoutly.

iv   So the wicked one   drenched in wine
the lords of his retinue   all the long day
30   the arrogant bestower of treasure   until they lay in a stupor;
he drowned his attendants all,   as if dropped in death they were
emptied of any lingering good.   So the lord of men ordered
that the revellers in the hall be filled   until the dark night fell
upon the sons of men.

III

i   Dazed with sins he ordered
35   that the blessed maiden   blazoned with rings
adorned with bracelets   be brought with haste
to bed in his tent.   The attendant messengers
quickly moved to perform   what their prince commanded
lord of armored men.   At once they marched
40   to the guest shelter   where the wearers of shields
met with Judith   prudent of mind,
and without delay   prepared to lead
this lovely maiden   to the lofty tabernacle
where Holofernes   hateful to the Savior
45   the powerful ruler   always rested
during the night.   A golden netting
surpassingly lovely   about the leader's
bed was hanging   so that baleful
the lord of men   might look through it
50   upon anyone   who entered there
of the sons of men,   but on him might none
of mankind look   except as the proud lord
commanded one of his men   mighty for evil
to approach for privy conference.   Then the prudent woman
55   they hastily brought to bed.

ii   The cruel-hearted men went
to make known to their leader   that the holy lady had

gebroht on his burgetelde.   Þa wearð se brema on mode
bliðe burga ealdor,   þohte ða beorhtan idese
mid widle and mid womme besmitan   —ne wolde þæt wuldres dema
60   geðafian þrymmes hyrde,   ac he him þæs ðinges gestyrde
dryhten dugeða waldend.   Gewat ða se deofolcunda
galferhð gumena ðreate
bealofull his beddes neosan   þær he sceolde his blæd forleosan
ædre binnan anre nihte   —hæfde ða his ende gebidenne
65   on eorðan unswæslicne   swylcne he ær æfter worhte
þearlmod ðeoden gumena   þenden he on ðysse worulde
wunode under wolcna hrofe.   Gefeol ða wine swa druncen
se rica on his reste middan   swa he nysta ræda nanne
on gewitlocan.   Wiggend stopon
70   ut of ðam inne   ofstum miclum
weras winsade   þe ðone wærlogan
laðne leodhatan   læddon to bedde
nehstan siðe.

IV

i   Þa wæs nergendes
þeowen þrymful   þearle gemyndig
75   hu heo þone atolan   eaðost mihte
ealdre benæman   ær se unsyfra
womfull onwoce;   genam ða wundenlocc
scyppendes mægð   scearpne mece
scurum heardne,   ond of sceaðe abræd
80   swiðran folme.   Ongan ða swegles weard
be naman nemman   nergend ealra
woruldbuendra,   ond þæt word acwæð:
"Ic ðe frymða god   ond frofre gæst
bearn alwaldan   biddan wylle
85   miltse þinre   me þearfendre
ðrynesse ðrym   —þearle ys me nu ða
heorte onhæted   ond hige geomor
swyðe mid sorgum gedrefed;   forgif me swegles ealdor
sigor ond soðne geleafan   þæt ic mid þys sweorde mote
90   geheawan þysne morðres bryttan,   geunne me minra gesynta
þearlmod þeoden gumena   —nahte ic þinre næfre
miltse þon maran þearfe—   gewrec nu mihtig dryhten

been led to his private tent.   The famed lord of cities
became blissful in fancy,   he intended with filth and sin
to defile the shining woman   —the Ward of majesty would not
60 allow it the Judge of glory,   the Lord Ruler of hosts
prevented his doing the deed.   Then the devil's kin proceeded
lecherous from the company of men
baleful his bed to seek   where his glory would fall abased
directly that same night   —then to his savage end
65 on earth he had attained   in token of what he had done
stern-minded lord of men   while he remained in this world
here under the roof of heaven.   The ruler fell across
his bed so drunk with wine   that he had lost all wisdom
in the chamber of his mind.   The warriors marched
70 sodden with wine   in sudden haste
from inside the tent   when for the last time
they had brought to bed   the breaker of troth
the hated tyrant.

IV

i   Then was the Lord's
glorious servant   sorely mindful
75 of how she might   take the monster's
life most effectively   before he awoke
loathsome in sin;   the Creator's lady
with woven hair   took hold of the sword
sharp and battle-hard,   drew it from the sheath
80 with her right hand.   The Ward of heaven
she summoned by name   the Savior of all
who dwell in the world,   and spoke these words:
"God the Father   Fostering Spirit
Son of the Almighty   Triune Majesty
85 I must beseech   of thee thy mercy
for me in my need   —now is my heart
sorely enkindled   and my soul troubled
greatly oppressed with sorrow;   grant me Prince of heaven
victory and true faith   so that I may have power to fell
90 with this sword this giver of death,   make gift to me of safety
stern-minded Lord of men   —I have never had more need
of thy mercy than I have now—   avenge mighty Lord

torhtmod tires brytta   þæt me ys þus torne on mode
hate on hreðre minum."   Hi ða se hehsta dema
95   ædre mid elne onbryde,   swa he deð anra gehwylcne
                herbuendra   þe hyne him to helpe seceð
mid ræde and mid rihte geleafan.

ii   Þa wearð hyre rume on mode
haligre hyht geniwod.   Genam ða þone haðenan mannan
fæste be feaxe sinum,   teah hyne folmum wið hyre weard
100   bysmerlice   ond þone bealofullan
            listum alede   laðne mannan
            swa heo ðæs unlædan   eaðost mihte
            wel gewealdan.   Sloh ða wundenlocc
            þone feondsceaðan   fagum mece
105   heteþoncolne   þæt heo healfne forcearf
            þone sweoran him   þæt he on swiman læg
            druncen ond dolhwund   —næs ða dead þa gyt
            ealles orsawle.   Sloh ða eornoste
            ides ellenrof   oþre siðe
110   þone hæðenan hund   þæt him þæt heafod wand
            forð on ða flore.

iii   Læg se fula leap
            gesne beæftan.   Gæst ellor hwearf
            under neowelne næs,   ond ðær genyðerad wæs
            susle gesæled   syððan æfre
115   wyrmum bewunden   witum gebunden
            hearde gehæfted   in hellebryne
            æfter hinsiðe.   Ne ðearf he hopian no
            þystrum forðylmed   þæt he ðonan mote
            of ðam wyrmsele,   ac ðær wunian sceal
120   awa to aldre   butan ende forð
            in ðam heolstran ham   hyhtwynna leas.

B: BLæd ıudıthe

I

            Hæfde ða gefohten   foremærne blæd
            Iudith æt guðe   swa hyre god uðe
            swegles ealdor   þe hyre sigores onleah.
125   Þa seo snotere mægð   snude gebrohte
            þæs herewæðan   heafod swa blodig

splendor-minded Giver of glory   what splinteringly is in my breast
burningly within my heart."   Then the Judge most high
95   inspired her at once with courage,   just as he speeds each one
            who dwelling here   looks to him for succor
with wisdom and right faith.

ii   Then to the holy woman's heart
came fortitude and hope renewed.   She took the heathen man
firmly then by the hair,   and with her hands drew him near
100   in scornful manner   and skillfully placed
            the man in the fullness   of his filth and evil
            so that she might manage   most easily
            the woeful wretch.   The woven-haired struck
            the fiendish enemy   full of menace
105   with hostile sword   and hacked his neck
            straight to the middle   so that he lay in a stupor
            drunken and wounded   —he was not yet drained
            entirely of life.   The courageous lady
            then struck terribly   a second time
110   the heathen hound   so that his head rolled
            along the floor.

iii   The body lay
            foul and lifeless.   The soul leaving it
            was bound for the abysmal cliff,   there to be abased
            and fettered in torments   eternally thenceforward
115   with serpents bewound   with sufferings bound
            grievously held   in the fires of hell
            after his going hence.   Engulfed in darkness
            he had no cause to hope   that he could return
            from the serpent hall,   for in the dark home
120   despairing joyless   he would spend his days
            for endless time   into eternity.

B: Judith's triumph

I

            Though victory given   to her by God
            the Lord of heaven   Judith in hard
            battle had won   abounding glory.
125   The prudent maiden   then hastily pressed
            the bloody head   of the battle hunter

on ðam fætelse   þe hyre foregenga
blachleor ides   hyra beaga nest
ðeawum geðungen   þyder on lædde,
130 ond hit ða swa heolfrig   hyre on hond ageaf
higeðoncolre   ham to berenne
Iudith gingran sinre.   Eodon ða gegnum þanonne
þa idesa ba   ellenþriste
oð þæt hie becomon   collenferhðe
135 eadhreðige mægð   ut of ðam herige
þæt hie sweotollice   geseon mihten
þære wlitegan byrig   weallas blican
Bethuliam.   Hie ða beahhrodene
feðelaste   forð onettan
140 oð hie glædmode   gegan hæfdon
to ðam wealgate.

II

i   Wiggend sæton
weras wæccende   wearde heoldon
in ðam fæstenne   swa ðam folce ær
geomormodum   Iudithe bebead
145 searoðoncol mægð   þa heo on sið gewat
ides ellenrof.

ii   Wæs ða eft cumen
leof to leodum.   Ond ða lungre het
gleawhydig wif   gumena sumne
of ðære ginnan byrig   hyre togeanes gan
150 ond hi ofostlice   in forleton
þurh ðæs wealles geat,   ond þæt word acwæð
to ðam sigefolce.   "Ic eow secgan mæg
þoncwyrðe þing   þæt ge ne þyrfen leng
murnan on mode.   Eow ys metod bliðe
155 cyninga wuldor;   þæt gecyðed wearð
geond woruld wide   þæt eow ys wuldorblæd
torhtlic toweard   ond tir gefeðe
þara læðða   þe ge lange drugon."

iii   Þa wurdon bliðe   burhsittende
160 syððan hi gehyrdon   hu seo halige spræc

into the pouch   in which her companion
pale of visage   accomplished in virtue
thither had fetched   food for them both,
130   and Judith gave it   gory with blood
into the hands of her servant   serious of purpose
to carry home.   In haste they went
the ladies both   bold in courage
maidens blithe   in triumph blessed
135   until they had left   the enemy legions,
and then they might see   clearly before them
the shimmering walls   of the shining city
blessed Bethulia.   Blazoned with rings
they hastened their pace   along the path
140   until they had gained   with gaiety of heart
the gate in the wall.

II

i   The warriors sat
the waiting men   and held the watch
within the fastness   as Judith before
had commanded the folk   sorrowful of mind
145   when the wise maiden   went on her journey
the courageous lady.

ii   Beloved of her people
the woman had returned.   And wisely mindful
she straightway commanded   one of the men
of the spacious city   speedily to approach
150   and give to her   passage through the gate
within the wall,   and spoke these words
to the victory-folk.   "To you I shall unfold
a matter for thanksgiving,   that you need to mourn
no longer in mind.   To you the Lord is gracious
155   the Glory of kings;   it will become known
through the wide world   that your reward is near,
great and splendid   glory granted
in place of the sorrows   which you long suffered."

iii   Then were they happy   the inhabitants of the city
160   after they had heard   what the holy one spoke

ofer heanne weall —here wæs on lustum.
Wið þæs fæstengeates folc onette,
weras wif somod wornum ond heapum
ðreatum ond ðrymmum þrungon ond urnon
165 ongean ða þeodnes mægð þusendmælum
ealde ge geonge. Æghwylcum wearð
men on ðære medobyrig mod areted
syððan hie ongeaton þæt wæs Iudith cumen
eft to eðle, ond ða ofostlice
170 hie mid eaðmedum in forleton.

III

i Þa seo gleawe het golde gefrætewod
hyre ðinenne þancolmode
þæs herewæðan heafod onwriðan,
ond hyt to behðe blodig ætywan
175 þam burhleodum hu hyre æt beaduwe gespeow.

ii Spræc ða seo æðele to eallum þam folce.
"Her ge magon sweotole sigerofe hæleð
leoda ræswan on ðæs laðestan
hæðnes heaðorinces heafod starian
180 Holofernus unlyfigendes
þe us monna mæst morðra gefremede
sarra sorga and þæt swiðor gyt
ycan wolde, ac him ne uðe god
lengran lifes þæt he mid læððum us
185 eglan moste; ic him ealdor oðþrong
þurh godes fultum. Nu ic gumena gehwæne
þyssa burgleoda biddan wylle
randwiggendra þæt ge recene eow
fysan to gefeohte syððan frymða god
190 arfæst cyning eastan sende
leohtne leoman; berað linde forð
bord for breostum ond byrnhomas
scire helmas in sceaðena gemong,
fyllað folctogan fagum sweordum
195 fæge frumgaras; fynd syndon eowere
gedemed to deaðe, ond ge dom agon

across the high wall   —the host was joyous.
To the fastened gate   the folk hastened,
men and women   together pell mell
in crush and rush   pressed and raced
165   toward the Lord's maiden   many a thousand
elders and children.   Cheered were the hearts
of all the men   of the merry city
after they had discovered   that Judith had come
again to her home,   and then humbly
170   they gave to her   hasty passage.

III

i   Then adorned with gold   sagacious she commanded
that her servant   serious of purpose
unwrap the head   of the battle hunter,
and in view of the citizens   reveal its bloodiness
175   as a sign to them   of her success in battle.

ii   The noble one then spoke   to all the nation.
"Victorious lords   leaders of the people
here you may openly   look on the head
of the much hated   Holofernes
180   a loathsome heathen   deprived of life
who upon our men   most murder inflicted
and sore sorrow   which he sought to increase
even more grievously,   except that God would not grant
that by length of life   he might longer
185   load us with afflictions; I took his life
with the help of God.   Now I give command
to all citizens   all men of the city
wearers of shields,   that straightway for war
you make preparation   when God the Maker
190   the glorious King   shall send a gleam
of light from the east;   carry your linden
shields before your breasts   your shining helmets
and coats of mail   into the enemy mass,
fell with hostile swords   the fated
195   lords and leaders;   laid on your enemy
is doom of death,   and your destiny in battle

tir æt tohtan   swa eow getacnod hafað
mihtig dryhten   þurh mine hand."

iii   Þa wearð snelra werod   snude gegearewod
200   cenra to campe.

c: blæd ebrea

I

i   Stopon cynerof
secgas and gesiðas,   bæron sigeþufas,
foron to gefeohte   forð on gerihte
hæleð under helmum   of ðære haligan byrig.
On ðæt dægred sylf   dynedan scildas
205   hlude hlummon.   Þæs se hlanca gefeah
wulf in walde   ond se wanna hrefn
wælgifre fugel,   wistan begen
þæt him ða þeodguman   þohtan tilian
fylle on fægum;   ac him fleah on last
210   earn ætes georn   urigfeðera,
salowigpada   sang hildeleoð
hyrnednebba.

ii   Stopon heaðorincas
beornas to beadowe   bordum beðeahte
hwealfum lindum   þa ðe hwile ær
215   elðeodigra   edwit þoledon
hæðenra hosp   —him þæt hearde wearð
æt ðam æscplegan   eallum forgolden
Assyrium   syððan Ebreas
under guðfanum   gegan hæfdon
220   to ðam fyrdwicum.   Hie ða fromlice
leton forð fleogan   flana scuras
hildenædran   of hornbogan
strælas stedehearde.   Styrmdon hlude
grame guðfrecan   garas sendon
225   in heardra gemang   —hæleð wæron yrre
landbuende   laðum cynne.

iii   Stopon styrnmode   stercedferhðe,
wrehton unsofte   ealdgeniðlan
medowerige.   Mundum brugdon

is glory and dominion   as the mighty Lord
has made manifest   by means of my hand."

iii   Then the ranks of the bold   and brave in battle
were quickly prepared.

c: the hebrew triumph

I

200   i   The companions marched
noble warriors,   forward they moved their banners,
straight forth they went   on their way to battle
heroes under helmets   from the holy city.
At crack of dawn   their shields made din
205   loudly clashed.   Of this the lean wolf
in the forest was glad   and gluttonous of carrion
the dark raven,   both had no doubt
that the warriors   wished to provide them
a fill of the fated;   and dun-feathered
210   the dewy-winged eagle   eager for feast
soared in pursuit,   the horned-beak sang
the song of war.

ii   The warriors marched
sheathed in the hollow   of linden shields
men seeking battle   who long had borne
215   heathen insult   and the hateful scorn
of a foreign host   —fiercely for this
and completely   at the spear play
the Assyrians were repaid   after the Hebrew people
had won their way   under their war banners
220   into the battle camp.   Then with boldness
they let fly forth   a flight of arrows
battle adders   from the horned bows
the hardened shafts.   The angry heroes
loudly stormed   delivered their spears
225   into the enemy ranks   —enraged were the men
who lived in the homeland   against the hated race.

iii   Determined they marched   resolute of mind,
they awoke an enmity   for the mead-weary
both hard and ancient.   With their hands the men

230   scealcas of sceaðum   scirmæled swyrd
        ecgum gecoste.   Slogon eornoste
        Assiria   oretmæcgas,
        niðhycgende   nanne ne sparedon
        þæs herefolces   heanne ne rice
235   cwicera manna   þe hie ofercuman mihton.

II

i   Swa ða magoþegnas   on ða morgentid
        ehton elðeoda   ealle þrage
        oð þæt ongeaton   ða ðe grame wæron
        ðæs herefolces   heafodweardas
240   þæt him swyrdgeswing   swiðlic eowdon
        weras Ebrisce.   Hie wordum þæt
        þam yldestan   ealdorþegnum
        cyðan eodon;   wrehton cumbolwigan,
        ond him forhtlice   færspel bodedon
245   medowerigum   morgencollan
        atolne ecgplegan.   Þa ic ædre gefrægn
        slegefæge hæleð   slæpe tobrædan
        ond wið þæs bealofullan   burgeteldes
        weras werigferhðe   hwearfum þringan
250   Holofernus.

ii   Hogedon aninga
        hyra hlaforde   hilde bodian
        ærðonðe him se egesa   on ufan sæte
        mægen Ebrea.   Mynton ealle
        þæt se beorna brego   ond seo beorhte mægð
255   in ðam wlitegan træfe   wæron ætsomne
        Iudith seo æðele   ond se galmoda
        egesfull ond afor,   næs ðeah eorla nan
        þe ðone wiggend   aweccan dorste
        oððe gecunnian   hu ðone cumbolwigan
260   wið ða halgan mægð   hæfde geworden
        metodes meowlan.   Mægen nealæhte
        folc Ebrea,   fuhton þearle
        heardum heoruwæpnum   hæste guldon
        hyra fyrngeflitu   fagum swyrdum

230   drew from their sheaths   their shining swords
            with edges tested.   They smote terribly
            that Assyrian host,   filled with hostile
            spirit of anger   they spared not one
            of the invading army   whom they might vanquish
235   no living man   mean or mighty.

II

i   So the retainers   in that morning time
            ever harried   the foreign host
            until in the vanguard   of the invading army
            the lieutenants in wrath   became aware
240   that the Hebrew men   gave violent menace
            of close combat.   With clamor of words
            they went to tell   the chief lieutenants
            the commanding warriors;   they awoke the leaders
            and told them in terror   the fearful tidings
245   of the menace of morning   to the mead-weary
            the dire sword play.   Then I heard that suddenly
            the warriors cast off sleep   and doomed to slaughter
            weary of heart   the men herded
            to the privy tent   of the baleful prince
250   Holofernes.

ii   They had in mind
            to announce war   to their lord in their need
            before the terror   fell upon them
            the Hebrew might.   All imagined
            that the two were together   in the shining tabernacle
255   the lord of men   and the fair maid
            the lady Judith   and the lecherous one
            dire and dreadful,   yet not one lord dared
            to awaken   the warrior within
            or seek to learn   what to the leader
260   had come to pass   with the pious lady
            the maiden of the Lord.   In might approached
            the Hebrew folk,   they fought vigorously
            repaid stiffly   the ancient strife
            the grudge of old   with grim swords

265   ealde æfðoncan —Assyria wearð
     on ðam dægeweorce dom geswiðrod
     bælc forbiged. Beornas stodon
     ymbe hyra þeodnes træf þearle gebylde
     sweorcendferhðe; hi ða somod ealle
270   ongunnon cohhetan, cirman hlude
     ond gristbitian gode orfeorme
   mid toðon torn þoligende —þa wæs hyra tires æt ende
   eades ond ellendæda. Hogedon þa eorlas aweccan
     hira winedryhten —him wiht ne speow.

275 iii   Þa wearð sið ond late sum to ðam arod
     þara beadorinca þæt he in þæt burgeteld
     niðheard neðde swa hyne nyd fordraf,
     funde ða on bedde blacne licgan
     his goldgifan gæstes gesne
280   lifes belidenne. He þa lungre gefeoll
     freorig to foldan, ongan his feax teran
     hreoh on mode ond his hrægl somod,
     ond þæt word acwæð to ðam wiggendum
     þe ðær unrote ute wæron:
285   "Her is geswutelod ure sylf forwyrd
     toweard getacnod þæt þære tide ys
   mid niðum neah geðrungen þe we sculon nu losian
   somod æt sæcce forweorðan, her lið sweorde geheawen
   beheafdod healdend ure." Hi ða hreowigmode
290   wurpon hyra wæpen ofdune, gewitan him werigferhðe
       on fleam sceacan.

III

 i   Him mon feaht on last
     mægeneacen folc oð se mæsta dæl
     þæs heriges læg hilde gesæged
     on ðam sigewonge sweordum geheawen
295   wulfum to willan ond eac wælgifrum
     fuglum to frofre —flugon ða ðe lyfdon
     laðra linde. Him on laste for
     sweot Ebrea sigore geweorðod
     dome gedyrsod —him feng dryhten god

265　　　　hostile weapons　—in the work of that day
　　　　　the Assyrians' fame　faded away,
　　　　　their pride tumbled.　Around their lord's tabernacle
　　　　　the soldiers stood　direly stirred
　　　　　their hearts darkening;　huddled together
270　　　　they began to cough,　and lacking of good
　　　　　to wail terribly　and to gnash their teeth
　　　suffering their tearing grief　—the end had come to their success
　　　to their lustre and bold deeds.　The leaders had in mind to awaken
　　　　　their friend and lord　—it availed them little.

275　　iii　　　　One man of battle　became emboldened
　　　　　tardily to venture　within the privy tent
　　　　　hardened in sin　as necessity drove him;
　　　　　his gold-giving lord　he found lying
　　　　　pallid on his bed　departed from life
280　　　　deprived of soul.　With sudden chill
　　　　　he fell to the ground,　furious in heart
　　　　　he began to rend　his hair and robes,
　　　　　and then these words　spoke to the warriors
　　　　　who in misery　had remained outside:
285　　　　"Here is discovered　disclosed as near
　　　　　our own ruin,　for directly upon us
　　　the time of strife is pressing　when we shall meet destruction
　　　and huddled together perish in battle,　here lies our ruler beheaded
　　　cut to pieces with the sword."　They then disconsolate of soul
290　　　cast their weapons down,　weary of heart they began
　　　　　to hasten their flight.

III

　　i　　　　　　　　The strengthened host
　　　　　fought in pursuit　until the most part
　　　　　of the heathen lay　hewn by the sword
　　　　　felled in battle　on the field of victory
295　　　　a festival for wolves　and for the feast-eager
　　　　　fowls a delight　—they fled who lived
　　　　　of the hated shield-wearers.　The Hebrew army
　　　　　followed in pursuit　glorified with favor
　　　　　honored with victory　—their help was the Lord

300   fægre on fultum   frea ælmihtig.
           Hi ða fromlice   fagum swyrdum
           hæleð higerofe   herpað worhton
           þurh laðra gemong   linde heowon
           scildburh scæron,   sceotend wæron
305   guðe gegremede   guman Ebrisce
           þegnas on ða tid   þearle gelyste
           gargewinnes;   þær on greot gefeoll
           se hyhsta dæl   heafodgerimes,
           Assiria   ealdorduguðe
310   laðan cynnes   —lythwon becom
           cwicera to cyððe.

     ii   Cirdon cynerofe
           wiggend on wiðertrod   wælscel oninnan
           reocende hræw.   Rum wæs to nimanne
           londbuendum   on ðam laðestan
315   hyra ealdfeondum   unlyfigendum
           heolfrig herereaf   hyrsta scyne
           bord ond brad swyrd   brune helmas
           dyre madmas;   hæfdon domlice
           on ðam folcstede   fynd oferwunnen
320   eðelweardas,   ealdhettende
           swyrdum aswefede.   Hie on swaðe reston
           þa ðe him to life   laðost wæron
           cwicera cynna.

IV

     i   Þa seo cneoris eall
           mægða mærost   anes monðes fyrst
325   wlanc wundenlocc   wægon ond læddon
           to ðære beorhtan byrig   Bethuliam
           helmas ond hupseax   hare byrnan
           guðsceorp gumena   golde gefrætewod
           mærra madma   þonne mon ænig
330   asecgan mæge   searoþoncelra.
           Eal þæt ða ðeodguman   þrymme geeodon
           cene under cumblum   on compwige

300   the great Master   who in grace protected them.
     The valiant heroes   with hostile swords
     boldly fashioned   a path of battle
     through the hated mass   hewed and slashed
     the linden phalanx,   fierce in combat
305   became the Hebrews   comrades and warriors,
     in that hour the thanes   for thrust of spear
     had furious desire;   the Assyrian nobility
     its highest lords   the largest part
     of the hated kin   by count of heads
310   fell to the field   —few made their way
     alive to their land.

ii   The lordly warriors
     turned back from pursuit   among the reeking bodies
     the shells of carnage.   They captured much
     the men of the land   from the unliving
315   their long and most   loathed enemies
     bloody booty   shining battle-gear
     their shields and glaives   and gleaming helmets
     a dear treasure;   triumphantly the protectors
     of the land had conquered   their long-time enemies
320   on the field of battle,   their foes with swords
     had put to rest.   On the path of pursuit
     rested those who alive   were the most loathed
     of living men.

IV

i   For one month's time
     all the heroic tribe   of woven hair
325   nation most celebrated   to the shining city
     fair Bethulia   fetched and carried
     belt-swords helmets   and gray byrnies
     garments of war   adorned with gold,
     much more treasure   than any man
330   however learned   might ever relate.
     All this the warriors   won into their power
     brave under banners   in the field of battle

þurh Iudithe   gleawe lare
mægð modigre.   Hi to mede hyre
335 of ðam siðfate   sylfre brohton
eorlas æscrofe   Holofernes
sweord ond swatigne helm,   swylce eac side byrnan
gerenode readum golde,   ond eal þæt se rinca baldor
swiðmod sinces ahte   oððe sundoryfes
340 beaga ond beorhtra maðma;   hi þæt þære beorhtan idese
ageafon gearoþoncolre.

ii   Ealles ðæs Iudith sægde
wuldor weroda dryhtne   þe hyre weorðmynde geaf
mærðe on moldan rice,   swylce eac mede on heofonum
sigorlean in swegles wuldre.   Þæs ðe heo ahte soðne geleafan
345 a to ðam ælmihtigan   huru æt ðam ende ne tweode
þæs leanes þe heo lange gyrnde.   Þæs sy ðam leofan dryhtne
wuldor to widan aldre   þe gesceop wind ond lyfte
roderas ond rume grundas,   swylce eac reðe streamas
ond swegles dreamas   þurh his sylfes miltse.

through the judicious counsel   of Judith
courageous maiden.   By merit of her venture
335   as her reward   the noble heroes
the gory helmet   of Holofernes
and his sword did bring to her,   as also his broad byrnie
adorned with red gold,   all the riches that the arrogant
lord of men possessed   the riches belonging to him alone
340   rings and shining treasures;   these they gave to the radiant
and most judicious lady.

ii   The glory of all this Judith
ascribed to the Lord of hosts   who gave nobility to her
glory in the kingdom of the world,   as also reward in heaven
and triumph in eternal glory.   Because she kept true faith
345   ever in the almighty Lord   indeed at the end she lacked not
the reward she long had desired.   For this to the dear Lord
who through his favoring grace   fashioned wind and sky
the firmament and the wide lands,   as also the wild seas
and the glad joys of heaven   may glory be forever.

the beginning of the *Judith* is lost, but how much is lost is a matter of debate. On the one hand the amount of loss is assumed by A. S. Cook to be negligible, the poem being "virtually complete as it now is." On the other hand, B. J. Timmer considers that the surviving lines constitute merely the last fourth of a poem of "about 1344" lines, and the editor of the *Anglo-Saxon Poetic Records*, E.V.K. Dobbie, is of a similar opinion.[1] To judge the poem the reader must decide between these two views; for a long, epic paraphrase of the Book of Judith must be judged differently from a compact heroic ode centering on the slaying of Holofernes.

On external evidence, Timmer and Dobbie make a strong case. The manuscript of *Judith* contains sectional numbers, the first of which, X, appears at line 15, followed by XI, line 122, and XII, line 236. It seems obvious that the portion of *Judith* which remains begins toward the end of section IX, with sections I–VIII preceding. But Rosemary Woolf has taken most of the decisiveness from this argument. She has observed that in Old English manuscripts the numbers are very irregular in occurrence (see, for example, the Vercelli Book), and more importantly, that in the Junius manuscript the numbering of the first three poems runs seriatim I–LV. Such numbering, considered as auctorial, would force us to consider three manifestly distinct poems as parts of one poem. The apparently solid evidence of manuscript numbering, then, provides no evidence for deciding on the length of the original *Judith*.

In the absence of solid external evidence Cook's argument from internal evidence cannot be dismissed as lightly as Timmer and Dobbie suggest in calling his argument subjective. In fact, their objections to Cook's views seem themselves superficial, being apparently based on the assumption that Cook's evidence consists entirely of the fact of the repetitions involved in the beginning and ending of the poem (lines 6–7 and 344–346). What they overlook—or disregard as "subjective"—is Cook's entire view of the poem as a work of art: "I have endeavored to present the poem, fragmentary though it be, as a work of art, being persuaded that unless philological scholarship tends to exalt life, and the noble aspects which life has assumed, or under which it has been conceived, the less we have of it the better."[2] In his introduction, Cook presents a reasoned and convincing view of the art of the poem, a piece of first rate criticism, however "old-fashioned" his critical vocabulary. He affirms as the poet's

---

1. B. J. Timmer, *Judith*, 2nd ed. (London, 1961), p. 2: "The poem is a fragment . . . the complete poem may be estimated at about 1,344 lines." E. V. K. Dobbie, *ASPR*, IV (New York, 1954), pp. lix ff.

2. A. S. Cook, *Judith* (Boston, 1904), Preface.

deliberate art his limitation of characters to three, Judith, Holofernes, and the maid. He shows how the poet has modified the biblical narrative to enhance "the importance of the protagonists" and to throw them "into relief upon a background formed by the two armies respectively." Cook's observation that the poet has limited the characters of his poem to three is not subjective. Objectively, as R. E. Woolf has argued, the view which holds *Judith* to be a long epic treatment of the Book of Judith fails to explain the absence in the extant poem of any mention of leading characters of the earlier part, Joabim, Achior, Ozias, Vagao, Nebuchadnezzar.[3] Moreover, if the poem is viewed as an epic treatment of the entire apocryphal book, the ending also presents a problem, since the extant poem omits the final chapter 16 with its striking Song of Judith and the account of her later life.

The poet's selection for his poem of the climactic episode of the Book of Judith does not perhaps require much explanation because the Old English poet characteristically dealt with biblical narratives selectively; as I have elsewhere shown, even the *Genesis* A, frequently called a paraphrase, turns out to be a poem providing *in extenso* a thematic development of a definite selection from Genesis. Even more clearly *Daniel* and *Exodus* are selectively thematic.[4] Latin precedents for the poet's handling of *Judith* seem to reinforce the likelihood that the poem as we have it is almost complete, and patristic examples provide a clue to the poet's thematic purpose.

By way of argument for the view that *Judith* may be virtually complete, R. E. Woolf has pointed out that Aldhelm makes highly selective use of the Judith story in his *De Virginitate*, affirming, but without explanation, that Aldhelm's selection of significant events is similar to that of the poet. On the other hand, Ælfric's metrical paraphrase of the entire Book of Judith seems to provide counter-evidence. The fact that his paraphrase was written more than a century after the poem does not in itself rule out its relevance to the problem of the length of the poem. For, if it appears that the last portion of Ælfric's paraphrase is in any way comparable to the poem, they might presumably derive from a common tradition. But no real similarities appear, other than their relation to the Book of Judith. Ælfric's account of Judith's exploit is a metrical paraphrase; *Judith* is free, heroic, narrative poetry. The latter provides heroic example; the former is a free but faithful version of the Book. To be sure, Ælfric does omit verses of *Judith*, transforms some, and makes phrasal additions, but his aim is simply to provide a faithful but concise, clear, and effective paraphrase.[5] The selectivity of *Judith* is too extreme to have its inspiration in a tradition of paraphrase; rather its tradition must have been one which treats the Book of Judith selectively as heroic example, a tradition exemplified in Aldhelm's *De Virginitate*.

3. R. E. Woolf, "The Lost Opening to the 'Judith,' " *MLR*, 50, pp. 168 ff.
4. B. F. Huppé, *Doctrine and Poetry*, pp. 131–226.
5. B. Assmann, "Ælfric's Book of Judith," *Anglia*, 10 (1887), pp. 87–104.

Significantly, whereas Aldhelm's selective exemplary treatment has many precedents, which together provide a significant background for understanding the poem, precedents for Ælfric's paraphrase seem to be lacking. The merest sampling suggests a thread of consistency in Latin patristic and poetic treatments of the Book of Judith from Jerome to the 8th century. In an index search and casual scanning of the *Patrologia Latina,* one finds a dearth of complete and systematic exegesis of the Book of Judith, with the single exception of one by the master of the compendious, Rabanus Maurus. This dearth, of course, is not surprising since the book is not part of the Hebrew canon. However, it is part of the Septuagint, and appears along with Esther to have been accepted very early as canonical. Clement of Rome seems to accept Judith without question along with Esther in his Epistle to the Corinthians (c. 90 A.D.): "Many women also, being strengthened by the grace of God, have performed numerous manly exploits. The blessed Judith, when her city was beseiged, asked of the elders permission to go forth into the camp of the strangers, and exposing herself to danger, she went out for the love which she bore to her country and people then beseiged; and the Lord delivered Holofernes into the hands of a woman." [6] There are also references to Judith in Clement of Alexandria, Origen, and Tertullian. By the time of the Latin fathers, Ambrose, Augustine, Jerome, the Book of Judith was considered, at the least, quasi-canonical. St. Augustine, *City of God,* Book 18, Chap. 126, notes that the work is not in the Hebrew canon, but in *On Christian Doctrine,* Book 2, Chapter 7, accepts the Septuagint Canon, including Judith. This quasi-canonical status is noted by the influential Isidore of Seville, who in his *Etymologiae,* Book 6, Chapter 2, includes Judith and Esther as addenda to the canon. In his *In Libros veteris ac novi Testamenti proemia* he states that although the Hebrews did not accept Judith "the Church nevertheless counts it among the canonical scriptures." However, in his ensuing discussion he omits any discussion of Judith (as in *De ortu,* he places Judith at the end with other apocryphal figures).[7]

Ælfric, in his metrical version of the Book of Judith,[8] suggests clearly what apears to be the traditional attitude toward the Book of Judith. He begins his paraphrase by placing the story historically, explaining that the Nebuchadnezzar of Judith had the cognomen Cambyses and is not to be confused with the earlier Nebuchadnezzar. Although he concludes his paraphrase with a brief exegetical passage, he finds it necessary to affirm vigorously the historicity of the Book of Judith: "This is no fictitious narration" (*nis þis nan leas spel*). He notes that it appears in the Vulgate (*hit stent on Leden*), although not in the Hebrew canon (*on ðære bibliothecan*). Appealing to the "scholars who

6. Translation by A. Roberts and J. Donaldson in *The Ante-Nicene Fathers,* Vol. I, (New York, 1908), p. 20.
7. Isidore of Seville, *PL* 83, 157–158.
8. Edited by Assmann, *op. cit.,* 76–104.

PLATE 5. Judith Going to Holofernes

From the Bible of San Paolo, Rome, 231 vo., reproduced from the Princeton University Index of Christian Art, with the permission of Professor Kurt Weitzmann.

know Latin," he repeats that he is not creating fiction (*we na ne leogað*). He adds that Judith is an example of Christ's saying that the exalted shall be humbled and the humble shall be exalted. Further, in his introduction to his translations of the Old Testament, he declares that, "the widow Judith, who overcame Holofernes, the Assyrian lord, has, among these books, her own book concerning her own victory; this was also written in English in our fashion as an example to you men that you with weapons should protect your land against the attacking enemy." [9]

Certainly her literal "reality" seems to have been accepted without question. Chromatius of Aquila, a contemporary of Ambrose, Tractate XV on Matthew 6, 16–18, cites her as a historical "example of humility in the observance of fasting." [10] Isidore of Seville in *De ortu et obitu patrum*, includes her among "the holy fathers and most noble men" whose origins, worthy deeds and deaths he gives synoptically; from the nature of this work, he gives special note to her birth and burial place; otherwise, his account accentuates the Holofernes episode. [11]

As will be seen, Jerome, Ambrose, and the poets, Prudentius, Dracontius, Aldhelm, make frequent exemplary use of Judith. The interest of each in the Book of Judith is in the climactic episode of the beheading of Holofernes, as it provided edifying example. They show no interest in the historical purpose of the Book of Judith as a work of Hebrew patriotism. Concentrating their attention on Judith and Holofernes, and ignoring the other main characters, like Nebuchadnezzar and Vagao, they celebrate Judith as the chaste widow, wise through her faith in God, whose triumph over Holofernes is the triumph of virtue. The hypothesis suggests itself that what they saw in Judith was a heroic example of Christian virtue.

Ambrose pays tribute to Judith as a historical figure of exemplary virtue. In the *Liber de viduis* he develops at length Judith's role in exemplifying, "true fortitude, the power of virtue and temperance, which through devotion of mind surpasses the course of nature, the infirmity of the sex, such as was in that one called Judith, who alone was able to recall from a rabble, to defend from the enemy, men broken by seige, shattered with fright, wasted with hunger. For, as we read, when Holofernes, terrible through the conclusion of many battles, constrained within the walls innumerable thousands of men, with the warriors shaking in terror, and now treating from fatal extremity, she proceeded outside the walls, more illustrious than that army she freed, and braver than that which she put to flight. . . ." [12]

In a similar vein, Aldhelm in his prose *De virginitate* celebrates Judith as an example of triumphant chastity:

9. In C. W. M. Grein, *Bibliothek der angelsächsischen Prosa*, I, p. 11.
10. *CCSL*, 24, 16–18.
11. *PL*, 83, 148.
12. *PL*, 16, 258–260.

Judith, daughter of Merari, after the death of Manasses, having put on the garments, and having rejected the nuptial peplum, despising the shining allurements of wooers,—not yet with the resounding trumpet sounds of the apostolic trumpet, *I say to the unmarried, good it is for them, if they remain* (I Cor. 7,8)—like a shining lily flowering in pious chastity, from public view concealing herself in a solarium of the upper story directed her mind to shamefastness: when with Abra following she undertook to frustrate the terrible prince of the Assyrians, who glorying in innumerable thousands of soldiers on horse and on foot terrified the trembling earth; by no means otherwise did she believe he would be deceived, nor otherwise did she think that he would be killed, unless her own countenance in its native beauty were contained in corporeal ornaments. Concerning which by the LXX translators it is written: *she clothed herself with the vestments of happiness, and put on sandals, and chains, and rings, and all her ornaments, and arranged herself excessively for the conquest of men.* Lo, not through our assertions but by the declaration of Scriptures the dress of women is called the conquest of men. Truly because in this narrow seige of Bethulia she became grieved through affection for her suffering fellow countrymen, it is not mentioned that it was done through a failing in chastity; for the reason of the preservation of chastity with honored reverence she reported to the fearful citizens the memorial of victory, and the renowned triumph to the trembling burgers in testimony through the tyrannical head and canopy.[13]

Aldhelm's verse *De Virginitate* contains a similar, although briefer, glorification of Judith. Here her exemplifications of the triumph of virginity, perhaps through condensation, approaches the emblematic, where Judith stands for, represents, what she exemplifies, lines 2560–2570:

Shall I record Judith born of noble stock, despising in her pure body to be prostituted of a king, trampling down in her heart the profane ravishing of evil? For the reason of the danger of death the citizens endured, she carried the bloody memorial of victory in a holy leather bag, observing intact shamefastness in her devout mind. Thus chaste purity in propitious triumph despises the vice of wicked flesh through polluted filth; with maidenly arrows repelling emulous, ghastly wars, the poison of prostitution was not able to infiltrate the fragile fibers with the firebrand of hearts set aflame.[14]

The emblematic form which Aldhelm gives to Judith has precedents, for Judith as a quasi-canonical figure was subject to the exegetical law which provides that each Old Testament figure is a type whose meaning is revealed through the New Law; that is, Judith represented certain Christian truths. Her moral (tropological) significance derives quite directly from her chief exploit, but also from the interpretation given to her name; according to Jerome, Judith may be translated *laudens, confitens,* "praising, confessing." The meanings given to her name provide a thread of thematic significance for her appearance

13. R. Ehwald, *Aldhelmi opera, MGH,* AA 15, pp. 316–317.
14. *Ibid.,* p. 457.

as a type of Christian chastity. Her strict observance of her widowhood is an act of penitential praise of God, (*laudens*), and her triumph is a triumph of faith (*confitens*). The beheading of a powerful but drunken, lecherous warrior by a weak woman strong in her faith emblemizes Christian faith and the life dedicated to chastity. Indeed, her beheading of Holofernes emblemizes the act of cutting away the Old Adam through faith in the New Law. Thus in Epistle 54, *To Furia*, Jerome gives counsel on the preservation of widowhood, as the second of the three degrees of chastity, and offers Judith not merely as an example, but as a type of Christian chastity:

> In the *Book of Judith*—if anyone is of the opinion that it should be received as canonical—we read of a widow wasted with fasting and wearing the somber garb of a mourner, whose outward squalor indicated not so much the regret which she felt for her dead husband as the [penitential] temper in which she looked forward to the coming of the Bridegroom. I see her hand armed with the sword and stained with blood. I recognize the head of Holofernes which she has carried away from the camp of the enemy. Here a woman vanquishes men, and chastity beheads lust. Quickly changing her garb, she puts on once more in the hour of victory her own mean dress, finer than all the splendours of the world.[15]

Granting Judith's quasi-canonical position, Jerome thus sees her in the characteristic role of the Old Testament figure typifying the New. Her widowhood represents the wedding to Christ; that is, it is the life of the dedicated contemplative, vowed to chastity which triumphs over the flesh by cutting it away.

It may be noted that Ambrose, too, is aware of Judith's moral typology, for in the *Liber de viduis* he speaks of her putting on the robes of allurement because she sought to please the Bridegroom with those "memorials of marriage which are the arms of chastity." But Prudentius provides the most interesting development of Judith's moral typology in the speech of Chastity triumphant in her victory over Lust, *Psychomachia*, lines 53–87:

> 'Here it is done,' exclaims the victorious queen. 'This will be the final end to you. You will always lie prostrate; no longer will you dare to scatter the deadly flame among the servants and handmaids of God, in whom the inmost vital part of the soul burns only with the wedding torch of Christ.
>
> Oh harasser of men, think you to be able among renewed men to revive with the breath of the destroyed head? As soon as the slashed neck of Holofernes moistened with cupidinous blood the Assyrian marriage couch, the stern Judith spurned the ornamental bed of the adulterous lord, and checked his impious madness with the sword, the woman bearing back from the host the infamous trophy, not with anxious hand, o my avenger, heavenly brave.
>
> But perchance then too little of strength [was] the woman, battling

15. Translated by H. W. Freemantle in *The Nicene and Post Nicene Fathers*, 2nd series, Vol. 6 (New York, 1897), p. 108.

under the shadow of the law, while yet prefiguring our times in which true virtue flowed into earthly bodies; through weak ministers the great head had to be cut off. What then does anything lawful now remain to you after the child-bearing of the unstained virgin? After the child-bearing of the virgin from which the first original [sin] departed the nature of the human body, arduous strength put on new flesh. And a virgin woman conceived Christ God, man of mortal mother, but God with the father. Whence now all flesh is holy, who conceives that one, he assumes the nature of God in the covenant of a brother. The Word, indeed, made flesh, does not cease to be what it was, the Word, while it joins to the nature of the flesh, in majesty, indeed, not degenerating, through making use of flesh, but in drawing wretches to the worthier-state.' [16]

Here Judith is not merely exemplary but almost completely figurative. She is the representation of Christ "under the shadow of the Old Law"; she represents the curative virginity of the New. Her typology for Prudentius seems to border on the allegorical, as her beheading of Holofernes suggests the more general triumph of the New Law through the incarnation of Christ. This ascription of an allegorical typology to Judith seems to have been commonplace. Thus in Epistle 22 one of Jerome's references to Judith is so allusive, even cryptic, as to suggest his assumption of an accepted understanding of her allegorical typology: "As soon as the Son of God set foot upon the earth, He formed for himself a new household; that, as He was adored by angels in heaven, angels might serve him also on earth. Then chaste Judith once more cut off the head of Holofernes." [17] We may adduce that Judith, in her role as destroyer of Satan's power, was on the allegorical level a type of Holy Church, Christ's new household. Jerome is even more explicit in Epistle 79: "[Judith] lived day and night in the temple and preserved the treasure of [her] chastity by prayer and fasting. [She] was a type of the church which cuts off the head of the devil." [18] And Isidore of Seville says: "Judith and Esther act as types of the Church; they punish the enemies of faith and the people of God bring forth from ruin." [19]

Before turning to the one complete commentary on the Book of Judith, that of Rabanus Maurus, we should note Ælfric's brief allegorical comment on his paraphrase on Judith. His paraphrase has no ready precedent, but his commentary does, and confirms the traditional attitude toward Judith. Affirming her historical reality, as noted, he makes clear that her importance for him is as prefigurative example. He continues from his affirmation of her historical reality:

16. *CCSL*, 126, pp. 153–154.
17. Translation by Freemantle, *op. cit.*, p. 30.
18. *Ibid.*, p. 168; *PL* 22, 732.
19. *PL*, 83, 116.

She, humble and chaste, small and weak, conquered the proud one and cast down the great one, because she betokened surely with deeds the holy congregation which now believes in God, that is, Christ's church in all Christian people, his one chaste bride, who with brave belief cuts off the head of the old devil, ever in chastity serving Christ. Judith promised first to the bloodthirsty lord that she would bring him within among her people. However, it was not entirely a lie that which she promised him, for she bore his head within the walls, and to the people showed how God aided her. To Him be ever praise eternally. Amen.

    She would not keep, as the story tells us, the war gear of the bloodthirsty one, which the people granted her, but cast aside entirely his garments; she would not wear them; she would not through his heathenness have sin. . . . Take example by this Judith how chastely she lived before the birth of Christ and never feign to God in the time of the gospel holy chastity which you vowed to Christ because he condemns secret fornications and foul shames.[20]

With Ælfric's customary mastery of concise exposition, he gives Judith's allegorical and tropological typology as well as her exemplary value. His commentary, not his paraphrase, is in the direct tradition of the selective concentration on the significance of Judith's virtue as the slayer of Holofernes.

    Finally, Rabanus' commentary on the Book of Judith is systematically maintained on the allegorical level with Judith representing Holy Church: "Judith, therefore, who is a type of Holy Church, reveals the tradition of the Judges; is to be interpreted 'confessing' or 'praising,' and is the daughter of Merari, that is, of affliction; because through the tribulation and afflictions of the present life one attains to future joys where the holy soul in corporeal flesh will praise God into eternity."[21] Along with the allegorical, however, Rabanus provides a tropological interpretation which may be illustrated by his commentary on the slaying of Holofernes which is developed in unusual detail in his running commentary on the Book of Judith:

The column which was at the head of Holofernes' bed signifies the hardness of the depraved heart and produced the errors of badly confident security. The sword which hung suspended is the ill will of evil intention. The hair of the head is the presumption of the proud mind; the neck in truth the contumaciousness of evil doing. And the canopy, that is the mosquito net [*rete muscarum*] signifies the snares of deceitful thought. . . . She herself prays with tears because supernal aid she asks in the most inner devotion of heart. She approaches the bed and draws out the sword, through which the head of the most wicked enemy was to be cut off, when the malice of the hard heart, having been laid bare, cuts off from the enemy the occasion of wanton temptation. She carries away the canopy because she lays bare his

20. Assmann, *op. cit.*, p. 103–104.
21. *Opera* (1627), III, p. 250.

frauds, with which, impious and reckless, he strove to involve her; The mutilated body of the enemy she rolled away. When the same enemy shows himself in every part infirm and weak, so Christian soldiers may trust to be able to conquer the worst enemy, who fully show themselves to be fragile and conquerable.[22]

In Rabanus' translation of *canopaeum*, (a word in Scriptures unique to the Book of Judith) as *rete muscarum*, may be noted a small, interesting, if indecisive, parallel with *Judith* where the canopy is called a *fleohnet*, a word otherwise found only in a gloss of *canopaeum*. Since Rabanus, the Old English glossator, and perhaps the poet, were simply providing the literal meaning of the word, there is no serious basis for considering Rabanus' gloss to be the source of the poet's word. Yet if the possibility does exist that the poet had read Rabanus' commentary, something very interesting results, not from the commentary itself, but from the prefatory poem which Rabanus wrote in place of his usual prose prefaces.[23] The structure of Rabanus' thirty-five line poem contains an interesting parallel with *Judith* in that it, like the Old English poem, is framed by an invocation of the Creator at the beginning and end:

> 1   Sumne Sator rerum, qui verbo cuncta creasti,
>   Atque opus omni tuum dextra tu rite parasti
>   Luminibus cœlum et ramis florentibus arva
>
> 4   Ornans. . . .
>
> 29   Fac nos velle, rogo, tua iussa implereque rite . . .
>   Scandamus læti, et capiamus regna serena,
>   Lux ubi perpetua est vitae, laus, gloria vera.
>   Quo Pater, ac Natus, regnat et Spiritus almus,
>   Vivus namque Deus verus summusque creator,
>   Parvos qui et magnos sanat per secula iustus
> 35   Omnium et est factor Iudex atque omnibus aequus.

However, since Judith signifies one who "praises" and "confesses" God, the frame of invocation is natural, and the parallel does not mean, any more than does the Old English poet's use of *fleohnet*, that the poet had made use of Rabanus. Indeed the commentary itself does not tend to shed much light on the poem, for which it has little or no relevance. Rabanus' commentary is itself without precedent, and the poet's tradition appears not to be Rabanus' commentary, but the pervasive tradition of selective exemplification.

Significantly, however, Rabanus had a special reason for his commentary on

22. *Ibid.*, p. 255.
23. *Ibid.*, p. 243, *PL*, 109, 541–542. The poem is preceded by a fulsome prose dedication to the Empress Judith. For the "paradigmatic" prayer, with reference to Old Testament figures, used at the marriage of Judith to Æthelwulf, see A. Katzenellenbogen, *The Sculptural Programs of Chartres Cathedral* (Baltimore, 1959), p. 31.

the whole Book of Judith, other than his encyclopedic zeal. As the body of his prefatory poem reveals, his commentary is addressed to the Empress Judith:

13   Te quoque deposco ni linquas lædere quemquam
      Reginam fraude, foveasque benignus amatam,
      Tu ut facias fortis Iudex regnare quietam
      Istic, sicque polo Iudith ipsa paretur adire.
17   Quo dignatque vocata ipsa sit munere Christi. . . .

Judith was the second wife of Louis the Pious; she was a lady of exemplary piety and of considerable knowledge of affliction. For a time the sons of the first wife succeeded in deposing their father and having Judith consigned to a nunnery. Although times were indeed troubled, Rabanus apparently remained unwavering in his loyalty to Louis and Judith, and he clearly sees something of high significance in the name of the Empress, the Christian embodiment of the typology of her name; protectress of her people, a true Christian, in her affliction confessing Christ so that she may gain the high estate of heaven. This is not to say that Rabanus' commentary is a piece of propaganda. It is not. Rather it is a straightforward development of the allegorical implications of Judith as representing the struggle of the Church against the devil; however this dedicatory poem to the Empress Judith, which makes clear Rabanus' recognition that the Book of Judith is noncanonical, suggests that the inspiration for his commentary was his reverence for the Empress rather than a unique desire for exegetical completeness. Similarly in his dedicatory epistle to Esther, he notes that he has "exposited in an allegorical sense" not the whole of the Vulgate Book of Esther but only the canonical portion.

> The remaining portions, in truth, which from the language and letters of the Greeks have been added over and above, and marked with an obelus, we have omitted to expound, but a reader most studious of the sense, when he had well delved into the preceeding [i.e. the canonical portion] he would have been able to know enough. You, however, O most noble Queen, when you will have well perceived the divine mysteries in the expositions, in the remainder what is to be understood you will properly perceive. Almighty God, who raised up the mind of the queen to releasing the calamities of her people, may deign to lead you, laboring in like zeal, to the heavenly joys.[24]

From this epistle, we may judge that Rabanus' dedicatory poem to his commentary on Judith, with its flattering reference to the Empress, is also intended to set off his commentary in a special way, and with a special sense of its contemporary relevance.

Rabanus' special purpose in his commentary, as this is expressed in the dedicatory poem, could have suggested to the Old English poet, assuming his knowledge of it, that a poem on Judith might have direct relevance to the situation of his own country. A. S. Cook has suggested that "the poem was prompted

24. *Ibid.*, p. 274.

by the arrival in England of that Judith whom Æthelwulf, the father of King Alfred, had married on the continent . . . in 856." But the date is probably too early for a poem with no early WS forms, and Cook later gave assent to Foster's hypothesis [25] that the inspiration for the poem is not the step-mother of Alfred, but his daughter Æthelflæd, Queen of the Mercians, a lady who was at least remembered as late as William of Malmesbury, who calls her, in words strikingly suitable to Judith, "*favor civium, pavor hostium*," "acclamation of her subjects, fear of her enemies." Henry of Huntingdon celebrates her in a poem. However, the most recent editors of the poem find this hypothesis unconvincing, and Timmer advances two arguments against it. He argues first that no contemporary evidence of adulation of Æthelflæd exists, and that, in fact, "Pre-Conquest England was not given to hero-worship." Be this as it may, Æthelflæd was the daughter of Alfred and step-granddaughter of Judith, who was the granddaughter of the Empress; moreover, she was involved in the defense of her country, and if she had not been venerated it is difficult to see why she should be remembered for two centuries. Timmer's second objection bears more weight. Because *Judith* belongs to a specific type of poetry, "the religious epic describing the deeds of a fighting saint," he argues that, "this makes it very unlikely that a religious heroine like Judith would represent a secular queen like Æthelflæd." He argues further that if the poet had wished to celebrate Æthelflæd, he would have written a poem of the type represented by *Brunnanburh, Eadmund,* etc. On the other hand, Rabanus could see the special relevance of the Book of Judith to the Empress, and could be impelled, in consequence, to write his commentary. The poet, similarly, could have been impressed by the relevance of Judith to the Queen of the Mercians, and be impelled, in consequence, to write a poem glorifying Judith. The frequent use of Judith as an example of Christian virtue would have provided ample precedent for him to write a poem on Judith's exploits as an example of the virtue of a Christian queen successfully defending her people against the heathen Vikings.

What Ælfric says in commenting on his paraphrase of the Book of Judith may have bearing on the poet's motivation. Speaking of a rendering into Old English of Judith he makes the point that, "It was also (*eac*) written in English in our manner (*in ure wisan*) as an example to you men, that you defend your country with weapons against the attacking army (*here*)." [26] Although Ælfric is speaking of his authorship of translations of the Old Testament, his mention of another Old English *Judith* does not make clear whether or not he is talking of his own work. His language seems to imply a reference to an already existent work. The implication appears to be that in addition to his translation (his or another's) there is also (*eac*) another written "in our manner" (*in ure wisan*). The ambiguity of this latter phrase causes the problem. Does it mean "some-

25. J. G. Foster, *Judith* (Strassburg, 1892); for Cook see his *Judith*, 2nd ed. (Boston, 1889), and edition of 1904.
26. Grein, *op. cit.*, p. 11.

thing written in the manner of Old English verse," or "something written in his own manner," i.e., in metrical prose? It seems quite possible, as Dietrich first argued, that Ælfric's reference is, indeed, to the Old English *Judith*.[27] However, Assmann, who disputed Dietrich's hypothesis, argues that Ælfric's paraphrase of Judith is written in four stress meter, not in metrical prose, and is thus distinct from his usual metrical prose, which is particularly "in the English manner." Assmann concludes that Ælfric meant to distinguish his Judith paraphrase from the rest of his translations.[28] However, even granting Assmann's doubtful contention about the difference between the Judith paraphrase and Ælfric's other translations, he misses the obvious point that Ælfric is writing an introduction to his own translations from the Old Testament, including his paraphrase of Judith, so that the simplest meaning to be attached in context to his reference to another version "in our manner" would be to a work other than his own paraphrase to which he would naturally be referring in his introduction. It would seem to follow that there is nothing unreasonable in the hypothesis that he is referring to the *Judith*. In that event he appears to be aware of a tradition which connects the poem with its value "as an example" to the English to defend their "country with weapons against the attacking army." However, even if he is not referring to *Judith*, his remarks suggest his awareness of the patriotic timeliness of a rendition of the Book of Judith. If Ælfric in the 10th century saw clearly the relevance of *Judith* to the struggle against the Viking invaders, it is not difficult to suppose that a 9th century poet might have seen just as clearly the relevance of his *Judith* to Æthelflæd's defense of Mercia against the heathen Vikings.

This review of the background against which the Old English poem must be placed does not provide us with a "source" for the poem, nor does it provide any certain clue to the immediate circumstances of the composition of the poem. On the other hand, it does suggest not only the unlikelihood that the poem is a fragment of a paraphrase of the Book of Judith, but also the likelihood that the poem is virtually complete as we have it; that it is a poem which celebrates Judith's slaying of Holofernes, the climactic episode of the Book, the episode which alone makes for her popularity as example. More than this, the survey of the background helps to suggest the theme the poet had in mind in writing his poem. For in the poem Judith's faith in God (*confitens*) and her praise of Him (*laudens*), and the diabolical nature of her adversary, are stressed. The poet's art, as will appear, is directed toward providing the spiritual significance of Judith's beheading of Holofernes. It is not the Hebrew patriotism of the Book of Judith which the poet recalls; rather the Judith celebrated by the poet is a type of Christian innocence triumphant over heathen bestiality. Her individual exploit and the rout of the Assyrians are given typological force. If the poet's art is seen only as it translates a few chapters of the Vulgate Book of Judith into

27. *Zeitschrift für die historische Theologie*, 26 (1856), p. 179.
28. Assmann, *op. cit.*, pp. 76–77.

the idiom and form of Old English verse, much of the subtlety, force and beauty of the poem is missed. It is perhaps because B. J. Timmer sees the poem as a fragment of a paraphrase that he casts cold water on those who have "lavishly praised it from the days of Sharon Turner down to the latest edition of Sweet's *Anglo-Saxon Reader,* where the poem is called 'one of the noblest in the whole range of Old English poetry.' . . . But though the poem deserves the high praise that has been bestowed upon it—even if one does not go quite so far as Henry Sweet did—it is the poet's character more than his art that wins it its high praise. His art is stereotyped and conventional. . . . Like *Maldon,* it is imitatory in its art, but, as in *Maldon,* one feels behind it the strong character of the man who made it." For myself, the poem has not taught me much about the character of the poet; he appears subsumed in his poem. In what follows, in the context of the background just sketched, the attempt will be made to demonstrate that Henry Sweet is right, and B. J. Timmer wrong. We will see again and again that the structure and language of the poem are at the service of a thematic design to which the background reading has given us a key; that the poet's art is subtle, profound, original, and that he creates a moving typological portrait of heroic virtue.

A. S. Cook, who was also one of those who "lavishly praised" the poem, divided it into thirteen "topics," an introduction, a conclusion, and eleven narrative units:

a) Divine assistance granted to Judith (1–7).
b) Feast (7–34).
c) Judith brought to Holofernes' tent (34–57).
d) Evil purposes and slaying of Holofernes (57–121).
e) Return to Bethulia (122–170).
f) Account of Holofernes' death and advice to the warriors (171–198).
g) Departure of the Hebrew army (199–216).
h) Surprise of the Assyrians and discovery of Holofernes' dead body (216–289).
i) Flight and defeat of the Assyrians (289–311).
j) Return of the Israelites and taking of spoil (311–334).
k) Recompense of Judith (334–341).
l) Judith's thanksgiving (341–346).
m) Poet's ascription of praise (346–349).

Cook's arrangement is perceptive although some of his topical divisions seem not entirely accurate. Thus Cook under d, 57–121, included two separate topics, Holofernes' evil purposes, and Judith's slaying of him. He perceived that the action of bringing Judith to Holofernes tent, c, 34–57, is a narrative and rhetorical unit, but failed to observe that the unit balances the action of Holofernes' going to his tent, 57–73. The two are complementary actions preliminary to the climactic scene of the slaying, 73–121. In marking the end of the preliminary action, the approach to the tent, lines 69–73 are conclusive, for they describe

Holofernes' men leaving his tent, an action which is preliminary to, and cannot be part of the narrative of the beheading. Their action completes the topic of the approach, narrated in two balanced paragraphs: i, the approach of Judith, 34–57; ii, the approach of Holofernes, 57–73. This two-fold action is preliminary to, and must be distinguished from the climactic action, Judith's beheading of Holofernes after the two are left alone.

Cook's e, Return to Bethulia, combines two topics: the actual journey to Bethulia, and the rejoicing of the people upon Judith's return. Both actions are distinguished by rhetorical frames and should be distinguished as separate narrative topics: the return to Bethulia, 122–141; the welcome to Bethulia, 141–170. Again, Cook's division of his topics g and h at line 216 appears to be wrong. Topic f, Judith's Revelation, is followed by a narrative unit, the battle, which is marked by a distinct rhetorical pattern involving the repetition of *stopon* in anaphora, 200, 212, 227. This action begins at line 200, and is clearly to be distinguished from the topic of the rout of the Assyrians, 236–291, a narrative unit also marked by a distinct rhetorical pattern. Cook's division at line 216 violates not only the narrative, but also the rhetorical structure of the two units. The correct division distinguishes the battle at dawn, 200–235, from the rout of the Assyrians, 236–291.[29]

Modification of Cook's topics j through m, 311–349, is required. Cook's j, 311–334, combines two topics, the return of the Hebrews, 311–323, and the gathering of the spoils, 323–341. His combination of the two topics is not defensible. The Vulgate clearly separates the two actions, and what is more important the two actions are clearly distinguished in the poem by their rhetorical structures. The return of the Hebrews, 311–323, balances their pursuit of the Assyrians, (Cook's i), 291–311. These are two verse paragraphs which together make up one topic, the vengeance of the Hebrews. This unit is marked rhetorically by repetitive variation throughout of the key word, *last*. At line 323 the beginning of a new topic is marked by a shift from plural to singular subject, and by the development of a new key word, *eall*. The narrative of the gathering of the spoils, 323–341, constitutes a verse paragraph which forms part of a single topic, the Hebrew triumph. In this unit are narrated the gathering and disposition of the spoils, 323–341, and the thanksgiving, 341–349. Cook's arrangement should be modified accordingly; his topic j should be divided, with lines 321–323 made part of the topic of vengeance, and lines 323–334, and his k, 334–341, made part of the unit narrating the gathering and disposition of the spoils of victory. Cook's topic l belongs to the general topic, the Hebrew triumph to

29. Cook edition of 1904, xx, ends his scene h at 289, but it seems better to end it at 291. The two lines in question complete the scene of the Assyrians' terror, as they fling down their arms. The transition at 291 is to the Hebrew warriors, so that a break at this point seems indicated. It should also be noted that at line 272 Timmer following Pope's suggestion, makes one line of what in Cook appears as two lines; Timmer's reading has been followed here, and the line numbering in Cook silently emended.

which Judith's speech of thanksgiving (1) provides an appropriate conclusion. Her thanks to God for worldly prosperity and for the heavenly reward toward which she looks serves also as a frame of conclusion for the entire poem, echoing, as it does, lines in the extant portion of the introduction. The explanation that she will find the reward for which she hopes because "she possessed true faith," 344–345 is a thematic, not a narrative statement, and leads directly to the final prayer, 346–349, which is accordingly made part of the final topic.

The simplification and modification of Cook's arrangement by narrative topics provides the following eleven topics (with Cook's divisions indicated parenthetically):

1	(a)	Introduction: God's aid to Judith	1–7	(1–7)
2	(b)	The Feast	7–34	(7–34)
	(c)			(34–57)
3		The Approach to the Tent	34–73	
	(d)			(57–121)
4		The Slaying of Holofernes	73–121	
5		The Return to Bethulia	122–141	
	(e)			(122–170)
6		The Welcome	141–170	
7	(f)	Judith's Revelation	171–200	(171–198)
8		The Battle at Dawn	200–235	
	(g)			(199–216)
9		The Rout of the Assyrians	236–291	
	(h)			(216–289)
10		The Hebrew Vengeance	291–323	
	(i)			(289–311)
11		The Hebrew Triumph	323–349	
	(j)			(311–334)
	(k)			(334–341)
	(l)			(341–346)
	(m)			(346–349)

This arrangement does very well in suggesting the narrative structure of the poem. However, to provide a view of the basic design of the poem, its thematic development, and its structural unity, it is necessary to do more than list the narrative building blocks seriatim. It is necessary to show how the narrative building blocks are assembled and organized. Even from the sequence of scenes it is clear that there are three major episodes: A, which culminates in the slaying of Holofernes; B, which culminates in Judith's revelation of her triumph in her address to the people; C, which culminates in the triumph of the Hebrew people and Judith's prayer. Within these episodes, still on narrative grounds alone, the basic scenes appear. Episode A, the Slaying of Holofernes, comprises four scenes: I (1), Introduction; II (2), the Feast; III (3), the Approach to the Tabernacle; IV (4), the Slaying. Episode B, Judith's Triumph, consists of three scenes: I (5), the Return; II (6), the Welcome; III (7), the Revelation of Triumph. Episode C, the Hebrew Triumph, comprises four scenes; I (8), the Battle at Dawn; II (9), the Terror and Flight of the Assyrians; III (10), the Hebrew Vengeance; IV (11), the Hebrew Triumph. Although a more detailed outline by paragraph, period, and clausule must rest on rhetorical analysis, for convenience of reference, a complete outline may be given in advance of the analysis.

A SCHEMATIC OUTLINE OF JUDITH

Lines	Units	Topics	Significant Words and Phrases
1-121	A	The Slaying of Holofernes	
1-7	I	Introduction	*tweode gifena in ðys ginnan grunde . . . heo ahte trumne geleafan a to ðam ælmihtigan*
7-34	II	The feast	
7-10	i	Introduction, command to the feast	*het gumena baldor*
10-21	ii	Warriors feasting	
10-14	1	(a) Hasty approach: (b) Fourth day	(a) *ofstum miclum . . . comon . . . feran:* (b) *ælfscinu*
15-19	2	(a) Sitting: (b) cups filled	(a) *sittan eodon:* (b) *fulle fletsittendum*
19-21	3	(a) Feasting: (b) Holofernes' unawareness	(a) *fæge þegon:* (b) *se rica ne wende*
21-27	iii	Holofernes' feasting	*goldwina gumena . . . hloh ond hlydde, hlynede ond dynede*
28-34	iv	Conclusion: command to gluttony	
28-32	1	Drowning men in wine	*Swa ofer ealne dæg drencte . . . oferdrencte*
32-34	2	Command to fill the men	*Swa het se gumena baldor fylgan fletsittendum . . . oð þæt nealæhte niht*
34-73	III	Approach to the tabernacle	
34-55	i	Judith's approach	
34-37	1	Introduction, Holofernes' command	*Het ofstum fetigan*
37-39	2	Men's obedience	*hraðe fremedon*
39-46	3	(a) Summoning of Judith: (b) Leading her to tent	(a) *Bearhtme stopon to ðam gysterne:* (b) *fromlice . . . lædan . . . to træfe*
46-54	4	Decorative insert, the canopy in the tent	*fleohnet*
54-55	5	Bringing of Judith to bed	*gebrohton snude*

Lines	Units	Topics	Significant Words and Phrases
55-73	ii	Holofernes' approach	
55-57	1	Introduction, report of warriors	*eodon cyðan*
57-61	2	(a) Holofernes' lustful expectation: (b) God's refusal	(a) *bliðe . . . þohte:* (b) *ne wolde . . . Dema geðafian*
61-67	3	(a) His seeking of bed: (b) Loss of glory	(a) *gewat . . . beddes neosan:* (b) *sceolde his blæd forleosan*
67-69	4	His falling senseless on bed	*Gefeol . . . swa nyste ræda nanne*
69-73	5	Conclusion, departure of drunken warriors	*Wiggend stopon . . . ofstum miclum*
73-121	IV	Slaying of Holofernes	
73-97	i	Preparation	
73-80	1	(a) Judith's planning: (b) taking of sword	(a) *Nergendes þeowen . . . gemyndig:* (b) *genam . . . mece*
80-94	2	Call to the Trinity	
80-82	a	Introduction	*Ongan nemnan*
83-86	b	Invocation of Trinity	*biddan . . . þrynesse þrym*
86-88	c	Statement of plight	*onhæted . . . geomor . . . gedrefed*
88-94	d	Threefold plea: for victory and faith; safety; vengeance	*sigor . . . geleafan; . . . gesynta; . . . gewrec*
94-97	3	God's favoring response	*hehsta dema . . . onbryrde swa he deð anra gehwylcne*
97-111	ii	The slaying	
97-98	1	Introduction: Judith's courage renewed	*rume on mode*
98-103	2	Preparation to strike	*Genam*
103-108	3	Striking of first blow	*Sloh þa wundenlocc*
108-111	4	Striking of final blow	*Sloh . . . oþre siðe*
111-121	iii	Damnation of Holofernes	
111-112	1	Lifelessness of the foul body	*Læg se fula leap*
112-117	2	Departure of soul for hell	*Gæst ellor hwearf*
117-121	3	Eternal despair of Holofernes	*hytwynna leas*
122-200	B	Judith's Triumph	
122-141	I	Return to Bethulia	
122-124	1	Introductory generalization	*blæd . . . æt guðe swa hyre god uðe*
125-132	2	Disposition of head	*heafod . . . on ðam fætelse*
132-138	3	Journey back	*Eodon . . . geseon . . . wlitegan byrig*
138-141	4	Arrival	*forð onettan . . . to ðam wealgate*

Lines	Units	Topics	Significant Words and Phrases
141-170	II	The welcome	
141-146	i	The watch	*Wiggend sæton . . . swa . . . Iudithe bebead*
146-158	ii	The arrival	
146-147	1	Judith's return	*Wæs ða eft cumen*
147-152	2	Command to open gate	*in forleton þurh ðæs wealles geat*
152-157	3	Preliminary speech	*eow ys metod bliðe*
159-170	iii	Judith's entrance	
159-161	1	Joyousness of people	*bliðe burhsittende*
162-166	2	Hastening to gate	*folc onette*
166-170	3	Opening of gate	*in forleton*
171-200	III	The revelation	
171-175	i	Revelation of Holofernes' head	*het . . . heafod onwriðan . . .*
176-198	ii	Judith's speech	
176-186	1	(a) "Look on Holofernes: (b) my victory came from God"	(a) *heafod starian:* (b) *. . . þurh godes fultum*
186-198	2	(a) "Prepare for battle: (b) victory ordained by God"	(a) *biddan wille . . . to gefeohte . . . eastan leohtne:* (b) *getacnod . . . dryhten*
199-200	iii	Hebrew preparation	*snude gegearewod*
200-349	C	The Hebrew Triumph	
200-235	I	Battle at dawn	
200-212	i	Premonitory action	*Stopon cynerof*
200-203	1	Advance under banners	*bæron sigeþufas*
204-205	2	Clash of shields at dawn	*On þæt dægred . . . dynedan scildas*
205-212	3	Omens of battle	
205-209	a	Eagerness of wolf and raven for the feast	*wulf . . . hrefn . . . wistan . . . fylle on fægum*
209-212	b	Eagle's battle-song	*on last earn . . . sang hildeleoð*
212-226	ii	Advance	*Stopon heaðorincas*
212-220	1	Advance under shields	
212-216	a	Advance	*bordum beþeahte*
216-220	b	Premonitions	*forgolden . . . under guðfanum*
220-223	2	Discharge of arrows	*flana scuras*
223-226	3	Attack with spears	
223-225	a	Yelling, and hurling of spears	*Styrmdon . . . garas sendon*
225-226	b	Anger of Hebrews	*yrre landbuende*
227-235	iii	Joining of battle	*Stopon styrnmode*
227-229	1	Determination and enmity of Hebrews	*wrehton . . . ealdgeniðlan*
229-231	2	Drawing of swords	*Mundum brugdon . . . swyrd*
231-235	3	Attack à outrance	*Slogon . . . nanne ne sparedon*

Lines	Units	Topics	Significant Words and Phrases
236-291	II	Terror and flight of Assyrians	
236-250	i	Awakening	
236-241	1	Arousing of the chiefs of watch	*morgentid . . . ongeaton . . . swyrdgeswing*
241-246	2	Awakening of drunken chief lieutenants	*cyðan eodon . . . medowerigum morgencollan*
246-250	3	Assembly of the doomed at the tabernacle	*gefrægn slegefæge . . . burgeteldes*
250-274	ii	Dilemma	
250-253	1	Introduction: realization of need to awaken Holofernes	*Hogedon . . . bodian*
253-261	2	Fear of disturbing him	
253-257	a	Their belief that he is with Judith	*Mynton . . . træfe . . . ætsomne*
257-261	b	Their fear	*nan . . . aweccan dorste*
261-267	3	Approach of Hebrew threat	
261-265	a	Approach	*Magen nealæhte*
265-267	b	Premonition of disaster	*dom geswiðrod*
267-274	4	Congregation at the tabernacle	
267-272	a	Helplessness	*stodon . . . cohhetan, cirman . . . gristbitian*
272-273	b	Statement of doom	*tires æt ende*
273-274	5	Conclusion (a) Hope (b) Hopelessness	(a) *Hogedon . . . aweccan:* (b) *. . . ne speow*
275-291	iii	Discovery and flight	
275-280	1	Discovery	
275-277	a	One man's courageousness	*sum . . . arod . . . in þæt burgeteld . . . neðde*
278-280	b	Discovery	*funde . . . blacne . . . goldgifan*
280-289	2	Revelation	
280-284	a	Despairing action	*gefeoll . . . feax teran*
285-289	b	Speech	*Her is geswutelod . . . getacnod . . . beheafdod healdend ure*
289-291	3	Flight	*wurpon hyra wæpen . . . on fleam*
291-323	III	Vengeance	
291-311	i	Pursuit	
291-297	1	Harrying of enemy	
291-296	a	Pursuit until enemy provided a carrion feast	*feaht on laste . . . se mæsta dæl . . . wulfum . . . fuglum to frofre*
296-297	b	Flight of living Assyrians	*flugon ða ðe lyfdon*
297-300	2	Following of enemy	
297-299	a	Pursuit	*Him on laste for*

Lines	Units	Topics	Significant Words and Phrases
299-300	b	God as protector	*god . . . on fultum*
301-311	3	Destruction	
301-304	a¹	Battle path made by Hebrews:	a¹ *herþað worhton:*
304-307	a²	their fierceness	a² *guðe gegremed*
307-311	b	Flight of few living Assyrians	*on greot gefeoll se hyhsta dæl*
311-323	ii	Return	
311-313	1	Turning back of Hebrews	*Cirdon . . . on wiðertrod wælscel oninnan*
313-321	2	Booty and glory	
313-318	a	Greatness of booty	*Rum wæs to nimanne . . . dyre madmas*
318-321	b	Glory of Hebrews	*domlice . . . fynd oferwunnen*
321-323	3	Resting of Assyrians on the path	*Hie on swaðe reston*
323-349	IV	Triumph	
323-341	i	Spoils of victory	
323-330	1	All booty gathered	*eall . . . wundenlocc . . . læddon to ðære beorhtan byrig*
331-334	2	All owed to Judith	*Eal . . . þurh Iudithe gleawe lare*
334-341	3	All Holofernes' possessions granted to Judith	*to mede . . . swylce eac eal*
341-349	ii	Thanksgiving	
341-346	1	Judith's thanksgiving	
341-344	a	Thanks for all, glory and hope of heaven	*Ealles . . . sægde wuldor . . . weorðmynde on moldan rice, swylce eac mede on heofonum*
344-346	b	Her reward gained through faith	*þæs ðe heo ahte soðne geleafan . . . ne tweode þæs leanes þe heo lange gyrnde*
346-349	2	Concluding prayer	*Þæs sy . . . wuldor . . . swylce eac reðe streamas*

In such an outline as this, subjectivity cannot be avoided, particularly in the division of the smaller rhetorical units; but its adequacy in general may be tested by the internal evidence of the poem itself. The analysis which follows will test the outline, as the outline will serve as a convenient point of reference for the analysis. If the procedure seems circular, at least the external evidence does suggest that the major elements of the outline are plausible. The outline highlights the theme, given at the beginning and end, that Judith is specially favored by God because of her faith; it also emphasizes three major episodes: A, the Slaying of Holofernes; B, the Triumph of Judith; and through her, C, the Triumph of the Hebrews. The theme and special emphases of the poem, suggested by the outline, appear to reflect patristic and poetic allusions to Judith. The earliest reference to Judith, that of Clement of Rome, celebrates her deed as a triumph owed to God's grace and performed by her for her people. Isidore of Seville notes the bravery of her act and that her triumph was a victory for her people. Ambrose remarks on her special dedication to God, her keeping of herself amidst the drunkenness of the camp, the greatness of her exploit, her triumph, and the liberation of her people, for "she raised their spirits, and dispirited the enemy." In *De officiis*, he speaks of her two triumphs—first, that she preserved her chastity, and second, that she, a woman, conquered a man and put the enemy to rout; he speaks eloquently of her bravery, alone as she was in the midst of barbaric enemies. He summarizes the thematic value of Judith's example: "How great the power of virtue, that she believed in God as her help, how great the grace, that she found it to be so." In *De Elia et jejunia*, he speaks especially of her victory as one of sobriety over drunkenness. Dracontius pictures her "clothed in faith," alone amidst the terrifying enemy; he speaks of her carrying the head to the city, and of her triumph which gave her people freedom. Aldhelm pictures her solitary bravery, surrounded by enemies, and speaks of the "renowned triumph" which she reports to her people. The interpretation of her name, of course, provides a clue to the thematic structure of the poem, with its opening and concluding statement of faith and praise. Jerome sees her, as does Ambrose, looking toward Christ, her salvation. He pictures vividly the moment of the beheading, the carrying away of the head, her triumph. Prudentius pictures the moment of the slaying and her carrying away the head. In his allegorical interpretation of Judith, she slays the devil, punishes the enemies of faith, and delivers the people of God. Finally, in Rabanus' dedicatory poem, we find, as in the Old English poem, a framework of praise of the Creator.[30] However, the similarities between the poem and earlier treatments of Judith do not suggest that the poet lacked originality in the structuring of his poem. He has no known "source," as such, for his ordering of events; rather he gives brilliant form and shape to the notable and traditional elements in the story which awaited his triumphant poetic imagination. The poet's mastery appears at every turn; the design of the poem is elaborately and effectively organized to serve the purposes of allegorical characterization, and metaphorical narrative. In his diction the poet makes many new, striking combinations, and adds a new dimension to the stock of traditional poetic formulas.

In the following detailed analysis, segments of the outline given above will not be repeated, so that occasional reference to it will be helpful.

30. For Clement of Rome see note 10; Isidore, see note 11; Ambrose, see note 12, and *PL*, 16, 128–129, *PL*, 14, 741–742; Dracontius, *De laudibus Dei*, ed. F. Volmer, Book III, 480–495, *MGH*, AA, 14, 105; Aldhelm, note 13; Jerome, note 15; Prudentius, note 16; Rabanus, note 21.

A The Slaying of Holofernes

1–7, I, The Introduction: The extant poem lacks all but the last fifteen lines of the beginning of Manuscript section IX. Of the remaining fifteen lines, the first seven belong to the introduction, the remainder to scene II. Manuscript sections X, XI and XII each contain a little more than one hundred lines. If section IX contains an equivalent number of lines, it would lack approximately ninety lines. From what we have observed in the traditional accounts of Judith, they might well give an account of Judith's devout widowhood and of her persuading the elders not to surrender, but to let her go alone to the camp of the enemy. The action proper would then begin with the thematic statement, which ends with the first seven lines of the extant poem. On the other hand, some of the divisions in the Junius manuscript contain far fewer lines, for example the 19 lines of section LI of *Daniel* 104–123; the 30 lines of section V of *Christ and Satan* 224–253; the 62 of XL, *Exodus* 1–62. Section IX, containing the beginning of the *Judith*, might then contain only twenty to thirty lines, and the poem would begin *in media res*, with a brief introduction balancing the brief conclusion.

Whatever the length of Section IX, the first extant lines of the poem are very clearly reflected in the last lines by a pattern of chiastic repetition: *tweode . . . þe heo ahte trumne geleafan/a to ðam ælmihtigan*, 1–7: *þæs ðe heo ahte soðne geleafan/a to ðam ælmihtigan . . . ne tweode*, 344–345. There is in addition an echoic repetitive variation: *tweode/gifena in ðys ginnan grunde*, 1–2, and *ne tweode/þæs leanes þe heo lange gyrnde*, 345–346. The theme of the poem, which is established in the introduction, is that Judith's triumph and good fortune are the reward of her faith. The thematic statement reflects the kind of statement about Judith that we find in Ambrose, "How great the power of virtue that she believed in God as her help; how great the grace that she proved it to be so." [31]

In a way Judith's "characterization" is also established in the introduction, or rather, the absence of anything that we could call "characterization." For to seek for Judith's personality, for her individuality, her identity, is to seek not only in vain, but mistakenly. Judith is a romanesque statue, chiseled in rigid simplicity, without personal expression, yet alive because she emblemizes the heroic virtue of faith and its triumph over the forces of evil. (See plate 5, following p. 138) The poet's art rests in his creation of an emblematic heroine, in his suggesting through her formalized actions and words their majestic significance in the drama of the triumph of faith over the devil.

31. *PL*, 16, 179.

The extant portion of the introduction is developed around two contrastive repetitions. First, in line 3, it is said that Judith found the protection of the highest judge when she had (*ahte*) the greatest need of it against the highest terror, and in line 6, that she was victorious because she had (*ahte*) steadfast faith in God. Second, in line 4, *hehstan Deman* is set in contrast to *hehstan brogan*. In the latter phrase terror is personified. The highest terror is Holofernes, and his eternal archetype, the devil, particularly in contrast to *hehstan Deman*, by whose decree those who *have* faith *have* protection from the doomed enemies of faith. Later the poet will make striking use of the contrast between Holofernes' god-like awesomeness and the true awesomeness of God. The epithet, *Deman*, "Judge," especially appropriate as suggesting his providential justice, is framed by two variants: *mæran þeodne*, "illustrious Lord" (3), suggesting his glory, and *frymða Waldend*, "Ruler of Creation" (5), suggesting his power. Framing the second sentence declaring Judith's faith are two epithets for God: *Fæder on roderum* (5), and *ælmihtigan* (7). The epithets are again appropriate to the subject, the faith, the knowledge of those spiritual realities of which the sense has no experience, as in the Creed, "I believe in God, the Father almighty." The epithets look forward to the conclusion where Judith is said to find her heavenly home because of a faith tried by her works.

7–34, II, the Feast: Scene II is introduced with the *Gefrægen* formula and is rhetorically framed by the repetition: *het se gumena baldor* (9, 32), giving Holofernes' command to the feast and his command that all continue the debauch until night falls. The framed narration is arranged in four paragraphs, the first and last containing the *het* repetition. These provide a frame of cause and effect: in i, 7–10, Holofernes causes his men to feast; in iv, 28–34, the effect is shown in their drunken sleep as darkness falls upon them. The central narrative paragraphs, ii and iii, develop the action of the men and of Holofernes. In paragraph ii a major pattern for the development of the action is established. Here, as throughout, the action is advanced in three steps, marked in paragraph ii by three periods:

1, 10–14,	The warriors approach the feast.
	Hie . . . ræfndon rondwiggende comon . . . feran.
2, 15–19,	They sit at the feast.
	Hie . . . sittan eodon . . . byrnwiggende.
3, 19–21,	They feast.
	Hie . . . þegon rofe rondwiggende.

The three periods are linked by repetition. Each begins with the initial proleptic pronoun *Hie;* each has a plural verb in the past tense; further, the delayed subject of periods 1 and 3, is the same, *rondwiggende*, and a repetitive variant in 2, *byrnwiggende*. In each period the proleptic plural clausule is balanced by a clausule in contrastive construction.

In period 1, the a clausule is balanced by a parenthetical b clausule in the impersonal singular: "—That was the fourth day after/ the lady Judith alluringly lovely ready in soul/ first sought him out—." The parenthetical clausule provides suspense by suggesting Judith's peril, the subject of the next scene in which Holofernes summons her to his bed. It also serves a premonitory purpose in suggesting the doom toward which Holofernes is leading his men: Judith's hour is at hand, and deadly in her allurement to the evil-minded, in her wisdom she waits; through pride and gluttony Holofernes is incited to thoughts of lust, and will lurch toward his death. The designation of Judith as *ælfscinu*, 14, "elvishly beautiful," is particularly effective here in suggesting her deadly allure for Holofernes. The word is found elsewhere only in *Genesis* A, lines 1827 and 2730, where it is used to designate Abraham's wife, Sarah, in the particular context of her dangerous attractiveness to a gentile prince. In *Judith*, *ælfscinu* suggests synoptically both the allure and the danger of the beauty to the evil who desire to possess it.

The narrative clausule a of period 2 is balanced by a parenthetical clausule in passive construction describing the feverish pouring of the wine, "Unceasingly along the benches/deep bowls were carried pitchers and cups as well / full for the revellers in the hall" (17–19). The concluding phrase, *fulle fletsittendum*, is echoed in *fylgan fletsittendum* (33) in paragraph iv which describes the effect of the feast on the warriors.[32] The repetition suggests an ironic chain of events resulting from Holofernes' command that the men be filled: the cups are filled with wine until the men are "drowned" (31); in consequence they are "emptied of every good" (32).

In periods 1 and 2 the feasting described in the a clausules stands in contrast to the suggestion of doom implied in the b clausules. This implicit contrast is made explicit in 3 by the ironic contrast in clausule a between the two adjectives, *fæge*, "doomed," and *rofe*, "fearless," which modify the delayed subject, *rondwiggende*, and in the b clausule through its indication that their powerful and fearsome leader was blind to the impending doom, *se rica ne wende/ egesful* (20–21). The blindness of Holofernes pictured in the b clausule also serves to make a transition to paragraph iii, which pictures the drunken madness of Holofernes as he encourages his men through exhortation and example to drunken stupor.

32. The translation of *fylgan fletsittendum* as "revellers in the hall be filled" is a sense translation and does not involve acceptance of Cook's emendation of *fylgan* to *fyllan*. If Timmer is correct, and the word here reflects the meaning of *fyligan* in *Genesis* B, 249, "to serve," the action concerned is directly parallel to the filling of the cups, with word play on the root syllable, *fyl-ful*. Further the suggested relation to *Genesis* B is interesting, for there the word is used in the context of Satan's belief that his angels would serve him, *þæt hie giongorscipe fyligan wolden*. It should be noted, however, that the meaning "serve" is derived only from context in *Genesis* B, and does not provide an exception to Cook's statement that it is "a sense otherwise unexampled in poetry." It may be added that *fyllan* is entirely appropriate in context in *Judith*.

In paragraph iv repetition of a key phrase in i, *het se gumena baldor* (9, 32), links the paragraphs to form a rhetorical frame for ii and iii, which narrate the feast: in i Holofernes' command to the feast, and in iv the results of the feast are given. By repetition of the connective of result, *swa*, to introduce the two periods of iv, 28–32, 32–34, the relation of the paragraph as effect to the cause expressed in i is underlined. The evil will of Holofernes is the cause; the result is the death-like drunkenness of his followers and himself. The framing paragraphs and paragraph iii, which focuses on Holofernes' mad wilfullness, relates the entire scene of the feast to him and his evil power.

The description of the feast (A II) characterizes Holofernes as representing arrogant pride, worldly power and debauched folly. His power is suggested by the way his bold warriors hasten (*ofstum miclum*, 10) to obey him, and by the epithets describing him; *gumena baldor* (9, 32), *rican þeodne* (11), *folces ræswan* (12), *se rica . . ./ egesful eorla dryhten* (20–21), *goldwine gumena* (22). In their number and variety they parallel the epithets for God in the introduction except that Holofernes' power is evil and in its consequences, destructive. The mention of Judith in the appositive clausule of ii, 1 implies that the power of Holofernes displayed at the feast is self-destroying, but the first overt suggestion of this is given in period 2 through the epithet *weagesiðas* (16), literally, "companions in misery," applied with deliberate and ironic inappropriateness to the proud, bold warriors (*wlance, bealde byrnewiggende*) as they sit down to a brimming board. The first premonitory epithet is followed in period 3 by the use of *fæge* (19), "doomed," to describe the feasters, and in the description of Holofernes, the powerful, terrible leader of nobles, is shown to be ignorant of impending doom (*ðæs se rica ne wende*, 20).

A graphic portrait is drawn in paragraph iii of the great man in his joyful carousing (*gytesalum*), the portrait of a mighty man become beast. All dignity vanishes; only the naked display of a mighty self-indulgence remains. By use of rhymes and a staccato rhythm the poet suggests his drunken madness, *Hloh ond hlydde, hlynede ond dynede . . . styrmde ond gylede/ modig ond medugal* (23–26). Premonitions of disaster are suggested through effective manipulation of formulaic expression. Holofernes' celebration is so loud *þæt mihten fira bearn feorran gehyran*, "that the sons of men for miles could hear them." He exhorts his men by shouting and example to drink *ofer ealne dæg*, "all the long day" (28), *oð þæt fira bearnum/nealæhte niht seo þystre*, "until the dark night fell upon the sons of men" (33–34). The temporal formulas of day and night have an ominous significance, particularly as they provide a frame for a metaphoric development of the action of Holofernes filling his men with wine, an action likened to his drowning of them. First, Holofernes, *se inwidda*, (28) "drenched (*drencte*) in wine/ the lords of his retinue . . . until they lay in a stupor;/ he drowned (*oferdrencte*) his attendants all, as if dropped in death they were/ emptied of any lingering good" (29–32). The structure of repetition underscores the metaphoric likening of the stupor of drunkenness to death by drowning. In effect Holofernes' feast creates in his men the simulacrum of the death which they—and he—will undergo.

Even beyond their obvious metaphoric implications the key verbs which the poet employs, *drencte* (29), and *oferdrencte* (31), are peculiarly appropriate. *Oferdrencan* appears only in *Judith,* and the uncompounded form, *drencan,* appears only in *Judith* and the Psalms, 59.3, 68.21, 106.17. In the first two occurrences in the Psalms, the verb has the meaning "drenched," "made to drink," but in the last occurrence, by metaphoric extension, it means "die," translating *et appropinquaverunt usque ad portas mortis.* The Old English translator's use of "drencan" with referent "to die" can be explained. Psalm 105 speaks of the Egyptian captivity and in verse 11 tells of God's drowning of the Egyptian host, *and heora feondas flod adrencte;* similarly in the Old English translation of Judith, 5.31, [God] *adrencte hi ealle,* and in Ælfric's paraphrase, line 108, *Ac god hine adrencte.* It must clearly be such a referent that the Old English translator had in mind when in the next psalm, 106, he translated verse 17, *et appropinquaverunt usque ad portas mortis, þæt hy wið deaða drencyde wæron.* The possibility that the *Judith* poet had a similar metaphoric referent for the word *drencan* is suggested by the earlier reference to the drowning of the Egyptians in *Judith* and the cross reference in the Vulgate of Psalms 105 and 106 to Judith 13.21. Since Holofernes was indeed offering his men the drink of bitter death, *poculum mortis,*[33] the analogue with the Pharoah would have been suggested. Holofernes, like the Pharoah leading his men into the Red Sea, drowned his men in their iniquities. Their stupefaction is the prelude to their death, literally and spiritually, for after their day (28) they will die emptied of all good (32), when their dark night comes (34).

34-73, III, The Approach to the Tabernacle: Scene III narrates the approach to the tabernacle of Judith and Holofernes. The two actions are given in two balanced paragraphs, each having a complex periodic pattern. Paragraph i is introduced in period 1, 34-37, by the command formula, *het,* which was employed to frame Scene II. The period tells how Holofernes commanded that Judith be brought with haste to his bed, and serves to introduce the narrative of the carrying out of his command. This action is developed in three periods: 2, 37-39; 3, 39-46; 5, 54-55, with period 4, 46-54, being a "decorative insert" describing the "canopy." The threefold action is parallel to that in II, ii, 1, 2, 3. There the men obey, sit, accomplish what they were commanded; here, they obey, they go to Judith's tent, they complete what they were commanded to do. Further, as in II, ii the men hastened to obey Holofernes, their haste to obey is given special emphasis in III, i by repetition of adverbs of haste in each period. Holofernes, 1, commands that Judith be brought in haste, *ofstum* (35, cf. 10); in 2, the men obey speedily *hraðe* (37); in 3, they march quickly, *bearhtme*

33. C. Brown, *"Poculum Mortis* in Old English," *Speculum,* 15 (1940), 389-399.

(39), and conduct her promptly *fromlice* (41); in 5, they bring her to bed quickly, *snude* (55).[34] Each of the narrative periods 2, 3, 5, has a plural verb, and the same subject, *Hie*, with which 2 and 5 begin, the subject being suspended in 3. All three periods are brief and serve to frame period 4 with its elaborate description of the canopy of Holofernes' magnificent couch.

Paragraph ii is framed by periods 1 and 5, 55–57, 69–73, both with verbs of motion in the preterite plural, the subjects being Holofernes' attendants: *Eodon ða stercedferhðe* (55); *Wiggend stopon* (69). In the introductory period the warriors go to inform Holofernes that Judith had been brought to his tent; in the concluding period they leave the tent. Within this framework are three narrative periods in the preterite singular with Holofernes as subject. As in II, ii, and III, i the device of triple narrative statement is employed.

2 (intent) Holofernes was joyous in his evil intention;
3 (approach) He proceeded to seek his bed;
4 (completion) He fell on his bed in animal-like stupor.

In periods 2 and 3 the narrative is advanced in the a clausules, against which are balanced b clausules of comment: 2a, 57–59, tells what Holofernes intended, 2b, 59–61, what God intended; 3a, 61–64, describes Holofernes' approach to his bed, 3b, 64–67, his end, which will be according to his deserts. Period 4 consists of only one narrative clausule which completes the action with a highly charged picture of Holofernes made senseless with wine, becoming like his followers at the end of the feast (II), a simulacrum of death.

The narrative function of Scene III is to provide a suspenseful transition from the feast (II) to the climactic scene of the beheading (IV). In II Holofernes ordered his men to the feast, and then ordered that they be drowned in wine (*het*, 9, 32); in III Holofernes orders that his men bring him the object of his lustful desires. The sequence suggests the moral platitude that gluttony leads to lust, "Lust is fed with feasts, nourished with delicacies, enkindled with wine, inflamed with drunkenness." [35]

The characterization of Holofernes as a man of wordly power is continued in III, i, which begins with a repetition of the verb of command, *het*, and which makes repeated use of the adverbs of haste, suggesting, as in II, Holofernes' effect upon his men who hasten to do what he commands. Most striking, however, in the continuation of the typifying portrait of Holofernes is the description of his bed chamber in III, ii, 4. In this "decorative insert" the two words used to designate Holofernes' tent are of special importance in suggesting his god-like, yet evil, power. These two terms are the unique compound *burgeteld*

---

34. Timmer's objection to the translation by Cook and Sweet of *bearhtme* as "instantly" because it "would be repetitious of *hraðe* in 37," clearly runs counter to the evidence of rhetorical design. Timmer, *op. cit.*, p. 19.

35. Ambrose, *De penitentia, PL,* 16, 509; see also his Epistle 63, *PL,* 16, 1248, "Excess therefore is the mother of lust."

(57, 248, 276) and the uncommon *træf* (43, 255, 268). They may reflect the Vulgate Judith where in addition to *tabernaculum* the more specific *cubiculum*, "bed chamber," is used in referring to Holofernes' tent. The coinage *burgeteld* serves admirably to translate *cubiculum*, and needs no explanation. However, more is involved in the use of *træf*, in addition to *burgeteld*, than faithfulness to the Vulgate with its use of two terms to designate the tent. First, there is no correspondence between the use of *træf* in the poem and the appearance of *tabernaculum* in the Vulgate: sometimes *træf*, as in its first appearance, (43) translates *cubiculum*; sometimes *burgeteld* appears as a translation of *tabernaculum*. Second, *træf* nowhere else has the meaning of tent or tabernacle. *Træf* is an uncommon word, found, except in compound, only in *Andreas* 842, *tigelfagum trafu*, where it refers to buildings (temples?) in heathen Myrmidonia. In *Andreas* 1641 the compound *helltrafum* signifies heathen buildings or temples; Satan laments that Andreas through his teaching has drawn the people *fram helltrafum*, i.e., both their heathen temples and their destined residences in hell. In *Beowulf* 175 *hærgtrafum* signifies the heathen temples to which the Danes repair to ask vainly for help. The only other use of *træf* in compound is in *Elene*, 926, *of þam wearhtreafum*, as in *Andreas*, part of the devil's angry speech: he threatens to return from the abode of the evil, i.e., hell. Thus *træf*, separately and in compound, suggests an abode of the evil, or of the devil.[36] This connotation suggests the primary reason for the use of *træf* in *Judith*. Holofernes' tent is the abode of the evil. The word gives a metaphorical level of meaning to the tent as a heathen temple serving the devil, and standing opposed to the temple of God. (In plate 5, which follows p. 138, it may be noted that the tent is clearly pictured as a temple, one, indeed, which appears to be topped by a cruciform symbol.) The word is given further density of meaning in the "decorative insert" through word play, the dative singular *hean* modifying *træfe* (43) being a homonym with the meaning "high" and "abject." The proud temple is also an abject one because it is evil; in the second sense it is also premonitory of the abasement of Holofernes' pride.

In developing his description of Holofernes' bed in period 4, 46–54, the

36. If Holthausen is right (*Altenglisches Etymologisches Wörterbuch, s.v.*) in considering *træf* a borrowing from Latin *trabs*, Cassiodorus' explanation of the significance of tabernacle in Psalm 14.1 may suggest the relation of tabernacle and temple. Tabernacle here signifies God's Church. He goes on, "But why is it called *tabernaculum* we should examine a little more diligently. Our elders did name the houses of the poor *tabernas*, because they were covered with wooden beams (*trabibus*), rather than tiles; as it were, *trabernas*. And because they lived and ate, as the old custom was to take food, from the two words, that is, from *tabernas and cenaculum, tabernaculum* may be considered to be made. Hence we now perceive tabernacles to be properly called expeditionary and sudden dwellings," *CCSL*, 97, pp. 132–133. See also Augustine's explanation, *CCSL*, 14, p. 88, "Although sometimes tabernacle is written for an eternal dwelling; nevertheless when tabernacle is properly understood, it is a thing of war. Whence soldiers are called *contubernales*. . . . For within the time we contend with the devil, the work is in the tabernacle in which we refresh ourselves."

poet concentrates on the *fleohnet,* creating for it the function of preventing any-one from gazing through it, but permitting Holofernes to look out. In the con-text of the analogy between *træf* and temple the description of the mysterious canopy suggests a further analogy. The netting with its suggestion of the mys-terious presence of a god-like figure, not seen, but seeing all, invisible except as it chose to make its presence visible, suggests an analogy to the veil of the holy of holies within the temple, as in Exodus 26.33, *the veil shall divide unto you between the holy place and the most holy.* This analogy between the canopy and the veil of the temple again suggests not only the mysterious power of Holo-fernes, but even more powerfully the falseness and self-destructiveness of this power. The canopy itself may represent, according to Rabanus, "the snares of deceitful thoughts," [37] and the analogy between the canopy and the veil carries with it an ominous implication, for when Christ died the veil of the temple was rent, Matthew 27.51. Holofernes is a simulacrum of God, but he is false, and the canopy cannot protect him against the daughter of God.

The emphasis on Holofernes' power in the transitional Scene III is accom-panied by an increasing emphasis on the wickedness and destructiveness of this power, and the scene throughout contains premonitions of the ensuing, and climactic scene of the beheading. These premonitions are managed first through the choice of epithets for Holofernes; second, through increased emphasis on the contrast between Judith and Holofernes; third, through emphasis, particu-larly in paragraph ii, on God's judgment of Holofernes. As in Scene II, the Feast, epithets for Holofernes continue to be piled up, but with a shift from epithets of power to those of evil. The change is marked immediately in III by the initial epithet used to designate Holofernes; when he commands that Judith be brought to him he is said to be dazed by sins, *niða geblonden* (34). The epi-thet is given emphasis by its immediate juxtaposition to the epithet for Judith, *þa eadigan mægð* (35). Her purity and his infection are thus sharply contrasted. Judith is next described as "blazoned with rings, adorned with bracelets," (36–37). These adornments are a snare for Holofernes, but the destruction which they bring upon him is self-imposed. A distinction between Judith's natural beauty and her allure is suggested by the poet. The distinction reflects that made, for example, by Ambrose and Aldhelm. The former observed, "She loaded her-self with the artifices of fraud; she clothed herself with the vestments of delight. . . . And well preparing for battle she resumed the conjugal ornaments because the memorials of marriage are the arms of chastity; for the widow may not otherwise please or conquer"; the latter, "By no means did she believe he would be deceived, nor otherwise did she think he would be killed unless her own countenance in its native beauty were contained in corporeal ornaments." [38] The cause of Holofernes' destruction is not Judith's beauty, but his own lust which finds in her beauty the allure of the flesh.

37. See note 22.
38. Ambrose, *PL,* 16, 259; Aldhelm, see note 13.

In the description of Holofernes' men hastening to obey him, the epithets of authority are reiterated; Holofernes is "their prince, lord of armored men" 38–39. But when the men come to Judith's tent they find her "prudent of mind . . . the lovely maiden" (41–43). Her prudence stands in sharp contrast to Holofernes' befuddlement in sin, and her maidenly resplendence to his dark power. She is brought to the *træfe hean* where Holofernes, *se rica* (44), is accustomed to sleep, but *rica* is set in apposition to the ensuing epithet, *lað nergende*, "hateful to the Savior" (45). The adjective *lað* suggests Holofernes' fate, the noun *Nergend*, Savior, suggests the converse, that is, Judith's salvation. In the description of the canopy, Holofernes is called by an epithet, *wigena baldor* (49), which is a variant of the framing epithet of the first section, *gumena baldor* (9 and 32), but here the epithet is modified by two adjectives which frame it *bealofulla*, "baleful," *modiga*, "proud" (48, 52). The final period, which completes the action of bringing Judith to the *træf*, concludes with an epithet for Judith, *ða snoteran idese* (55), which again sets her in her godly wisdom against the evilly befuddled Holofernes.

Paragraph ii begins with the resolute warriors, *stercedferhðe hæleð*, announcing to their lord, *heora hearran*, that they have brought the holy maiden, *halige meowle*, to his *burgetelde* (55–57). There is obvious irony involved in calling the attendants who escort a defenseless woman "resolute of heart," *stercedferhðe*, but the irony reveals the truth that because Judith is holy she is stronger than any evil man, however powerful, as Ælfric says, "She, humble and chaste, small and weak, conquered the proud one and cast down the great one because she betokened with deeds the holy congregation which now believes in God." [39]

In period 2 of ii the two clausules set in opposition Holofernes' hopes and God's plans. Clausule a presents Holofernes as the "famed lord of cities/ blissful in fancy" (57–58). Ironically his bliss is unreal because it rests in his desire" to defile with filth and sin the shining woman" (58–59). His desire will remain unfulfilled because as clausule b declares, "God would not allow it" (59–62), or as Dracontius puts it, "The Lord [Holofernes] strong and audacious perished with the edge of the woman's sword; he whom war did not subdue, the anticipated pleasure subdued; the anticipations he was permitted, but his lust was not accomplished, and the adulterer suffered punishment for the self-promised nocturnal embrace." [40] Notable in clausule b of period 2 is the piling up of epithets for God, overwhelming, as it were, all Holofernes' proud titles. The epithets are entirely appropriate in suggesting the emptiness of Holofernes' power which is nothing in the house of God, for God is the "Judge of glory," "Ward of majesty," "the Lord Ruler of hosts" (59–60). Conversely in the a clausule of period 3 the formulas which describe Holofernes strip him of all pretense; as he approaches the bed, "where his glory will fall abased," he

39. See note 20.
40. *MGH*, AA, 14, 105 (lines 491–495).

is called "devil's kin," "lecherous," "baleful" (61–63). In the b clausule the premonitory comment is explicit, "the stern-minded lord of men," as he deserved, "had attained his savage end" (64–67). In period 4 which describes Holofernes' falling into a drunken stupor, bereft of reason, with appropriate irony, he is called, "the powerful one," *se rica* (68).

Period 5, in completing the action of period 1, frames the paragraph; the "warriors sodden with wine," who have conducted Judith to the bed of "the breaker of troth, hated tyrant," leave him with "sudden haste . . . for the last time" (70–73). The final adverbial phrase suggests the image of entombment, which may have been suggested to the poet by St. Ambrose who described Holofernes at the moment of the beheading as entombed, "He lay entombed in wine, so that he was not able to feel the blow of the wound." [41] There has been a steady build up from the hasty first to the hasty final action. As the narrative step by step reveals more and more clearly the strength of Judith's purity and God's watchful protection of her because of her faith, so in parallel steps it reveals the emptiness of Holofernes' pride, his degradation into a senseless creature. Through his urging, Holofernes' men at the feast became like dead men; now he himself becomes like one dead.

73–121, IV, The Slaying of Holofernes: The poet organizes the climactic Scene IV in a complex formal structure. The action has a beginning, i, 73–97, middle, ii, 97–111, and end, iii, 111–121. The beginning of the action, Judith's preparation, paragraph i, 73–97, has as its focus her prayer to God, period 2. In period 1, clausule a, 73–77, Judith prudently considers how she may best carry out her act, and in clausule b, 77–80, she takes Holofernes' sword from the scabbard. In period 2, 80–94, sword in hand she calls upon the Trinity. This period consists of four clausules, and is intricately contrived. Clausule a, 80–82, serves as an introduction. In clausule b, 83–86, the invocation to the Trinity is given, and in clausule c, 86–88, a statement of her plight. Clausule d, 88–94 is compound, and gives a threefold plea: d^1 consists of a plea for victory and true faith; d^2 consists of a plea for safety, and includes a parenthetical restatement of her plight; d^3 consists of a plea for vengeance. Period 3, 94–97, provides a conclusion, stating God's favorable response, and generalizing upon the relation between faith and God's favor.

The central action of the scene, the slaying, paragraph ii, is developed in three narrative steps, with an introduction, period 1, 97–98, which states Judith's resolve. In 2, 98–103, she seizes Holofernes by the hair and prepares to strike; a rhetorical link with the first paragraph appears in the repetition of *genam* (77, 98), and *eaðost mihte* (75, 102). In period 3, 103–108, she strikes the first blow, and in 4, 108–111, she strikes the second and final blow. The concluding paragraph iii, 111–121, tells of the corpse of Holofernes and of the departure

41. *PL*, 14, 741, "Ille vino sepultus jacebat, ut ictum vulneris sentire non posset." See also *PL*, 16, 260.

of his soul for hell where in eternal punishment he must abandon all hope.

Hitherto Holofernes has been the mover of the action; he issues commands and his men hasten to obey him. However, he creates for himself a doom he does not anticipate but of which we are with increasing emphasis reminded. In the beheading scene, Judith, under the wing of God, is the mover. She becomes a "manly woman," to use Dracontius' phrase, in contrast to Holofernes, because lust, as Ambrose notes, had "softened that warlike man, terrible to the people, and temperance in food made the woman stronger than the man; nature was not conquered in her sex, but conquered in his gluttony." [42] Holofernes is reduced to an object, (both literally and grammatically), so that Judith handles him in his stupor like an animal at slaughter, moving his head till it is convenient to the sword. Only in the conclusion does he again become the subject, but in final ignominy, he becomes a divided subject, his head rolling on the ground and his soul descending into hell. The epithets for Holofernes strip him of all the trappings of power. Either they directly categorize him as evil or they are ironic. In i, 1 he is called *þone atolan*, "the terrible" (75), but the effect of this is purely ironic in the context of Judith's planning how most conveniently she may slay him (*eaðost*, 75, repeated in line 102.) In her prayer to God Judith asks that she behead this *morðres bryttan*, "giver of death" (90). This phrase suggests his diabolic powers. (It is a formula which elsewhere signifies the devil.) However, in the context of the event the phrase is ironic; it is his own death that he is granting. In the beheading scene Judith seizes *þone hæðenan mannan . . . þone bealofullan . . . laðne mannan* (98–101). The final simple phrase, "evil man," emphasized by word-play: *alede laðne . . . unlædan* (101–102), recalls the earlier epithets *Nergende lað* (45) and *laðne leodhatan* (72). She strikes him, "fiendish . . . full of menace (104)," so that he *on swiman læg, druncen ond dolhwund* (106–107). Literally the poet says that Judith's blow caused him to lie in a stupor, drunk and gapingly wounded, an example of hysteron-proteron; his drunkenness is the cause, not the result. The hysteron-proteron makes possible a repetitive pattern; Holofernes is dead drunk just as his men, egged on by their lord, became as if dead, *hie on swiman lagon . . . swylce hie wæron deaðe geslegene* (30–31). The repetition is most effective in suggesting the retribution which falls upon the evil. Because Holofernes' power is evil it leads to his death, and that of his followers. In addition to the hysteron-proteron which establishes the relation between cause and effect, sin and its consequences, paranomasia appears involved in *dohlwund* 107 (a unique compound): *dolh*, "gash," and *dol*, "foolish, heretical"; Holofernes is wounded through his heretical folly. In the final period of the second paragraph when Holofernes receives his quietus, he is designated by one mean epithet, *hæðenan hund*, 110, "heathen dog."

In the concluding paragraph, iii, although Holofernes again becomes the grammatical subject, he is referred to only by the pronoun, except at the begin-

42. *PL*, 16, 1248.

ning of the paragraph in the contemptuous, *se fula leap* (111), which reduces him to the status of mere bodily object. His body is left behind by his soul which sinks into hellfire, "despairing, joyless into eternity" (120–121). The famous Holofernes, *se brema* (57), who rejoiced in the anticipation of lecherous pleasures, found instead the hopelessness of hell of which he is an unexceptional, a merely pronominal inhabitant. In place of the epithets of power and mystery in the description of Holofernes' inner sanctum, his bed, the description of his dissolution relies on the terror of his punishment. His body is a sack, and the soul makes its terrible journey under the deep headland, an image perhaps suggesting the plunge into hell. With terrifying economy the abasement of Holofernes is pictured through descriptive concentration on his imprisonment and loss of hope. In contrastive echo of the repetitive, rhyming description of Holofernes' unbridled gluttony at the feast, the description of his imprisonment in hell is underscored by a pattern in which a heavily rhyming line, *wyrmum bewunden witum gebunden* (115), is framed by rhyming echoic lines, *susle gesæled syððan æfre* (114), and *hearde gehæfted . . . æfter hinsiðe* (116–117). Finally, Holofernes' hopelessness is described through the prominence given to the formulas of eternity with which the period concludes, *awa to aldre butan ende forð . . . hyhtwynna leas* (120–121), formulas which echo the *Gloria,* "now and ever more shall be, world without end." The echo suggests the ultimate irony of the confrontation between God and Holofernes which was established at the beginning of the poem, *hehstan Deman—hehstan brogan* (4). His hopelessness is also suggested by his being enveloped in darkness, a darkness which recalls the temporal movement of Holofernes' feast from day, *ealne dæg* (28), to night, *niht seo þystra* (34). Holofernes has achieved his dark night; overwhelmed in darkness, *þystrum forðylmed* (118), joyless, *hyhtwynna leas* (121), he lives not in the winehall, but in the serpent hall, *wyrmsele* (119), the dark home, *heolstran ham* (121). Vividly compact and complete, the description of Holofernes' damnation has terrifying effectiveness through its masterful handling of formulaic expressions.

The descending rhetorical line which has been traced for Holofernes, hateful to God, is balanced by the ascending line of Judith's triumph through God. In period 1 of IV, i she is designated as the "Lord's glorious servant" (73–74), and in 2 as "the Creator's lady" (78). In the same phrase she is called *wundenlocc* (77), meaning apparently "curly haired" or "with braided locks," an adjective repeated in line 103, in paragraph ii, period 3, which describes the slaying. This repetition occurring at the beginning of the action and at the culmination of the action serves a framing purpose. The term is later used to designate the Hebrew people gathering the spoils of victory, perhaps to suggest the adornment of victory.[43] Similarly the repetition of the adjective to describe Judith in the

43. The only other use of *wundenlocc* is in *Riddle* 26, "the Onion," Tupper, *The Riddles of the Exeter Book* (Boston, 1910), pp. 19–20, and note, p. 125. Its meaning here is obscure.

act of slaying Holofernes is intended to suggest her adorned deadly beauty, and to remind the reader of the earlier epithet, *ælfscinu* (14), and the description of Judith's allure in III, lines 36–37, both of which suggest Judith's enticing beauty, destructive to the man of evil desire.[44] The poet's emphasis is so completely on Judith as holy maiden of God, that the note of allurement must be introduced to suggest how she made herself externally alluring, while remaining pure at heart.

In contrast to Holofernes who sought his bedchamber joyous in mind, *on mode bliðe* (58), at the thought of lecherous fulfillment, Judith is bitter at heart and comforted only through prayer (87), which renews her hope (97–98). Curiously in the slaying sequence, Judith is designated by only one epithet and that appears in the last period: *ides ellenrof*, "courageous woman." She, like Holofernes, has in this scene something of a pronominal anonimity, appropriate to her role as executioner of God's will. As Holofernes becomes a slaughtered animal deprived of all human identity, except for his damnation, Judith has the impersonality of an agent carrying out God's purpose. Indeed, in her prayer, her typological significance as daughter of the faith, confessor, *confitens*, is clearly suggested since she, the Hebrew woman, begins with an address to the Trinity, and her representative and general significance is suggested in the poet's comment on God's response to her, that God so answers all of the dwellers here who seek him with reason and true faith, *anra gehwylcne/herbuendra þe hyne . . . seceð/mid ræde ond mid rihte geleafan* (95–97). Judith thus typifies the congregation of the faithful, the Church.

Similarly, the epithets for God are clustered in the first paragraph and disappear in paragraphs ii and iii, when his judgment is executed and Holofernes finds himself the self-willed victim of fate. In the first period of paragraph i appear (as part of the epithets for Judith) *Nergendes* and *Scyppendes*. In Judith's prayer of i, 2 the epithets for God become heavily clustered. Judith calls by name on the Ward of heaven, Savior of all earth's inhabitants, *swegles Weard . . . Nergend ealra/ woruldbuendra* (80–82). She prays to the three persons of the Trinity, the Father, *frymða God*, the Holy Ghost, *frofre Gæst*, and the Son, *Bearn Alwaldan*, and then, with word play, to the triune majesty, *ðrynesse ðrym* (83–86). In her threefold plea to God the epithets she uses are appropriate to each plea. In asking for victory she calls upon the Lord of heaven, *swegles ealdor* (88); in her plea for safety upon the Lord of men, *þeoden gumena* (91); in asking God for vengeance she calls upon the mighty and splendor-minded Giver of glory, *mihtig dryhten/ tires brytta* (92–93). The last phrase, *tires brytta*, echoes the phrase, *morðres brytta* (90), which Judith has just applied to Holofernes. The echo is particularly effective in juxtaposing the princely power of light, which gives life, against the princely power of darkness, which gives death. Finally, in period 3, which describes God's favorable response, he is called the most high Judge, *hehsta dema* (94). The phrase repeats

44. See note 38.

the epithet which was used in line 4 to contrast God and Holofernes, *hehstan brogan*. In the context of God's promise of aid to Judith in vanquishing the heathen, the repetition of the epithet is highly effective.

B *Judith's Triumph*

Episode B, quietly undramatic in contrast to A, gives a remarkable sense of miraculous deliverance, as unexpected as it is joyous. The ensuing victory of the Hebrew people is made to appear an inevitable and necessary consequence of Judith's faith. Judith's deed which appeared spectacular against the norm of Holofernes' overwhelming power now appears as a simple act in the unrolling of God's design.

122–141, I, The Return to Bethulia: This scene consists of one paragraph, which is divided into one introductory, and three narrative periods. Period 1, 122–124, is transitional, and in summary states Judith's achievement of glory through God's gift. Period 2, 125–132, tells of Judith's placing the head in the provision sack, and giving it to her servant to carry. In period 3, 132–138, there is a shift from the singular subject, Judith, to the plural, Judith and the handmaiden; it tells how the two passed through the army (*Eoden*) until they saw the walls of Bethulia. Period 4, 138–141, also in the plural with verb of motion, *forð onettan*, tells of the two coming to the gates of the city.

In effect the scene of Judith's return is transitional. The mood is quiet; the escape is told in straightforward narrative, and the reader is permitted a descent from the high intensity of the scene of the slaying. The tripartite division of the narration, periods 2, 3, 4, is echoic of the earlier narrative structure of preparation, action, completion, but the structure here is rhetorically plain, except for the piling up of descriptive adjectives which give emphasis to the role of the handmaiden, who is thereby made to reflect Judith's triumph. Thus in the first period Judith is defined as wise maiden, *seo snotere mægð* (125), but thereafter the descriptive adjectives apply to the servant; she is called fair, excellent in virtue, prudent, *blachleor ides . . . / ðeawum geðungen . . . higeþoncolre* (128–131). In the next period she shares equally with Judith in the concentrated adjectives of praise. The two women are courageous, bold in spirit, blessed, *ellenþriste . . . collenferhðe . . . eadhreðige* (133–135). In the third period only two adjectives are employed, again with reference to both: they are adorned with rings, *beahhrodene* (138), and joyous, *glædmode* (140). Although the adjectives, strictly speaking, are appropriate chiefly to Judith, by being shared they tend to generalize Judith's triumph, perhaps, indeed, to make it more human. Her deed was fearful, awesome, above and beyond the nature of her sex, indeed of humanity. By reflecting Judith's superhuman glory in the handmaiden, the poet succeeds in the simple narrative of the return to cast into a softer light the barbarous horror of Judith's slaughter of Holofernes. The scene thus contributes importantly to the poet's triumphant creation of a heroic, yet believable, almost sympathetic character, embodying the virtues of Christian faith. Even in the slaughter scene Judith always appears as the handmaiden of the Lord; the scene is introduced by Judith's prayer, which places it in the context of God's punishing the wicked through her; it is followed by the humanizing scene of her return with her companion.

Exceptional in the otherwise plain scene is the description of the two women gazing from afar on "the shimmering walls of the shining city/ blessed Bethulia" (137–138). The description is apparently original with the poet since it does not appear in the Vulgate. It is an effective addition not only in its dramatic suggestion of the joy the women feel in seeing their home, all dangers past, but also in its thematic suggestion that Bethulia represents the true shining city, the eternal Jerusalem. Their journey is thus made the antithesis to the Babylonic journey of Holofernes to hell pictured at the end of the preceding scene, so that the paths of the damned and the blessed are subtly juxtaposed. Salvation, as we are told at the end of the poem, is Judith's goal; her vision of her native city prefigures her spiritual vision. Rabanus makes the point in his commentary, "She came to the gate of the city because that relates to the entrance of the kingdom of heaven." [45]

141–170, II, The Welcome: This scene consists of three paragraphs. Paragraph i, 141–146, describes briefly the watchful waiting of the warriors at the city gate, obedient to Judith's command, but without hope. Paragraph ii, 146–158, tells of Judith's arrival, her command to open the gate, her preliminary speech. Paragraph iii narrates the joy of the people when they discover that Judith has returned, of their hastening to the gate, of their giving Judith entrance. In this narrative action the characteristic tripartite structure appears: i, preparation (the watching); ii, action (Judith's appearance and speech); iii, conclusion (the opening of gates to admit her). Together, scenes I and II, both with simple narrative structures, prepare for the climactic moment of Judith's revelation of triumph to her people, narrated in scene III.

A. S. Cook has noted that the wording of the description of the sight of the city in the Scene I may reflect *Beowulf*, lines 221–223, the Geats' view of Denmark. In paragraph i of Scene II the picture of the men waiting at the gate seems even more significantly to reflect *Beowulf*, lines 1602–1605, the waiting of Beowulf's men for his return from his encounter with Grendel's dam:

Gistas setan

modes seoce   ond on mere staredon
wiston ond ne wendon   þæt hie heora winedrihten
selfne gesawan.

45. *Opera*, III, p. 235.

These notable lines suggest both the despairing hope of Beowulf's retainers, and their faithfulness to his command that they wait. Later, of course, as in *Judith*, their rejoicing at the return of Beowulf is redoubled because of their despair. The Hebrew warriors stand watch, but from duty and concern. Paragraph i thus serves brilliantly to introduce the ensuing paragraph of rejoicing. The intensity of the passage in *Judith* lies in its very simplicity and possibly in its allusive gain from the parallel with *Beowulf*.

The men of Bethulia, however devoid of hope, were kept at the gate through the force of Judith's command at her departure, *Iudithe bebead . . . þa heo on sið gewat* (144–145). This statement at the end of paragraph i provides a transition to paragraph ii which begins with Judith's return and her command, *Wæs þa eft cumen . . . het* (146–147). Characteristically in her speech, ii, 3, Judith declares that her victory is that of her people through God's grace to them.

Paragraph iii, period 1, is linked to i by its portmanteau echo in *burhsittende* (159), of the first phrase of i, 1, *wiggend sæton* (141). As before they sat watching in care, now the city dwellers rejoice, having heard the holy one speak. For special effect, in the manner of the descriptions of Holofernes feasting and of his descent to hell, rhyme is used in iii, 2 to point up the rejoicing of the people, *here wæs on lustum/ . . . wornum ond heapum/ ðreatum ond ðrymmum þrungon ond urnon/ . . . þusendmælum/ ealde ge geonge* (161–166). The actual entrance of Judith is held off until the end of iii, 3, *wæs Iudith cumen/ eft to eðle ond ða ofostlice/ hie mid eaðmedum in forleton* (168–170). This holding off of Judith's entrance until the very end serves to make a suspenseful unit of the entire scene II, and prepares for the climactic scene of revelation.

171–200, III, The Revelation: The scene consists of three paragraphs, with the characteristic tripartite structure of beginning, action, conclusion. Paragraph i, 171–175, is introductory and briefly describes Judith's command to her servant that Holofernes' head be revealed. The body of the scene appears in paragraph ii, 176–198, which consists of Judith's speech of triumph. Paragraph iii, 199–200, briefly gives the conclusion; emboldened by Judith's speech the Hebrew warriors make preparation for battle.

In the introductory paragraph of III the handmaiden, as in I, shares in the action, with Judith commanding her to reveal the head. This represents a change from the Vulgate where Judith is the sole actor. Paragraph ii, Judith's speech, consists of two periods: in the first she speaks of the death of Holofernes: in the second she issues the command to battle. In period 1, clausule a, 176–185, Judith reveals to the Hebrew people the downfall of their tormentor through the will of God; in clausule b, 185–186, she declares that she took his life through the help of God. Judith's command in period 2 is structured in the prevailing pattern of preparation, action, conclusion. In clausule a, 186–191, she commands that the men make preparation for battle when the dawn breaks; in clausule b, 191–195, she commands that they carry the battle to the enemy; in c, 195–198, she declares that the conclusion of the battle, the defeat of the enemy and the Hebrew triumph, has been revealed through her success, *swa eow getacnod hafað/ mihtig dryhten þurh mine hand* (197–198).

The result of her speech is given briefly and simply in paragraph iii, 199–200: the Hebrew warriors prepare for battle. Her revelation and counsel have been effective. As Ambrose explains; "Her deed is not so much a monument of strength as of wisdom. For with her hand she conquered Holofernes only; in her counsel she conquered the whole army of the enemy. For in holding up the head of Holofernes, which could not be contrived in the counsel of men, she raised their spirits, and dispirited the enemy, exciting hers to shame, casting down also in terror the enemy; thus they were put to flight. Therefore the temperance and sobriety of one widow not only conquered her nature, but what is greater, made, indeed, men more fearless." [46]

C The Hebrew Triumph

Episode B, which has served as a transition between A and C, is effective in its simplicity. Episode C, like A, is effective in its complexity.

200–235, I, The Battle at Dawn: This scene has no counterpart in the Vulgate, which expressly states that no battle took place, only the Hebrew threat of attack, and the consequent flight of the Assyrians. Thus the battle scene in the poem, done in the traditional formulaic style of Old English poetry, actually involves an extended use of hysteron-proteron, the function of which is to intensify the description in II of the terror of the Assyrians when they discover Holofernes dead, and more importantly, to establish the spiritual and providential nature of the Hebrew victory. Judith has prophesied that their victory over the Assyrians is assured, *Fynd syndon eowere/ gedemed to deaðe* (195–196). Scene I in describing a battle which did not take place is pure fiction, designed to emphasize the presence of God's hand. The Hebrew warriors, like Judith, are clearly established as agents of the Lord, his executioners, as it were. The battle, in fact, is reminiscent of the highly symbolic battle of Abraham against the five kings in *Genesis* A. It is God who dooms the heathens; the battle is purely symbolic; it sounds and clashes are the outward representations of the spiritual triumph of faith.

Characteristically, the action of the scene shows a tripartite division: i, premonitiory action; ii, advance; iii, joining of battle. The structure of scene I, as Adeline Bartlett has noted, involves incremental repetition of the verb

46. *PL*, 16, 259–260.

stopon (200, 212, 227) with subject variation. This incremental repetition introduces the three paragraphs which comprise the scene. Paragraph i, preparation, 200–212, consists of three periods: 1, 200–203, the moving out of the banners; 2, 204–205, the sound of shields clashing at dawn; 3, 205–212, the arousing of the carrion raven and wolf, and the eagle, who sings the battle song. The same kind of period division and narrative progression as in i is found in paragraph ii, the advance, 212–226: 212–220, the advance of the warriors under shields; 2, 220–223, discharge of arrows; 3, 223–225, the casting of spears. Paragraph iii, 227–235, is also constructed on the same plan: 1, 227–229, the determination of the Hebrews; 2, 229–231, the drawing of swords; 3, 231–235, the attack *à outrance*.

The design of the scene is intricate. Each paragraph, introduced by *stopon* with subject variation, marks a step in the progression of the action by a sequential list of war objects and accoutrements: i, 1, banners; i, 2, noise of shields; i, 3, omens of battle; ii, 1, shields and banners; ii, 2, arrows; ii, 3, spears; iii, 2, swords. Particular attention is given to the sounds of war which are also arranged to mark a progression. The sounds in i are premonitory, the shields resound, awakening the carrion eaters so that the eagle sings the battle song; in ii, the Hebrew warriors give their battle cry, *styrmdon hlude* (25). In iii no verbs of sound appear, except the unexpressed sounds of the swords being drawn (*brugdon*) and of blows being struck (*slogon*). Another thread which binds together the three parts of the scene is the motif of the doom of the Assyrians. In i their doom is unexpressed but strongly suggested through the ominous carrion beasts, particularly in the phrase describing their expectation of their fill on the doomed, *fylle on fægum*. (The phrase appears ironically to echo phrases describing the filled and doomed Assyrians at the feast, and phrases, marked by word play, in Judith's speech: *fulle fletsittendum. Hie þæt fæge þegon*, 19; *fyllað folctogan fagum sweordum/ fæge frumgaras* (194–195). In C, I, ii, the doom of the Assyrians is expressed, "at the spear-play the Assyrians were repaid," and in iii their doom is completed as the Hebrews strike down without quarter the drunken Assyrians, *medowerig* (229), a word which again recalls the premonitory simulacrum of death produced in the Assyrians at the feast (32), as well as the drunken death of Holofernes (106–107).

In the rhetorical design of the battle scene the diction is of great importance. Dominating the scene is a profusion of variants, kennings, descriptive compounds, formulaic expressions to designate battle and the objects of battle. Surprisingly, although the list of battle words which follows suggests the traditional and formulaic, a number of them (indicated by preceding asterisks) are uniquely attested. Clearly the poet's style is anything but "stereotyped," as B. J. Timmer calls it, for without losing the sense of the traditional, the poet shows originality in the variety of epithets he chooses and in the creation of a number of new compounds to suit his own design. He uses seven words or phrases to designate battle and battlefield: *foron to campe, to gefeohte; stopon* *to beadowe; æt ðam *æscplegan; wrehton unsofte ealdgeniðlan; slogon eornoste; fyrdwicum.* To designate banners he uses two unique words, **þufas, *guð-fanum;* of the two phrases used to designate shields, one is unique, *scildas bordum, *hwealfum lindum;* of the three phrases designating arrows, one contains a uniquely attested word, *flana scuras, hildenædran, strælas *stede-hearde.* To designate swords he uses a phrase which contains a unique adjective, *of sceaðum *scirmæled swyrd/ ecgum gecoste.* Four phrases are used for the sounds of battle, one of which contains a unique noun, *dynedan scildas, hlude hlummon, sang *hildeleoð, styrmdon hlude.* To designate spears only the simple noun, *garas,* is used. In the scene the poet displays a considerable in-genuity in designating the Hebrew and Assyrians, for he manages a set of epithets which he has not used before, no easy task in view of the earlier pro-fusion of variant designations for warriors. (Epithets not used before are designated by a preceding dagger.) The enemy is called variously: *fægum; †elþeodigra; hæðenra; Assyrium; †heardra gemang; laðum cynne; †medo-werige; †oretmæcgas; †niðhycgende; þæs herefolces.* The Hebrews are called: *snelra werod; cenra to campe; †cynerof; †secgas ond gesiðas; hæleð under helmum; †þeodguman; heaðorincas; †beornas to beadowe; Ebreas; †grame guðfrecan; hæleð; †landbuende; †styrnmode; †stercedferhðe.*

The poet makes functional use even of the traditional battle setting of carrion wolf and raven, suggesting through echoic structure that they replace the Assyrians, the *fæge,* as feasters. The concatenation of phrases is as follows: in the feast the cups are *fulle fletsittendum* and the Assyrians *fæge þegon* (19); Holofernes orders *fylgan fletsittendum* (33); Judith prophesies that the Hebrews will *fyllað . . . fæge* (194–195); finally, the carrion creatures *þoh-ton tilian/ fylle on fægum* (208–209). Ironically they wait to take their fill at a feast of the feasters which the Hebrew warriors will serve to them when they slaughter the fleeing Assyrians. The interlocking of Holofernes' feast, Judith's prophesy, and the carrion hope for a feast functions to suggest further that the battle is representative, a spiritual victory preordained in God's providential scheme. The grouping of wolf, raven, eagle is equally functional. There are precedents in *Elene* and *Beowulf* for this grouping, precedents close enough to suggest direct borrowing. In *Elene,* 27–30, 52–53, 110–113, Cynewulf uses the motif in incremental pattern (as in *Judith*) to mark three rhetorical divisions in Constantine's battle against the heathens:

1		fyrdleoð agol
	wulf on wealde	wælrune ne nað
	urigfeðera	earn sang ahof
	laðum on laste.	
2		hrefen uppe gol
	wan ond wælful.	
3		hrefn weorces gefeah
	urigfeðra	earn sið beheold

> wælhreowra wig,   wulf sang ahof
> holtes gehleða.

In *Beowulf*, Wiglaf's speech after Beowulf's death contains a prophecy of defeat in battle, and in this context includes a reference to the three companions of slaughter, 3024–3027,

> ac se wonna hrefn
> fus ofer fægum   fela reordian
> earne secgan   hu him æt æte speow
> þenden he wið wulfe   wæl reafode.

Implicitly in *Elene*, explicitly in *Beowulf*, a distinction is made between the raven and the wolf, who seek carrion, and the eagle, who is, as in *Riddle* 24, the warbird, *guðfugol*, perhaps through association with the Roman war eagle.[47] In *Beowulf* the distinction between the eagle and the carrion seekers is made by the eagle's remaining aloof, above the battle, with the raven reporting the slaughter to it. In *Elene* the eagle raises its cry in pursuit of the defeated enemy, and gazes on the battle. The distinction is maintained in *Judith*, and nothing more clearly illustrates the poet's functional handling of poetic formulas than a comparison with the way the poets of *Maldon* and *Brunnanburh* make use of the traditional companions of slaughter.

In *Maldon* when the battle is joined, the eagle and the raven make a joint appearance, 106–107,

> Þær wearð hream ahafen   hremmas wunden
> earne æses georn.

In *Brunnanburh* all three companions are introduced together at the end of the battle, 60–65:

> Letan him behindan   hræw bryttian
> saluwigpadan,   þone sweartan hræfn,
> hyrnednebban,   and þone hasewanpadan,
> earn æftan hwit   æses brucan
> grædigne guðhafoc   and þæt græge deor,
> wulf on wealde.

The later Old English poets use the traditional elements effectively as poetic battle formulas, but they use them decoratively, not functionally. In contrast to *Elene*, where the carrion companions are used as part of the structure, and to *Beowulf*, where they provide a conclusion of dark foreboding, in *Maldon*, economically, in *Brunnanburh*, profusely, they are used somewhat mechanically to provide heroic atmosphere for the ensuing and completed battle scenes

47. The other appearances of the eagle in Old English poetry have no relevance for *Judith*: in *Seafarer* 24, *Andreas* 865, the eagle is associated with the sea; in *Phoenix* 235, 238, *Riddle* 40, 67, Psalm 102.5, they serve as elements in comparisons; in *Solomon and Saturn* 472, the *blodige earnes* constitute one of the punishments of Hell.

respectively. In *Judith*, 205–212, to the contrary, the traditional patterns of *Beowulf* and *Elene* are used functionally to relate the carrion wolf and raven to the doom of the Assyrians in a pattern which represents the operation of God's justice: the feasters become the feast of the retributive creatures through the agency of the Hebrew avengers:

> Þæs se hlanca gefeah
> wulf in walde   ond se wanna hrefn
> wælgifre fugel,   wistan begen
> þæt him ða þeodguman   þohtan tilian
> fylle on fægum;   ac him fleah on last
> earn ætes georn   urigfeðera,
> salowigpada   sang hildeleoð
> hyrnednebba.

The eagle, although also eager for the feast, is carefully distinguished from raven and wolf. It is said to follow "them" on the path, presumably the Hebrew warriors, but possibly the carrion creatures, since the *him* of 209 is ambiguous as to its reference. The concept of the eagle following *on last*, which may be a borrowing from *Elene*, is used functionally, for in the episode of the flight of the Assyrians, as will be seen, the motif of the path is structurally important. The anticipation of this motif in the battle scene is a reminder that the reality of the battle at dawn is a premonition of the destruction of the Assyrians.

Also functional is the statement that the eagle sounds the battle cry, for this cry is an integral part of the sounds of the Hebrew advance: The shields resounded, *dynedan scildas* (204), and awoke the creatures of omen; then the warriors attacked, giving the battle cry, *styrmdon hlude* (223). The two verbs echo the mad shouts of Holofernes at the feast, *dynede* (23), *styrmde* (25); furthermore, in its context—*On þæt dægred sylf dynedan scildas/ hlude hlummon*—*dynedan* embraces a special set of symbolic connotations,[48] parallel to those in the description of Christ's harrowing of hell in *Christ and Satan*: *þa com engla sweg . . . dyne on dægred* (401–404); *þis wæs . . . ær dægrede . . . þæt se dyne becom hlude of heofonum* (463–467). The association of the crack of doom with the crack of dawn, and the dawn coming up like thunder is perfectly clear in *Christ and Satan*. It has had a curiously long survival, the dawn coming up like thunder still seeming perfectly natural. Yet as a lady asks in a recent novel, "The sun doesn't come up like thunder, does it?"[49] Since there is nothing in the dawn to suggest the crack of thunder it seems likely that crack of dawn is a product of association with the crack of

48. Ignoring the association of *dægred* and *dynedan*, editors have concluded the period of the advance from the city with line 204b, on *ðæt dægred sylf*. The time is actually more appropriate, quite apart from the association of dawn and din, to the period which describes the first sounds of battle.

49. V. Bourjaily, *The Man Who Knew Kennedy* (New York, 1967), p. 243.

doom, perhaps specifically at the time of Christ's harrowing of hell. In the poet's phrase, *dægred sylf*, the use of the intensifier may possibly be intended to suggest the actual association of Christ with the dawn. *Dægred sylf*, "the very dawn," could be taken as a reference to Christ through whom the battle is won, for the battle symbolizes the triumph over evil, as in the harrowing of hell. Relevant to this symbolic purport is the poet's use of the unique *þufa* and *guðfanum*, which may well represent the Latin *vexilla* and its standard association with the banner of Christ, the cross through which he triumphed over evil.[50] The symbolic overtones of *dægred, dynedan, þufa, guðfanum* would serve to strengthen the underlying metaphoric meaning of the battle which never took place. The spiritual significance of the battle is the triumph of faith over the heathens, of good over evil. The battle scene is the visualization of Judith's prophecy.

The battle at dawn is an intricate scene, highly charged with symbolic suggestion, carefully intertwined into the structure of the entire poem, with its echoes of the feast, of Judith's speech, and with its repeated tripartite division of the action.

236–291, II, The Terror and Flight of the Assyrians: In this scene the Assyrians awake to their peril too late. The battle is already lost, and the simulacrum of their drunken death becomes reality. The scene is again constructed with beginning, middle, conclusion: i, 236–250 relates the awakening of the Assyrian outposts to their peril; ii, 250–274, the paralyzing dilemma of the Assyrians, torn between fear of the Hebrews and fear of Holofernes; in iii, 275–291 their dilemma is resolved by their discovery of Holofernes and their flight. The periodic structure of each paragraph is similarly tripartite, except that in paragraph ii, the narrative action is framed by an introductory and a concluding period.

First, in paragraph i, period 1, 236–241, the chiefs of the guard are aroused; then, period 2, 241–246, they awaken the chief lieutenants; finally, period 3, 246–250, all assemble before the tent of Holofernes. The subject

---

50. For example, in Aldhelm, *De Virginitate* (Ehwald, *op. cit.*) pp. 364 ff, 2022–2023:

> 276 Idcirco simul ad belli certamina cruda
>   Contra Antichristum gestant vexilla Tonantis. . . .
> 2022 Dum vincunt sancti fallentis proelia mundi
>   Atque coronatis gestant vexilla maniplis. . . .
> 2456 His adversantur vitiorum castra maligna,
>   Spissa nefandarum quae torquent spicula rerum,
>   Aemula ceu pugnat populorum turma duorum,
>   Dum vexilla ferunt et clangit classica salpix.
>   Ac stimulant Martem legionum cornua cantu.

See also Dracontius, *De laudibus Dei*, II 506, *MGH*, AA, 14, 83, "Per vexilla crucis hostis populando cohortes."

of period 1 remains the Hebrew warriors. The effect is to make a transition from Scene I to Scene II which reinforces the symbolic character of the intricate battle scene, the reality of which is simply the Hebrew show of force, directed by God through Judith. Thus period 1 states that the Hebrews pursued the invaders, *ehton elðeoda* (237), a phrase which continues the extended hysteron-proteron of the battle-scene, for the actuality of the pursuit occurs only in the ensuing scene. Ironically the battle at dawn has revealed the doom of the Assyrians, but it suggests to the chiefs of the guard only that the Hebrews were making a show of force, *ongeaton . . . heafodweardas/ þæt him swyrdgeswing . . . eodon/ weras Ebrisce* (238–241). Although the outcome has been decided, and the symbolic battle has revealed God's intent, the heathen Assyrians, stupefied by their feasting, do not grasp the truth. They are not aware that they are already being pursued; they perceive only the "sword brandishing" of the Hebrews. In support of the irony implicit in the period, the designation of the Assyrians who first perceive the assault is particularly effective. The chiefs of the guard are called, "head guardians," *heafodweardas* (239),[51] a grim play on words which suggests that these head guardians have not been able to guard the head of Holofernes, so that they have become headless head guardians. They are puppets walking out a scene already preordained, seen and declared prophetically by Judith, and revealed in the battle at dawn.

In period 2 a similar ironic designation occurs. The *heafodweardas* arouse Holofernes' lieutenants who are first called *yldestan ealdorþegnum* (242), the highest lieutenants, then *cumbolwigan* (243), a unique compound literally meaning banner warriors, i.e., standard bearers, about whom the troops rally in the forefront of battle. The term is ironically effective as a reminder that the Hebrew warriors were emboldened, awakened as they moved out under their banners, the *vexilla regis*, whereas the Assyrian standard bearers are "exhausted by wine," *medowerigum* (245), a compound also unique to *Judith*. Thus these leaders of the vanguard, who might rally the Assyrian forces, have themselves to be aroused by the terrifying urgency of the message which the *heafodweardas* bring to them. This message is given special prominence by repetition: *Wordum . . . cyðan eodon . . . bodedon . . . færspel . . . morgencollan . . . atolne ecgplegan* (239–243). Period 3 is introduced by the *gefrægn* formula, as in lines 7–8, introducing the feast. The repetition underlines the ironic parallel between the summons of the Assyrians to the feast, which results in their death-like sleep, and their present fearful assembly at Holofernes' tent. The men are designated by a unique compound, *slegefæge*, "doomed to slaughter," which echoes the thematic use of *fæge* established in the feasting scene (19), in Judith's prophecy (195), and in the premonitory motif of the carrion seekers' expectation of a feast (209).

51. These are the chiefs of those called in the Vulgate *exploratores*, i.e., outposts; in the Vulgate these outposts go to the chiefs. The compound is found only here and in Psalm 77.19. In *Beowulf* 2909 *heafodweard* signifies a death watch.

The subject of paragraph ii is the paralysis of the Assyrians, torn between two terrors, the fury of the Hebrews and the fury of Holofernes. The introductory period 1, 250–253, tells of their hope of arousing their leader, but 2, 253–257, reveals their fear of disturbing Holofernes at what they suppose is his pleasure. In 3, 261–267, the central fact of their dilemma is unfolded in the reminder of the Hebrew approach; in 4, 267–273, the upshot of their dilemma is described as they stand helpless before the tent. In the concluding period 5, 273–274, their plight is revealed as the hope expressed in period 1 is said to be false. The introductory and concluding periods, 1 and 5 are linked by the repetition of the verb of expectation *hogedon* (250–273), to introduce both periods. The verb in the first period expresses their hope, a hope which is repeated in period 5, only to be dashed with the laconic clausule, "it availed them little," *him wiht ne speow* (274). Period 2, in contrast to the expression of hope of 1, pictures the Assyrians' fear of Holofernes, with the terms designating Holfernes reflecting their attitude; he is the leader of men, *beorna brego* (254), licentious, *galmod* (256), but also terrible and fierce, *egesfull ond afor* (257). Although he is their hope, he is also a man not to be interrupted in the pursuit of the pleasure which they thought, *mynton* (253), he was enjoying with Judith. In contrast to Holofernes Judith is called *seo beorhte mægð* (254), *seo æðele* (256), *halgan mægð* (260), *meotodes meowlan* (261). These terms, particularly the last, indicate whom the Assyrians should fear, yet still fearful of their diabolical leader, they do not dare interrupt the defilement of the holy maiden. Period 3 relates the other terror which faces them, the approach of the Hebrews, *mægen nealæhte* (261), and foreshadows the doom of which the Assyrians are as yet unaware.

Period 4 describes their paralysis as they stood, *stodon*, before the tent. The verb marks the sharp contrast between their irresolution and the purposeful activity of the Hebrews as they moved, *stopon*, to battle, their might approaching, *mægen nealæhte*. Standing before the tent, *þeodnes træf* (269), the symbol of Holofernes' diabolical power, they make a despairing effort to arouse their leader. First they begin to cough, *cohhetan* (270), a neologism designed for ludicrous effect. Then, as now, the cough appears to be a delicate way to catch someone's attention. The boudoir cough (cf. Pandarus) proving ineffective, they try stronger measures; "lacking in good," they begin to shriek loudly and to gnash their teeth, *cirman hlude/ ond gristbitian gode orfeorme/ mid toðon torn þoligende* (270–272). The picture of their frustration is both ludicrous and terrifying in its realism: the lack of response to the timid cough leading to the desperate wailing and grinding of teeth by men paralyzed through their inability to act. Moreover a symbolic significance is given to the picture of their frustration by the phrasing of the clausule. It suggests the sounds of the damned in the exterior darkness. The gnashing of teeth of the men "deprived of good" is obvious, and the connotations of *cirman hlude* is equally unambiguous. In *Exodus* 462, *laðe cyrmdon* has reference to the shrieks of the Egyptian warriors as they are engulfed in the waters of the Red Sea, symbolic, it should be noted, of the engulfing of the damned in Hell; *Guthlac* 908, *swa wilde deor/ cirmdon on corðre* has reference to the screams of the devils attempting vainly to terrify Guthlac. The noun, *cyrm*, is equally clear. Of all the uses in poetry only one, *Exodus* 107, has reference to anything but the shrieking of the devils and evil-doers. Thus in *Guthlac* 264 and 393 *cearfulra cirm* refers to the lament of the devils at Guthlac's defiance. In *Genesis* 2409 and 2549 *synnigra cyrm* and *cirm arleasra* have reference to the Sodomites, first in God's words to Abraham threatening destruction, and second in the shrieks of the Sodomites as destruction falls. *Christ* 835 and 997 *cwaniendra cirm, cirm ond cearu*, refer respectively to the cries of the doomed at Judgment Day and in Hell. *Andreas* 1125 1155, *cyrm up astah, hlud heriges cyrm* refer to the cries of the heathen Myrmidonians before and after the foiling of their attack.[52] The Assyrians of *Judith* are similarly poor devils; they are banned from entering Holofernes' holy of holies, which, unknown to them has lost its false god; this is why they wail and gnash their teeth to awaken their hope. In terms of the only true reality, God's purpose, they will fall before the swords of the avengers and will be cast into the exterior darkness where eternally they will wail and gnash their teeth, following their leader in his fearsome journey. An additional but interesting juxtaposition may be noted. As a result of the "work of the day," *dægweorce* (266), the hearts of the Assyrians are dark, *sweorcendferhðe* (269). This picks up a motif from the feast, the darkness approaching the sons of men (28–34), and stands in contrast to the dawn when the Hebrews began their advance, that dawn which is accompanied by the sound of the crack of doom.

In period 1, 275–280, of paragraph iii, one man with the courage of despair enters the tent to find his headless lord; in 2, 280–289, he makes known his discovery, the result of which is the flight of the Assyrians, briefly noted in 3, 289–291. Paragraph iii has ironic parallels with Judith's actions seeking Holofernes. Like Judith one Assyrian alone finds the courage to face Holofernes. His act is underscored with wordplay: *nið-, neð-, nyd; blacne, goldgiefan*; strong in iniquity and driven by need, he found his resplendent gold-giver shining with the pallor of death, *niðheard neðde swa him nyd fordraf/ funde . . . blacne licgan/ his goldgiefan*, 277–278.[53] Like Judith he reports to his people. He reveals to them the headless trunk of Holofernes. His speech ironically reflects Judith's speech to her people, not only as revelation, but also in parallel wording. Judith revealed the head as a symbol of the

52. The connotations of *cirman* in the Riddles, 9 and 49, are not clear.

53. The word play involved in *blacne* rests on more than the contrast of meaning between it and *goldgiefan* (pallid: gold). *Blacne* has a root meaning, "shining," particularly with reference to fire and lightning. (Bosworth-Toller *s.v.*) The derived meaning "pale" appears in a reference to the light of the moon, one must suppose because of the contrast of darkness and light. A further meaning, "pallor of death," is attested, and derives presumably from the pale shine of death in contrast to the ruddiness of life.

doom of the Assyrians, *Her ge magon sweotule . . . on . . . heafod starian/ Holofernes unlyfigendes . . . swa eow getacnod hafað mihtig dryhten* (177–198); the Assyrian reveals the headless trunk also as a symbol of their destruction, *Her ys geswutelod . . . toweard getacnod . . . her lið . . . beheafdod healdend ure* (285–289). The last epithet, "our savior," is devastatingly ironic in its contrast between Judith's Savior and their lord who not only cannot save them, but who has himself led them to destruction. Finally in response to Judith's prophecy the Hebrew people took up arms; in response to the Assyrian his people throw down their arms and take flight.

291–323, III, Vengeance: Scene III contains two balanced paragraphs; i, 291–311, which describes the pursuit of the enemy by the Hebrews, ii, 311–323, which describes the return of the Hebrews.

Paragraph i, the pursuit, contains three periods, each introduced by a re-statement of the image of the path of pursuit: 1, *Him mon feaht on last* (291); 2, *Him on laste for* (297); 3, *Hi . . . / herpað worhton* (301–302). The narrative action of the pursuit is contained in the three a clausules of the three periods. In periods 1 and 3 this narrative action is followed by a statement of the result of the action in the b clausule: 1, a, 297–299, the Hebrews pursued, leaving most of the Assyrians as a feast for the carrion creatures, and in 1, b, 296–297, those who escape flee; 3, a, 301–304, the Hebrews create a battle path through the enemy, and 3, b, 307–311, the few surviving Assyrians flee. In period 2, however, the statement of pursuit in the a clausule, 297–299, is followed not by a statement of effect in b, 299–300, but by a statement of cause, that God is their protector. In effect the cause and effect relationship between the a and b clausules of 1 and 3 is reversed in 2. Standing at the center of the paragraph, clausule b of 2 gives the ultimate cause of the victory of the Hebrews. The flight of the Assyrians has as its immediate cause the show of force at dawn, but the ultimate cause of their flight is God, who has ordained their defeat.

In period 1, clausule a, the pursuit of the enemy is described with a grim reminder of the expectations aroused in the wolf and the raven by the Hebrew advance at dawn; the pursuit continues until these expectations are realized, and the feasting Assyrians lie on the "field of victory/ a festival for wolves and for the feast-eager/ fowls a delight" (295–296). The b clausule simply adds the laconic comment, "those of the hated warriors who lived fled."

In period 2, clausule a begins with a repetitive variant of the beginning of clausule a of 1, *Him on laste for*. Clausule a is completed by the causal statement that the God took the Hebrews under his protection. This b clausule is linked to the a clausule by anaphora, both clausules beginning with *Him*. The use of anaphora results in an abrupt shift of reference because the first *Him* refers to the Assyrians, the second to the Hebrews, but with no hint of the shift except in the context of clausule b, which demands that the reference be to the Hebrews. This abrupt shift of reference, which, as will appear, occurs again in paragraph ii, is probably not the result of a careless use of anaphora; rather the anaphora causes attention to be paid to a deliberate ambiguity like that given to Judith and Holofernes in the beheading scene, 97–111, 111–121. The pronominal ambiguity given here in the pursuit scene to both friend and foe suggests how completely the tide of battle is in the hands of God.

In period 3, clausule a, 301–304, the variant on the introductory path formula, *Hi . . . herpað worhton* indicates the pains the poet takes with the smallest details. In 1 and 2 simple chiastic repetition and verbal variations are involved; *feaht on last* (291), *on laste for* (297). The variant is logical; the first verb, "fought," suggests the actual attack; the second, "followed," suggests the pursuit itself. In 3, semantic repetition with complete structural and verbal variation is involved; they "fashioned a path of battle," *herpað worhton* (302). The Hebrew army, now indicated in the plural, no longer follow a track, "last"; they literally make it, hew it out. This action suggests the completion of the rout; the "track" is cut and paved, as it were, with the slain enemy.[54] The a clausule is completed, clausule 3, a^2, 304–307, with a notice of the warlike disposition of the Hebrew warriors, a disposition which is the result of Judith's words and example. The implied relation of cause and effect follows naturally from the statement in period 2 that the ultimate cause of their bravery is God's having taken them under his protection. Periods 1 and 3 are linked not only by their introductory phrases, but also by echoic reference to the slaughtered Assyrians: in 1, *se mæsta dæl/ þæs heriges læg . . . on ðam sigewonge* (292–294); in 3, *ðær on greot gefeoll/ se hyhsta dæl* (307–308). The literal *greot*, "dust," of period 3 adds to the irony involved in the hysteron-proteron, *sigewong*, "field of victory," of 1. Both periods are concluded with brief parenthetical clausules: 1, b, *flugon ða ðe lyfdon/ laðra linde* (296–297); 3, b, *lythwon becom/ cwicera to cyððe* (310–311). The flight of the Assyrians noted in 1, b, the living fled, is thus completed in 3, b, few returned home.

In paragraph ii, the Return, 311–323, the completion of the Hebrew victory is celebrated. The paragraph is framed by two complementary periods, 1, 311–313, and 3, 321–323, which develop the image of track or path of the first paragraph. In period 1, some ambiguity exists in the word *wiðertrod*, 312. The second part of the compound, *-trod*, is clear. Its meaning, "track," is a continuation of *last* of 1. *Wiðer-*, however, may mean either "opposite," or "hostile"; in the first sense the compound would mean "back-track," i.e., the return of the Hebrews, in the second, "hostile track," the retreat of the enemy. The only other recorded use of the compound is in *Genesis* A, 2084, where its meaning is clearly "retreat." The *Judith* poet apparently selected the word both for the linking connotations of *-trod*, and for its double meaning: the Hebrews turn back from the retreat on the return path. As with the ambiguous reference

---

54. The word *herpað* is found only here and in *Daniel* 38, where its meaning is literal, not figurative as in *Judith*.

of *him* in the preceding paragraph, the word has double reference: to the Hebrews' return, and to the Assyrians' retreat. There is also a difficulty with *wælscel*, 312, one of the hapax legomena in which the poem abounds. Although the compound has been emended by some, Cook, Dobbie, and Timmer appear to agree upon the meaning "carnage," with the second element of the compound derived from *scelle*, a gloss for *concisium*, "cutting." However, *-scel* may have the meaning "husk" or "shell," as in *scealu*, or *scill, scell*.[55] The meaning for the compound would then be "slaughter-shells," i.e., "corpses." Such a meaning seems probable, not only as directly parallel with *hræw* in the following line, but also in reflecting the earlier image of Holofernes' lifeless trunk, the shell left after the soul has departed. In the context of a similarly formed compound, *stanscealu*, "stony soil," *wælscel*, would be echoic of *greot* of i, 3, and would anticipate the leading subject of the next period, the despoilment of the Assyrian dead.

Period 2, 313–321, is central in the paragraph, being framed by the brief periods 1 and 3, which restate the motif of the path. The period emphasizes two aspects of the Hebrew triumph: in clausule a, 313–318, the quantity of the booty; in b, 318–321, the greatness of the victory. This emphasis on riches and glory prepares for the final scene, the Triumph, where Judith is awarded much riches, where she attributes the glory to God, and where are distinguished the treasures of the world and the treasures of heaven.

Period 3, 321–323, serves with period 1 to frame the central period 2 which describes the taking of the booty. In period 1 the return of the Hebrews amidst the corpses of the Assyrians is briefly described; in period 3 the Assyrian dead lying on the path are even more briefly noted, *Hie on swaðe reston/ þa ðe him to life laðost wæron/ cwicera cynne.* The phrasing of period 3 has the further function of echoing passages in paragraph i which speak of the slaying of the Assyrians: *flugon ða ðe lyfdon/ laðra linde* (296–297); *lyhtwon becom/ cwicera to cyððe* (310–311). The echo provides a conclusion to the motif of the slaughter of the Assyrians, a conclusion given special emphasis in period 3 by the ironic use of the verb, *reston*, and by the sudden shift in pronominal reference. The introductory pronoun in *Hie on swaðe reston* at first reading is taken as referring to the Hebrews, the subject of the preceding period, but the rest of period 3 corrects this reading when the actual reference is given; those who rest on the path are those who while they were living were most hateful to them, that is, to the Hebrews. The pronoun thus refers to the Assyrians, whose corpses rest on the path. These corpses the Hebrew people will

55. See Bosworth-Toller *s.v., scill.* If *scealu* is the word from which the second element is derived, *e* for *ea* may have a parallel in *stercedferhð* (see Timmer, p. 5); if *scell*, the single *l* of the MS would involve the same simplification as is posited in deriving the word in the poem from *scelle*. Since both *scealu* and *scell* are feminine, an ending in *e* would appear likely, but the absence of the *e* in *scelle* would also have to be explained. It is possible that the scribe (or poet) took the word to be neuter, perhaps influenced by the neuter *hræw*.

busy themselves in unshelling, as they strip them of their accoutrements of war, an action described in the next and final scene.

323–349, IV, The Triumph: The scene consists of two paragraphs, i, the spoils of victory, ii, thanksgiving. Paragraph i, 323–341, narrates the taking and dividing of the spoils. It is developed in three periods tied together by the repetition of *eall:* 1, 323–330, *þa seo cneoris eall . . . wægon . . . to ðære beorhtan byrig;* 2, 331–334, *Eal þæt þa ðeodguman . . . geeodan;* 3, 334–341, *Hi to mede hyre . . . eal þæt se rinca baldor . . . ahte.* The first *eall* is ambiguous; its reference is either to the Hebrews (*cneoris*), or to the treasure, probably treasure to which *eall* unambiguously refers in its repeated use. The ambiguity of the first *eall,* which points both to the treasure and to the Hebrew people, leads to the establishment of a parallel between the radiance of the treasure and the corresponding radiance which the city and its people share with Judith. This strikingly effective parallel is achieved through the repetition of *beorhtan;* the treasure is brought to the shining city, *beorhtan byrig* (326), and shining treasure, *beorhtra maðma* (340), is given to the shining woman, *beorhtan idese* (340). The parallel is also suggested through the piling up phrases listing the booty and a similar piling up of phrases designating the Hebrew people and Judith, who thus share a common richness and radiance. Without listing all the variants, special note can be taken of *wundenlocc* (325), used to describe the Hebrew warriors. Because it was used twice earlier to describe Judith (77, 103), and is clearly a beautifying designation, the effect of its use here is to have Judith's people share in her radiance. One interesting deviation from the adjectives of brilliance used to describe the booty may also be noted. In the description of the splendid war gear given to Judith the helmet of Holofernes is called blood-stained, *swatigne* (337). The intrusion serves effectively to recall the head which the helmet encased, the object of Judith's triumph. The helmet cannot in fact be stained with blood—it is rather the bloody head which is suggested by metonymy.

Paragraph ii, Thanksgiving, contains two periods, the first giving Judith's thanks, the second giving a concluding prayer of praise. The *Ealles* of period 1, 341–346, *Ealles ðæs Iudith sægde/ wuldor weroda dryhtne,* serves as a transitional tie to the key word of the preceding paragraph, the phrase *sægde wuldor,* which is found only in *Judith,* defines the true end of her triumph, her true reward. In praising God for her earthly reward, but also for the reward of heaven, *swylce eac mede on heofonum/ sigorlean in swegles wuldor* (343–344), Judith reveals her ultimate hope. Through its structuring, the phrase is made to stand in contrast to the preceding, *swylce eac side byrnan* (337), which appears in the list of earthly treasures given to Judith. The contrast suggests that the gift of treasure is simply the outward manifestation of the reward for which she truly yearned, and which, in her faith she did not doubt she would receive; *þæs ðe heo ahte soðne geleafan/ a to ðam ælmihtigan huru æt ðam ende ne tweode/ þæs leanes þe heo lange gyrnde* (344–346). These lines also recall that at the beginning of the poem she was given earthly reward and the Lord's grace. Earthly reward is significant only as it follows from the triumph of good over evil; that is to say, as it reflects the reward of heaven.

In name and example Judith signifies faith and the praise of God. Period 1 states appropriately why God's grace was shown to Judith; period 2, 346–349, developing the phrase, *sægde wuldor* of period 1, consists of a prayer of praise (*wuldor*, 347) to the Creator: "For this to the dear Lord / who through his favoring grace fashioned wind and sky / the firmament and the wide lands as also the wild seas / and the glad joys of heaven may glory be forever." This prayer of thanksgiving, as in Rabanus' verse dedication of his commentary on Judith, is appropriate because the story of Judith is the story of faith, of belief in God, the Creator of heaven and earth. One phrase, however, seems out of keeping with the theme of praise, that is the mention of God's creation of the wild seas, *swylce eac reðe streamas* (348). The phrase takes on particular significance as the third phrase in a pattern of repetition which binds together the two paragraphs of the final scene:

> i, 3, 337,   *swylce eac side byrnan*
> ii, 1, 343,   *swylce eac mede on heofonum*
> ii, 2, 348,   *swylce eac reðe streamas*

Here again the prominence given to a difficult word or phrase calls attention to something of thematic significance. A double theme is developed in *Judith*— God's punishment of the oppresser proud in his worldly power, and God's reward of those who remain steadfast in faith through all tribulation, so that the image of the wild seas is probably intended as a reminder of the earlier bold metaphoric picture of the Assyrians drowned in wine. The image of the worldly life as a sea which one must cross is commonplace. One striking development of the figure is in the standard exegesis of the crossing of the Red Sea, where the crossing of the Hebrew people is taken to represent the salvation of the just, and the drowning of the Egyptians, the damnation of the evil. Judith is a type not only of triumph of the faithful, but also of the destruction of the wicked. Good and bad alike must face the rough seas, the world. The rough seas represent those tribulations which man must overcome in order to earn the reward appropriate to his deeds. The byrnie of faith bears him up on these seas; the byrnie of worldly pride weighs him down and drowns him. Judith has journeyed over rough seas, for the devil's head is not cut off except through faith and Christian fortitude. Some such message seems implicit in the poet's calling special attention to the two aspects of God's creation, his justice and his mercy. Because Judith converts the bright byrnie of Holofernes into the armour of faith by attributing all to God in praise, she gains the bright city.

* * * *

The preceding analysis of the structure of *Judith* has not been free from subjective judgement, particularly in the determination of the smaller rhetorical units, the clausules, and periods, but what can fairly be claimed for it is that it does suggest the complex rationale of the poet's design. The design shapes the narrative so that what emerges is the theme that God aids those who are resolute in faith.

In the course of the commentary, the poet's skill in the use of striking word or phrase and in the use of the counter-pointing of metaphor and motif has been noted: for example, Holofernes' tent prominently featured in Episode B as a kind of diabolical holy of holies stands in contrast to its appearance in Episode C where it is revealed for what it is, the empty temple of evil; or, the functional use of the formulaic attendants of battle, the wolf, raven, and eagle, to recall with fatal irony Holofernes' feast—the feasters have become the feast. Finally, how completely the structure of the poem is organized may be suggested by a schematic diagram (see page 189) of what has already received notice, the overall design of the narrative action in a fixed tripartite pattern: (1) beginning or preparation for action, (2) action, (3) conclusion or completion of the action. Even in the framework of the introduction and conclusion to the poem a similar progression may be noted. The extant introduction tells of God's protection of Judith, and of the glory granted to her. The conclusion tells of Judith's thanks for her victory and of her trust in the promise of salvation. Thus the introduction states the premise of the action of the poem, and the conclusion completes the meaning of the action by revealing its true, spiritual import, the gift of God's protection and the promise of salvation.

The structure of Judith is complex, ornate, schematic, but its effect is essentially that of pious simplicity, for morally the confrontation of Judith and Holofernes is white and black. Her heroism is that of the daughter of the faith; his evil that of the prince of darkness. The overwhelmingly contrived and mathematically organized structure serves the end of spiritualizing the narrative it embodies as does the creatively used traditional vocabulary. The mind is engaged to perceive the bent and direction of Judith's triumph and Holofernes' punishment, and to perceive God's rational order in the simulacrum of the poetic order. Although each narrative unit is constructed on a simple principle, the variations, the ornamentation, the decorative inserts, prevent any potential monotony, while, at the same time, they lead back to a recognition of a primary unity of structure. The poem is full of echoes, particularly of *Beowulf;* these echoes always reinforce the particular effect *Judith* is intended to create. The poem recalls a traditional heroic poetry, but the heroism is that of a simple and profound piety in which a woman standing alone because she is strong in faith demolishes an overwhelming military power because this power has been made weak in the winehall of gluttony and the bedchamber of lust. The ultimate hero of the poem is God, and the heroic action involves the working out of his just and merciful providence.

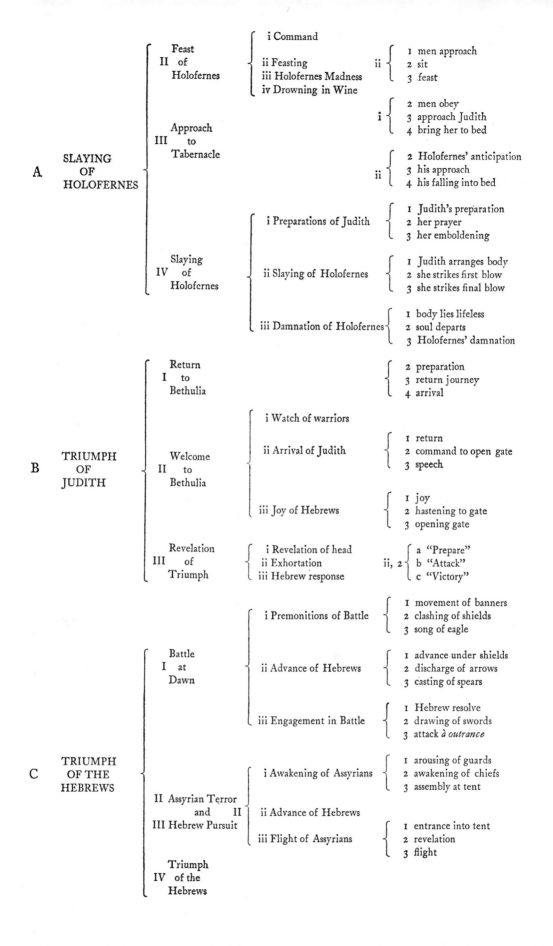

Index

For convenience, Old English words discussed in the text have been separately indexed, and will be found following the standard index. The four poems discussed in the text are not indexed because the texts, the translations, and the running commentary in the analyses facilitate easy reference to these poems.

For their good-humored and painstaking assistance to me in the preparation of this index, and in proofreading, I am greatly indebted to Miss Marla Mudar and Mr. Thomas Miles.